Toward a Sociological Theory
of Information

Toward a Sociological Theory of Information

Harold Garfinkel

Edited and Introduced by
Anne Warfield Rawls

Routledge
Taylor & Francis Group

LONDON AND NEW YORK

First published 2008 by Paradigm Publishers

Published 2016 by Routledge
2 Park Square, Milton Park, Abingdon, Oxon OX14 4RN
711 Third Avenue, New York, NY 10017, USA

Routledge is an imprint of the Taylor & Francis Group, an informa business

Library of Congress Cataloging-in-Publication Data

Garfinkel, Harold.
  Toward a sociological theory of information / by Harold Garfinkel.
    p. cm.
  Includes bibliographical references and index.
  ISBN-13: 978-1-59451-281-0 (hardcover : alk. paper) 1. Information theory in sociology. I.
Title.
  HM651.G37 2008
  306.4'201—dc22

                                                                      2007052292

Designed and Typeset by Straight Creek Bookmakers.

ISBN 13: 978-1-59451-281-0 (hbk)
ISBN 13: 978-1-59451-282-7 (pbk)

Contents

Editor's Introduction

Anne Warfield Rawls

Introduction[1]

THIS LONG OVERDUE PUBLICATION OF HAROLD GARFINKEL'S *TOWARD A Sociological Theory of Information* makes available for the first time a manuscript completed by Garfinkel in April of 1952—as Memo #3—for a seminar he was teaching at Princeton University on information and formal social organization—in conjunction with the Organizational Behavior Project.[2] In the manuscript, Garfinkel outlines an inherently *social* theory of information—maintaining that information is not only put to social uses—but becomes information in the first place through situated social processes, in details. Thus, he argues, it is impossible to understand information, either intrinsically, or

---

1. *Acknowledgments:* I would like to express my thanks to those who attended my May 12, 2006 talk on Garfinkel's theory of information at MIT for their many helpful comments and questions. My special thanks to John Van Mannen and Peter K. Manning in this regard and to Peter especially for many helpful discussions along the way. To Jeff Coulter for his early and sustained critique of classic information theory. I need also to thank JoAnn Brooks and the team of researchers at MITRE, Dave Mann, Matt Burton and Deb Bodeau. I learned so much about information from our work together. And, finally, to Harold Garfinkel, without whose ideas a great deal of progress would never have been made and to whom I owe a great deal. As always, I know that it is not possible to do justice to these ideas that are so brilliant and ahead of their time. But, I have tried.
2. Background given in Part One.

in application, without addressing its social—and by social Garfinkel means primarily its organized—character. In several accompanying manuscripts Garfinkel outlines theories of communication, self, and social order that support his theory of information (Memos #1 and #2 and two research proposals written in 1951–52, included as appendices to this volume). Far from being outdated, in the 55 years since it was written, the argument has become increasingly relevant as technical worksites and computer mediated interaction have become more prevalent, traditional approaches more problematic, and ethnomethodologically (EM) informed studies of those issues—inspired by Garfinkel—have made a significant contribution.

In the manuscript, Garfinkel launches a serious critique of classic information theory and the semantic and linguistic theories of communication it assumed—a critique that was further elaborated by his later research and also by his students and colleagues. The critique focuses on aspects of interaction and sensemaking that ethnographies of work and workplace studies inspired by Garfinkel have shown to be the key to current work practices and research.[3]

More importantly, Garfinkel not only criticizes classic approaches to information theory—a line of argument pursued by some of his students and colleagues—but, he also offers an alternative theory of information. As he points out, information theory has, from the first, been informed by theories of language. Therefore, changing the theory of language changes information theory. Garfinkel grounds his theory of information on a theory of communication and objects, that treats both as constituted by the order properties of the situations in which they are perceived—and as having no other "objectivity" (by which Garfinkel means mutually intelligible coherence). This alternative theory remains innovative and is the real heart and soul of the manuscript. Garfinkel's alternative theory not only casts information in a new light, but also promises to clarify the role of Ethnomethodology (EM) and Conversation Analysis (CA) in contemporary detailed studies of the workplace—and also to highlight strengths and limitations of existing approaches to information— thereby more adequately grounding current research and design efforts.[4]

By the early 1950s—when Garfinkel did this work at Princeton—the information age had ushered in a new focus on information, the design and

---

3. Studies by Orr, Suchman, Heath, Luff, Lynch, Harper, Hughes, Whalen, and Knorr-Cetina in particular.

4. Known variously as workplace studies, ethnographic studies of work, and "Hybrid Studies of Work" (Garfinkel 2002), there are researchers focused on such studies at Xerox PARC (now the Palo Alto Research Center and Cambridge, and at Microsoft research centers in the UK. There will be a new journal devoted to Workplace Studies.

management of information systems, and the need for easy information retrieval. Because signals must be paired with codes, and "noise" distinguished from information, in order for any of this to work, theories of information necessarily raise the problem of the relationship between ideas and their alleged symbolic representations. In other words, information raises the classic problem of language and meaning in a new and very pragmatic form. Thus, from the beginning, information theory has addressed deep philosophical issues of epistemology and ontology and has been closely tied to theories of language. In fact, this may have been one of the driving forces behind what has been called the "linguistic turn" in modern scholarship.

Representations in information systems must match the content assigned to them in ways that are easily accessible by many different people. Theories about how people are believed to ordinarily manage a process of transferring ideas from one "mind" to another—through ordinary language and communication—are invoked in designing such systems. In this way, assumptions (many of them problematic) about language, epistemology, ontology—and the nature of mind, cognition, categorization, and classification—have found their way into technical specifications of work and information.

From the beginning, there have been many confusions about meaning—the relationship between words, meaning and objects and the role of logical systems in ordering, creating and enabling meaning. Questions about whether meaning is a matter of "mind" or public "use" have been debated.

Information theorists have wanted language to work in logically driven and referential ways that can be easily engineered, but which do not match up well with the way language and meaning actually work. Because of this, information theory continues to struggle with theories of meaning and classification, and with epistemological and ontological assumptions, that are untenable. Research is hampered by these assumptions and advances tend to be unpredictable and difficult to explain theoretically.

Thus, the contemporary turn toward language in philosophy and social science intersects with the pragmatic organization, management and retrieval of information in a profound way. Frustrated researchers in information sciences sometimes appeal to philosophers and social theorists to take seriously the problems of meaning, categorization and epistemology they face as if they had not already done so.[5] Ironically, problematic assumptions made by such researchers about definitions, categories, semantics, and grammars that get

_____

5. Geffrey C. Bowker and Susan Leigh Star, *Sorting Things Out: Classification and Its Consequences* (Cambridge, MA:MIT Press, 1999).

caught up not only in definitions of information—but in the organization, access and retrieval of information—have been seriously contested for centuries. The educational process has become so specialized that the essential debates are not in touch with one another. The judgment of philosophy and social science has been for more than a century that these issues are deeply problematic as currently formulated. What is new is that such "theoretical" questions have in the last two decades finally been recognized as practical problems for workers and systems designers in the world of information. More contact between disciplines is required to recognize the amazing conjunction between esoteric questions of theory and practical relevance that inhabit information.

Garfinkel's manuscript is an important piece of this historical debate that helps to situate and clarify the current state of both research and theory and to put information theory in touch with the philosophical and socio-theoretical issues. Those inspired by Garfinkel—along with followers of James, Durkheim, Levy-Strauss, Wittgenstein, Foucault and others—have for years engaged in a sustained critique of conventional information theory as based on a cognitivist and individualist model of communication that does not take the Wittgensteinian critique of referential (linguistic/semantic) meaning into account, does not reflect the anti-positivist critique of pragmatism (the fallacy of misplaced concreteness—Whitehead), or consider social aspects of information (Coulter, Hacker), or the social character of categorization and classification (Durkheim, Levy-Strauss, Derrida, Foucault).

That Garfinkel's position on information, along with his earlier position on communication, is intrinsically theoretical—constitutes an answer to the currently pressing question of how to theoretically situate research based on his work. Given the success of studies inspired by his work, the question of how to do EM informed studies, debates about their theoretical relevance and grounding, and how to incorporate their implications into a broad understanding of the issues surrounding technical work and information, have become a topic of some importance.

The answer is a rather simple one. The problems and practices which EM researchers so demonstrably turn up are intrinsically bound up with Garfinkel's theoretical argument that order is the essential property of mutually coherent objects. Paired with theories that treat objects as independent of constitutive practices, or which take things (words and objects) out of context and treat them as abstractions—EM inspired studies quickly become irrelevant—the detail ambiguous and misleading. Garfinkel's main point is that objects—things—of *any sort* must be "thingified" in the context of some shared practice in order to be rendered in mutually intelligible ways—made recognizably and mutually coherent for more than one person at the same time—and thus become objects. It is order that gives them coherence. Studies inspired by Garfinkel should keep this point clearly in view.

The argument of this early manuscript promises to clarify these concerns and offer further inspiration to those working to bring EM studies of detailed order to bear in highly technical areas of work and interaction.

In Garfinkel's view, it is not possible to adequately apprehend information, objects, or information exchange, without situating objects, meanings, and actions in the ordered social processes that constitute them. Other currently popular approaches that seem to take the situated character of action and perception into account escape into abstraction at some point. The currently popular idea of "boundary objects" for instance—objects that are allegedly the "same" across many contexts—solves the problem of "same object" by positing abstractions that escape the constraint of constitutive practice.[6] I believe Garfinkel would maintain that if there are objects that cross situated boundaries, it is not because some objects are common to more situations than others, but rather, because the practices which constitute them as objects—mutually intelligible objects—are common across many situations and memberships. It is not the objects that have the alleged "durability," as ontological presences, but the practices which constitute them. Furthermore, the practices that are doing the boundary crossing likely constitute fundamental boundary objects in their own right as practices with some inherent necessity.[7]

Because of his unusual marriage of theory and practice, the theoretical issues raised by Garfinkel's critique of information theory have also turned out to be the crucial pragmatic issues, as the limitations of logical, rational and semantic approaches to information systems have become apparent. Given Garfinkel's insistence that theory be based on practice—and tied to just those order properties of practices that participants need in order to make mutually intelligible sense—it should not be surprising that his theoretical insights continue to run so true—but it is—and I believe he had not anticipated it, expecting that later, more empirical work, would entirely supersede these early attempts to theoretically specify interaction orders. They have not. In

---

6. Bowker and Star (1999); John Seely Brown and Paul Duguid, *Documents as Boundary Objects: Patrolling and Controlling* (1996).

7. The argument that some practices should turn out to be fundamental in this respect is one of the arguments of the "Turntaking" paper (Sacks, Schogloff and Jefferson 1974). I have elaborated the argument in various of my own articles (Rawls 1987, 1989, 1990). Doug McBeth's work on teaching illustrates how some conversational practices can be used to create the mutual apprehension of objects. Thus, these practices are functioning as boundary objects.

fact, the reverse has been true. The empirical work stands in serious need of theoretical contexting.

This introduction will proceed by way of four major sections. *Section One* provides some background for the manuscript (Memo #3) and the development of information theory. It also considers the relationship of Garfinkel's argument to information theory, to contemporary studies of high-tech work, and to the development of Garfinkel's later work—in particular what he referred to as "Hybrid Studies of Work" (2002). This is followed in *Section Two* by a summary discussion of Garfinkel's theoretical position. *Section Three* provides a detailed analysis of Memo #3, and *Section Four* takes up a discussion of the appendices.

SECTION ONE: Background and General Discussion

Background of the Manuscript

The seminar for which the manuscript was written, and the work which Garfinkel did at Princeton in the years 1951–53, were organized under the auspices of the Organizational Behavior Project—a project funded by the Ford Foundation, the sociological aspects of which were administered by Wilbert Moore. Moore was a member of the Department of Economics and Social Institutions and the Office of Population Research, at Princeton University (in the years before most universities had sociology departments). The relationship between Moore and Garfinkel is one interesting aspect of the project. Garfinkel had undertaken a field study for Moore in 1942, just after completing his MA thesis at North Carolina, which explored the effects of temporary military industry on the social organization of the town of Bastrop Texas. The study was part of a continuing analysis of the war effort and part of an extensive research project on the effects of industry on society that Moore was engaged in writing at the time. Moore's influential book *Industrial Relations and the Social Order* was completed in 1944 and first published in 1946.

Garfinkel's preliminary report of his study to Moore, included in the appendix to this volume, takes up several issues that are relevant to an understanding of the development of Garfinkel's ideas, and also raises interesting issues regarding Moore's approach and its relationship to the development of Garfinkel's ideas. As in his later work, Garfinkel's analysis in 1942 relies heavily on performative aspects of self and details of social interaction to get at issues of status and social hierarchy, as well as to evaluate social changes that could be attributed to the proximity of the army camp. Garfinkel insists in his letter to Moore, dated June 24, 1942 (see Appendix 5), that the observed actions of individuals are more "real" and say more about social change and constancy than the sorts of institutional measures that he expects Moore would prefer and explains that differences in their respective approaches to what order is may have led Garfinkel to design his study in ways that will be a "disappointment" to Moore. It is interesting, in light of this concern—and the real differences between them—that Moore turned to Garfinkel again five years later to work on the prestigious Organizational Behavior Project.

Garfinkel's work for the project included organizing conferences and presentations by visiting scholars, in addition to undertaking field studies of formal organizations, writing up research proposals, and teaching seminars at Princeton.[8] The manuscript on information, distributed to one of these seminars, was originally titled "Notes Toward a Sociological Theory of Information," headed Memo #3 and dated April 17, 1952. It was preceded by two shorter manuscripts—headed Memo #1 (no date) and Memo #2 October 4, 1951—which were distributed to his seminars at Princeton in the fall of 1951. Memo #3 was followed by two short proposals written for Moore based on Garfinkel's own field research (both of which reference that memo).

To provide a context for the information manuscript (Memo #3) and make Garfinkel's previously unknown writings from the years 1951–52 available to readers, these four documents, along with the field study of Bastrop Texas, are included as appendices to this volume.

Memo #3 represents a significant piece of work—laying the groundwork for a sociological approach to information—that has been essentially lost to scholarship since it was first written. The manuscript came to me through Rod Watson, of Manchester Metropolitan University in the UK, who had gotten it from a

---

8. Garfinkel organized two conferences for The Organizational Behavior Project, one in March 1952 ("Problems of Model Construction in the Social Sciences") and the other June 18–19 of 1952 ("Theory of Organization"); the second of which was sponsored jointly with The Social Science Research Council. The conferences were reported in the *American Sociological Review* (October 1952), volume 15 (5): 622–25 and in the *American Political Science Review* (September 1952), volume 46 (3): 930–31. Among the notable figures attending one of these conferences were Alfred Schutz, Kurt Wolff (who mentions it in a short note titled "My Brush with Phenomenology"), Kenneth Burke, Elliot Mischler, Paul Lazarsfeld, Gregory Bateson, Herbert Simon, Philip Selznick, Marion Levy Jr., James Sykes, Frederick Mosteller, James Duesenberry, George Lombard, William Starbuck, Floyd Mann, Nancy Morse, Carroll Shatle, E. Wight Bakke, Harold Stein, Robert Bush, Neil Chamberlain, Harold Garfinkel, and Wilbert Moore.

friend on the continent along with a note attesting to its importance. The copy I received from Rod was a photocopy bearing the stamp of the Goffman archives at the University of Pennsylvania. Like the manuscript for *Seeing Sociologically,* Erving Goffman had obtained an early copy and kept it in his files.[9]

After I had received and read the memo, I realized that I had in my own files Memos #1 and #2 (which I had read in conjunction with preparing an earlier 1948 manuscript on communication for publication ([1948] 2006). Garfinkel later gave me access to his original Memo #3 and the accompanying studies. Differences between these shorter Memos #1 and #2 and the earlier 1948 manuscript on communication should be seen, I believe, as oriented toward laying the groundwork for Memo #3. The two short papers—or research proposals—that explicitly mention Memo #3 were written after Memo #3, but during the project for Moore for submission to the Ford Foundation, and thus, serve as initial explorations of the basic approach Garfinkel was working out at the time.

Because they were written before Garfinkel's insight that interaction was rather more finely detailed than he, or anyone, could have imagined—an insight that came when he began working on tape-recorded conversations with Harvey Sacks in 1962—these studies are not properly speaking EM. Because they rely on what Garfinkel can imagine—theorize—they are not as empirically grounded as his later work. Nevertheless, they stand as important attempts to blaze the way toward a study of meaning as order: a principle that Garfinkel insisted on from the start, but most fully articulates theoretically in this manuscript.

During the time Garfinkel was working out his sociological theory of information at Princeton, other prominent scholars were working on similar problems: albeit in very different ways. Although these scholars were scattered around the world, some of the most influential worked in conjunction with the Organizational Behavior Project and/or were affiliated with other departments and projects at Princeton. These included, in particular, important work on game theory and economic theories of behavior by von Neumann and Morgenstern and Alan Turing's earlier work on computing at the Princeton Institute for Advanced Studies. Gregory Bateson and Deutsch also made presentations to the seminar. In contrast to Garfinkel, however, the others tended to neglect the social elements of "information," modeling instead a rational individual in a context of either rules, values, or individual reason (in which words or numbers designated specific ideas). The success of information

---

9. I have been told that there may be similar materials related to Garfinkel, particularly with regard to early conference presentations, in the Parsons archive at Harvard.

systems modeled on these ideas thus depended on the completeness of both reason and information.

Garfinkel's position should be seen as a concerted argument against these approaches. As Garfinkel points out, in real situations none of these conditions can be met. Actual persons are never perfectly rational, words are endlessly indexical, and the condition of completeness of information can in principle not be met. In fact, in situations where information is very incomplete people usually have little trouble communicating. Consequently, the classic approaches have had limited and problematic practical application (and when applied to computers, constrain them in ways that humans are not constrained). Garfinkel's sociological approach, by contrast, treats information as a thoroughly socially organized phenomenon in a way that addresses, and in many cases eliminates, these shortcomings.

In the manuscript, Garfinkel lays out the characteristics that information and the situation must both have in order for information to be mutually intelligible. The condition is not completeness and it is not rationality. Rather, it consists of shared ways of constituting the order properties of situations. Information and the conditions for something being recognized as information are order properties, he says. These order properties are also the conditions for its being mutually intelligible—plus whatever makes it new (information is by definition new). But, Garfinkel points out that the newness of a thing, or perception, cannot be assessed except against a background of expectations and orders.[10] Thus, his theory of communicative intelligibility is directly relevant to his theory of information.

Although famous as a sociologist of everyday life, Garfinkel focuses in this manuscript on large-scale organizational concerns with decision-making and the perception, retrieval, transmission, storage and management of information. In the research proposals that followed he addressed the implications of his approach for studies of formal organizations and leadership.

The Development of Information Theory

The classic age in information theory began in the 1930s and extended through the early 50s. Important work by mathematicians, logicians, and linguists that would lead to the development of modern computers began to congeal

---

10. Like the "scruff" (description of "evidence") in his pulsar paper—with Mike Lynch and Eric Livingston, "The Works of the Discovering Sciences Construed with Materials from the Optically Discovered Pulsar," *Philosophy of the Social Sciences* 11 (1981): 131–158.

at this time. The war brought funding to this work during the 1940s in an effort to improve communications, the accuracy of weaponry and information transmission and storage. After the war, with new developments in computers and improved communication transmission systems—and as a hedge against future wars—money poured into the development of information systems. "Information" became important as a transmittable, computable thing, that could be quantified, bought, sold and managed, and on the basis of which decisions about complex organizations could be made. And with that we entered the "information age."

The first theories of information—between 1935 and 1955—formulated for the most part in the languages of mathematics and engineering—focused on problems like the carrying capacity of telephone wires which had no obvious social component—although even then the *impact* of the new technologies *on society* was an immediate topic of interest—an early conference at MIT on the impact of the telephone on daily life standing as an example. Talking on the telephone was a distinctly new social form and it took time for people to develop expectations regarding its use. At first they tended to just talk at the receiver—placing an order with the grocer for instance—and then hang up without waiting for a reply.

But, as information systems began to develop, in attempting to formulate the ways in which messages—or information—could be discriminated from everything else—engineers and mathematicians had to begin theorizing about signs and signifiers—to formulate theories about redundancy in language— generally defining information (at least initially) as inhabiting the realm of the non-redundant. Information is the thing you don't yet know—the thing that is different and can be discriminated from other things by that difference—that in some basic sense fails the identity test and thus is not itself.

Not surprisingly, then, social patterns (which—being patterns—are necessarily repetitive) tended to be seen as extra—redundant—nonessential—and the goal from the beginning seems to have been to pare information back to its alleged "essence," by getting rid of any socially determined redundancies. The social aspects of information were treated as extra—as inefficient—and as if they not only could, but should, be reduced to problems of pure mathematics, logic, and engineering.

This led almost inevitably to a cognitivist and individualist approach toward information.[11] The focus was on linguistics (semantics and logic) and a

---

11. That EM/CA by contrast refuses to deal with "lexical" meaning stands at the crux of the difference— and explains why, in terms of this argument, people not understanding this and focusing on symbols has been tragic.

representational theory of meaning—although Wittgenstein had already effectively argued for the impossibility of such a system. Later approaches improved on the problem by adopting, or adapting Searle's *Speech Act Theory* (1968). But, even so, in focusing on the attributes of types of speech acts needed to transcend particular situations and cases—to be generalizable—the coherence of objects was treated as having an independent existence, situated differences were bypassed, and the classic problems with redundancy and reference remained.

While information is that which is not yet known, it is only the known, Garfinkel argues, the socially recognizable, that has meaning and can be given form: an important paradox.

Over the past several decades the degree to which information is socially imbedded—and cannot simply be reduced to math or logic—has come to be increasingly recognized. Partly, this is due to failures in existing theories, but it has also been driven by engineers trying to design systems, who find that existing semantic—or schema based—approaches limit their effectiveness (and the effectiveness of their designs).[12] This has resulted in a practical understanding of why treating word meaning as a matter of reference, logical grammar, or rules, is a problem. The resulting focus on language as a sequentially ordered practice has increased the appreciation of CA and EM.

However, in spite of these insights, information is still usually treated as something that has existence in its own right—that social things are done *to* and *with*—that existing independently, information also comes to have a social life. Garfinkel, by contrast, has since 1952 treated information as almost entirely dependent on constitutive social elements for its existence.

The classic examinations of the intersection between language and information by Shannon, Weaver, Bateson, etc., that Garfinkel makes creative use of in this manuscript, date from just before and after the second world war. Technical and theoretical aspects of information and its relationship to communication were critical to war strategy—and after the war it became clear that the balance of power and wealth would come increasingly to rest on information.

---

12. I am greatly indebted to my colleagues at MITRE for an understanding of what these theoretical insights mean in practice. Prior to reading this manuscript I had not seriously considered "information" to be a topic at the center of sociological theory. In keeping with Garfinkel's dictum that understanding comes only through practice—I undertook a field study of and with an information systems design team while writing this introduction. It has been through working with them, Dave Mann and Matt Burden in particular, that I have come to appreciate in particular that designers confront the problem more specifically than words like "linguistic theory" would allow for. Even the word "semantic" does not capture their dilemma, as for some designers the problem is more properly one of "schema" and the constitutive relationship between any "schema" and the "data" that it defines.

According to Garfinkel, this also impacted the drive toward quantification in sociology—a problem he addressed in 1948 in his theory of communication (*Seeing Sociologically* [1948]2006). As Garfinkel points out, the drive toward quantification—and its reduction of social order to general trends—eliminates details about precisely those constitutive and non-generalizable—and therefore inherently qualitative and detailed processes—involved in social orders of understanding that are crucial to information theory and management. Thus, social science and philosophy are crippled, just as their relevance to practical problems increases exponentially.

Garfinkel and Information Theory

Garfinkel's social theory of information belongs to the classic period in the development of information theory—1935–1955—but as a heretofore unrecognized alternative voice. Written and distributed by Garfinkel to a seminar he was teaching at Princeton University in the spring of 1952, the manuscript (Memo #3) builds on his earlier theory of communication ([1948] 2006) represented in the set of manuscripts by the first two memos (#1 and #2). Broadly consistent with his later work, the information manuscript is nevertheless more explicitly theoretical and, as such, sheds light not only on the relationship between information theory and communication, but also on the development of Garfinkel's general line of thought.[13]

The manuscript outlines a comprehensive sociological theory of information, and positions that theory in relation to other prominent theories at the time; in particular, the arguments of Claude E. Shannon, Norbert Weiner, G. A. Miller, E. Deutsch, Gregory Bateson and Ruesch, and John von Neumann and Oskar Morgenstern: several of whom participated in the Princeton project. In the manuscript, Garfinkel also positions his theory of information in relation to his own developing approach to communicative intelligibility as a matter of order, and discusses its relationship to what he refers to as phenomenology, by which he means the "rules," or constitutive orders, governing any approach to work, or social order, of any kind.

While a wide variety of approaches to information developed in the 1940s and 1950s, as information increased in importance, these theories treated the

---

13. It was not until after 1954 that Garfinkel began to use the term "ethno-methods" and not until the late 1950s and early 1960s that he began to realize the amazing extent to which the ordered detailed properties of interaction—and language in particular—constituted its meaning. Nevertheless, in these early manuscripts he explicitly equates order with meaning in ways that anticipate his later discoveries.

social aspects of information as relatively unimportant, focusing instead on the symbolic, cognitive and logical aspects of information.[14] Although there has been a sustained critique, and symbolic, logical and cognitively based approaches to information face serious limitations, an adequate alternative has not been recognized. Even contemporary approaches that treat social aspects of information as important, tend to treat the social as something that happens *to* and *with* information, rather than treating social processes as essential to the constitution of information as such.

Garfinkel's argument, by contrast, is distinctive in insisting that information is constituted—not just interpreted—or symbolically represented and exchanged—but actually constituted *as* information by the social (cooperatively ordered) aspects of the situated social orders in which it occurs. Objects, for instance, on his view, can only be perceived as objects of a particular sort within a particular constitutive social practice. Instead of treating meaning as a cognitive matter of ideas that must be matched up with representations in order to be exchanged—Garfinkel treats meaning as constituted by mutually ordered public processes of interactional exchange: sequences of action and interaction that are reflexively tied. Sequences of ordered actions constitute the coherence of things. Things that happen after have implications for the meaning of what went before and vice versa. As with anything mutually understood—or mutually apprehended—objects, words, ideas, or things—Garfinkel argues that information only exists in and through the ways in which it is constituted and apprehended cooperatively in social situations, according to mutually oriented processes of sequential order production. Meaning is posited as order, and ordered relations between next moves, instead of as a relationship between ideas and symbols.

Information, represented by Garfinkel as (in part IV) $e(p_n)$, is entirely given by the ordered relations that constitute it. If, as most theories assume, communication between people were a matter of exchanging meanings (ideas) attached to representations (symbols)—a relation of reference—then the problem for information systems would be simple: to design an analogous system that relates representations to ideas that can be easily assessed by people: one that accords with the cognitive organization of understanding

---

14. On the face of it this makes sense, particularly since the advent of computers, since computer code would seemingly have to represent something specific. But as computers have become more complex and have increasingly come into contact with other computers, (interaction) problems have emerged and designers and programmers have begun to experiment with new "ontologies."

that these theories assume. Many information systems proceed in just this way (and their problems and limitations are attributable to this approach).

But if, as Garfinkel argues, communication between people—mutual intelligibility—is not a matter of matching cognitive ideas with symbols— if it is more like what Wittgenstein called a language game—with complex ordered properties—sequences of next moves—that need to be seen in the ordered context of moves in which they are produced—and if a primary need of communicants is to be able to see how next moves will be seen by the other—that is, if mutual intelligibility requires a more interactive, reflexive, and social explanation in this sense, then the attempt to design information systems based on a representational theory of meaning burdens information systems with problems they don't need to have.

As Wittgenstein argued, treating meaning as a matter of reference, when it is not, creates the impression that there are massive issues of ambiguity that cannot be overcome, when in actuality this is not a problem in ordinary situations.[15] The problems in the case of information are also caused by the theoretical approach taken, according to Garfinkel, and not by any inherent difficulty in making mutually intelligible sense. People make mutually intelligible sense all the time.

It is one of the staples of Garfinkel's position that people manage to make sense in spite of theories that suggest they should be having problems. His argument is that the only way to explain how this is possible is to revisit the process of mutual intelligibility—as a process in empirical and social details—forgoing theoretical assumptions about cognition—and finding out how—just how—mutually intelligible sequences of action are made recognizably coherent for one another and mutually understood. Instead of accepting the problematic character of meaning, Garfinkel urges us to discover why it is not a problem.

Thus, Garfinkel's sociological theory of information is consistent with his overall approach to communication, interaction, and the pervasive achieved orderliness of social life generally. Treating all intelligible social phenomena as achieved orders—the intelligibility of which depend on their mutually recognizable and cooperatively built ordered properties—has been Garfinkel's unique and original contribution. Accordingly, this manuscript is important not only as a theory of information, but also as an essential piece of Garfinkel's overall approach to the problem of social order.

---

15. Wittgenstein also argued that treating meaning as reference has caused the appearance of many of the classical "problems" in philosophy.

Ethnomethodology and Studies of Work and Information

Over the past two decades, information sciences, artificial intelligence, and studies of work and organization have been confronted with a growing body of studies inspired by Garfinkel which show that organized activities at the level of face-to-face interaction, machine-mediated interaction, or human machine interaction, are intrinsic to information processes. Studies by Christian Heath, Lorenza Mondada, John Hindmarsh, Jack and Marilyn Whalen, Eric Vinkhuzen, Julian Orr, Lucy Suchman, Richard Harper, John Hughes, Angela Garcia and Dave Randall, among others, demonstrate that information processes and social interaction are interrelated in essential ways. Mutual intelligibility—communication—involves more than the exchange of concepts and symbols, although that too is involved. It requires cooperation in achieving ordered sequences of action into which symbols can be recognizably placed to facilitate their mutual recognition on particular occasions.

A word—or symbol—placed in one ordered sequence means something quite different from the same word placed in a different ordered sequence: It has a different relevance and calls up different "category members" even when the grammar of the utterances is the same.[16] Garfinkel refers to this quality as "indexicality."[17] Some theories assume that motives and intentions are needed to sort out the ambiguity of such sequences. But, in most cases—unless the relationship between the word/action and the constitutive practice in which the ordered sequence occurs is clear—as an ordered sequence—intentions cannot be "read off" in the first place. In other words, intentions—in the public mutually intelligible domain—are not known,

---

16. Membership categorization does several things. As Sacks (1964) demonstrated, it can connect indexicals in a single utterance as in baby/mommy. It can organize relevancies with regard to a particular group or category of person such as "hotrodders." It can orient participants to the "we" character of some speakers as opposed to others (Sacks's counseling lectures). While Sacks is the one who is given credit for the idea of membership categorization devices—Garfinkel reports that he and Sacks had been discussing the possibility of such devices. Sacks was working with the police and the question was whether or not there could be categorization devices that would change the looks of things—and the implications for action. Sacks came back from his field research one day and said to Garfinkel "I have a pair." The first membership categorization pair, as Garfinkel reports it, was "possessibles" and "possessitives." The distinction designated cars that were abandoned versus cars with owners. The two categories defined two completely different categories of police relevant business according to Sacks. That the police learned to "see" this difference was therefore crucial to their work.

17. Indexicals have meaning in relation to an ordered sequence of utterances, objects, parts, or an index.

they can only be attributed to people—and therefore cannot explain mutual understanding.

Other researchers working in areas designated "information" have a strong bias for theories that treat the logical and conceptual aspects of words and symbols—their grammar and syntax—as most important in facilitating mutual intelligibility.

Given the prevalence of these two schools of thought, focusing on motives and/or semantics, the EM focus on constitutive and sequential order has typically been treated as superfluous, or even irrelevant. The tendency is to say that while studies of interaction in detail enhance the understanding of communicative processes—they do not offer a solution to the problem of mutual intelligibility. The idea is that EM studies have a "place," but that it is a subordinate place—and that EM insights must be incorporated into existing theories. As a result, the main criticism of detailed EM studies tends to be that they focus on the details of interactional order instead of concerning themselves with issues of structure, related demographics, the study of beliefs, values and motives, and the logic of concepts, which the mainstream schools of thought presume are "more important."[18]

According to Garfinkel, however, structure is exactly and only the exhibited details of order—the order properties of objects, words, things—on each next occasion. Structures, motives, and so on, as traditionally conceived are secondary, and can be invoked only after the fact to explain what has happened—but cannot be used to do it—that is, to produce coherent action prospectively.

If Garfinkel were given to defending his position, which he is not, he would strongly disagree with the conventional assimilation of his insight. His argument is not intended as an addendum to mainstream theories, and as work inspired by his approach becomes more widespread he worries that it will be assimilated instead of challenging and changing mainstream thinking.[19] He does not agree that issues of structure and demographics are more important than order properties in details. He thinks on the contrary, that focusing on structure

---

18. The recent issue of *Organization Studies* devoted to Julian Orr's *Talking About Machines* serves as a good example. Everyone is reading and talking about Orr. His research is a great success. Nevertheless, the discussions are critical of Orr for "ignoring" the more important issues of "structure" and so on. Orr neatly sidesteps such issues in defending his work by claiming status as an Anthropologist. But the real problem is much deeper. Orr could only do this rich research because he did not do as his critics suggest. Like Garfinkel—who also found no "hearable to others" way of responding—Orr sidesteps the issue.

19. Garfinkel has been largely silent with regard to the many critics of his work. This is not because he is indifferent—in fact there are several unpublished early responses to critics in

and demographics makes it impossible to see the essential order that is there. Nor is his a theoretically neutral position—or theoretically indifferent—as is often claimed.[20] Garfinkel's theory of information is intended to supply the missing link—to offer a theory of social and communicative order which will reveal the ways in which information is actually socially constituted, making it clear that it is not a matter of structure, motives, intentions or beliefs. For Garfinkel, it is just those details of order that conventional researchers treat as trivial that explain mutual intelligibility. The mutual ordering of those details, shared in common constitutive orders of practice, explains how recognizable orders are rendered coherent in situ. The studies of interaction, work in details and oriented objects[21]—inspired by Garfinkel's work—were designed as a way of addressing exactly those issues and limitations of traditional approaches which researchers in the domain of information now face. Thus, it is no coincidence that the studies he inspired are being embraced as increasingly relevant to theories of formal organization and information.[22] But, they need to be treated as a theory in their own right.

Relationship to Garfinkel's Later Work on Basic and Constitutive Rules

Garfinkel's early efforts in 1951–1952 to develop a way of formulating both information and formal organization theoretically will come as a surprise to most scholars—even many who are familiar with his work. But, the argument is

---

his archive. The problem is that his argument is extremely complex and no one—not even his closest supporters—understands all of it. The fact that everyone gets pieces of the theory wrong, and Garfinkel can't explain is frustrating. His approach has been to retreat from this—often into silent anger—rather than attempting to respond.

20. The idea of "ethnomethodological indifference" is much misunderstood. It means that the researcher will be indifferent to the presuppositions of existing sciences—and even to their own assumptions prior to entering a situation. The commitment is to finding the ordered properties of the situation at hand—with which to explain how the work of making sense is getting done there. Of course, once having found this order one would have a "theory" about how it worked. Additionally, no one would ever engage in research in just this way unless they assumed that meaning was to be found in ordered details rather than in concepts. So, there is a serious theoretical presumption behind the approach.

21. Calling objects "oriented objects" is Garfinkel's way of highlighting the fact that they are only objects when and how they are oriented by some identified actor in some local order of practice.

22. See my paper titled "Harold Garfinkel, Ethnomethodology, and Workplace Studies" in *Organization Studies* (Rawls, 2008).

entirely consistent with his overall position. *Studies in Ethnomethodology* (1967) did not develop because of an interest in individual—as opposed to institutional or collective action—as many have alleged. Ethnomethodology has never been "micro" and in spite of its empirical focus it has never been theoretically indifferent. It was in the context of Garfinkel's explicit theoretical focus on information and communication—in both formal and informal organizations and as practical accomplishments—that he began to formulate his overall approach.

Garfinkel proposes a form of study—focused on what he calls "members' methods" for producing recognizable "constitutive" orders—that not only ignores existing mainstream theoretical formulations of information and organizations—but gets underneath them. He asks what those theories were assuming—but not examining—that explained the possibility of mutual intelligibility. The "missing what" as he refers to it. There was in these other theories much talk of "norms" and "conventions" and "ideal types" toward which action was said to orient, but which it nevertheless always deviated to some extent from. Hence, deviation and "normal curves" became a preoccupation of social science.

Garfinkel asked a different question. In the face of inevitable deviation and difference, what explains the mutual recognition of things, words and actions, even though they are never exactly the same twice—or exactly like any ideal types—no matter how hard actors might try to conform?

The mainstream focus on "norms" is a focus on averages. Norms indicate the net result of a large number of individual actions. People are presumed to be trying to act in a normative way because most behavior can be described as approximating some set of norms, and there are often sanctions when behavior falls too far from the expected mark. Norms are, like basic rules, not rules people follow to make action. They are not constitutive of action, and actions that deviate from "norms" nevertheless have coherence and are mutually intelligible to others.[23] In this sense, norms are like what John Rawls (1955) referred to as "summary rules." These are rules, formulated after the fact, that describe tendencies to act in a particular way which can be formulated as rules or norms. But, these tendencies, or summary rules, are not constitutive of the orderly and meaningful properties of action.[24] And, it is a huge mistake to confuse the one with the other.

Garfinkel realized that to focus on social order in this way—to treat the average of action over time as the organizing force behind the social order—

---

23. For instance, when a person robs a bank we don't say "what are they doing?" but rather we say "Why are they robbing the bank?" or just "Look at them robbing the bank."

24. The argument is complicated by the fact that the word "norm" is often used loosely and some things described as norms might in fact be constitutive and should not be called norms.

was to fall into a tautology. Treating the average result as if it had organized the action—when it had not—is what he called a "heads you win tails I lose" approach that can't fail. Garfinkel maintains that there must be something organizing, or constituting, the mutual sense of actions *in the first place* before they could even be organized as types or "seen as" oriented toward norms. Focusing on aggregations of individual "normative" action—or summary rules—obscures this from view.

Garfinkel argues that what makes an action recognizable to others as an action of a particular sort are constitutive aspects of the orderliness of action—a sequential and reflexive order—that constitutes the action as a recognizable action—for this group of identified actors—engaged in just this practice together. This also requires trust in both competence and commitment, to the order in hand, on the part of the participants.

Such orders, Garfinkel argues, are necessarily based on "trust" with regard to both commitment to the constitutive rules/practices that comprise them and the competence to enact those practices. For Garfinkel a "group" consists of members of a local order of practice: those who are bound by a commitment to constitutive trust relations—for the moment—with regard to a particular constitutive practice. This is a completely different notion of trust and of group than the usual. This idea of groups has nothing to do with trusting *people,* or even with collections of people, but rather with trusting the commitment and competence of participants as working members of a practice: as actors who are identified only by their membership in and commitment to a particular local situated order, never as whole demographic persons.[25]

In pursuing this notion of a constitutive and sequential order, Garfinkel formulated a method of working with anomalies. It is the unexpected that brings the "taken for granted" order into view—something that Gestalt psychology had pointed out in the 1930s and 40s. In the absence of the unexpected we produce very complex orders of action without noticing. The anomaly makes us notice.[26] One interesting thing about this insight—which Garfinkel got originally from Aaron Gurwitsch—is that it was already present in information

---

25. Trust does not involve whole persons—but rather what Garfinkel refers to as "identified actors." In any given situation, or practice, an actor inhabits—or enacts—a particular identity. This is not an artificial theoretical way of separating out parts of persons but is rather the way we ordinarily deal with one another. For instance, we might say about a person that he is a drunkard and a cheat—but also that he is the best computer programmer we know and that we trust his work.

26. There may even be aspects of brain function involved in this focus on the new. But, noticing "newness" would nevertheless always occur against a backdrop of "not new" socially patterned recognizability.

theory—but in a different way. For information theorists anomalies were the key to knowledge—the what is new—while for Garfinkel they were the key to locating the constitutive features of local constitutive sequential orders—as a constant against which anomalies appear. But, in both cases, information is to be found through the presence of anomaly.[27]

Because the original connection between Garfinkel and these classic questions has remained unknown, ethnomethodology is generally treated as having no theoretical assumptions of its own, and the attempt has been to ground it in some other theory. Untenable marriages of detailed studies to more formal and conceptual theories abound. Even ethnomethodologists often cite incompatible theories—when they do feel the need to cite theory. But, the study of details cannot be married to traditional theories—based on the idea of norms, habits and/or summary rule orders—without insurmountable contradictions. It cannot be tied to theories that treat formal abstractions as primary organizers of action. The world that such theories assume *is entirely different in every fundamental respect from the one we live in.* It is a fictive world organized by norms, institutional constraint, and activated by individual purposes.

Real people, by contrast, spend their lives in constantly shifting social situations that require the constant achievement of local orders and in each instance require participants to identify with the situation in a particular way in order to achieve that order. Traditional theories don't consider that there is an actual world of achieved order that creates the appearance of a social structure organized by norms and purposes. Against the foundation of this achieved order, and in the absence of anomaly, it is possible to think and act to some extent in terms of norms and purposes. But, it is the achieved order that makes this possible as a "taken for granted" position.

What a theory of social order would have to assume about mutual intelligibility as a process, and about action as constitutive—rather than normative—in order to be compatible with detailed ethnomethodological studies—and how and where those detailed studies fit into the classic theoretical tradition—is the business of Garfinkel's manuscript. It is not only a social theory writ large—but Garfinkel's insight is that social theory finds itself at the heart of the information question and not the reverse. We do not have to teach social science to

---

27. Consider my toaster. When I push the lever on the toaster it does not go down. It keeps popping back up. This anomaly gives me information. I look and see that it is not plugged in. I do not know that this is why it keeps popping up. But the anomaly makes me look, and then I see. It has been designed to produce this anomaly.

engineers—but, rather *learn the sites of social science from engineers*—and yes, take their problems very seriously as social science and social theory.

SECTION TWO: Main Elements of the Theory

Although I have always maintained that Garfinkel's position was deeply theoretical, albeit in empirically grounded ways, it was still something of a surprise to find that he had written such a comprehensive theory of information—and that it remains current after so many years. When I first read the manuscript (Memo #3) I had just finished editing the 1948 manuscript outlining Garfinkel's theory of communication for publication (Garfinkel [1948]2006). I recognized the main argument of that manuscript in Memos #1 and #2 of the Princeton set. But I also realized immediately that this argument went much further—delving deeply into general theoretical questions that thrust Garfinkel's approach to mutual sensemaking to the core of contemporary theoretical issues. The ensuing analysis attempts to pull out several of these issues and their contemporary relevance.

Phenomenology and the Continuity of Objects

The theory of information as a whole offers ways of approaching important current theoretical issues with regard to information, formal organizations, rationality, epistemology, ontology and theories of order and meaning in general that are still new because they have not yet been explored. We seem to be still struggling with the same issues. I was struck particularly in this regard by Garfinkel's reference to phenomenology as the current panacea in 1952: a way of escaping theory into fact. The passage reminded me of a comment one of my colleagues made several years ago after returning from an "Information" conference in Europe. Now again phenomenology was being presented as the "new" solution to the information problem. Garfinkel's comment on page 116[28] could just as easily have been made today:

> Much talk has recently been going the rounds of social scientists about phenomenology. A prevailing accent in this conversation depicts phenomenology as a *new* philosophy of social scientific method. Phenomenology is thereby frequently proposed as a touchstone by which one may get away from theoretical superfluities to the world of actual fact.

28. Page numbers are hereafter enclosed in parentheses.

As scholars grapple with the relevance of detail to the problem of information, intelligibility and the problem of social order generally—it has seemed repeatedly that phenomenology is more "in touch" with details than other approaches. Garfinkel's point could have been that phenomenology was not new in the sense that it dates from Husserl (1933), Hegel (1817) or even Kant (1754). But, this was not his point. Rather, he is arguing that there is a fundamental mistake in this way of thinking that has nothing to do with whether or not it is new. "What is not seen, by and large," he says (116):

> is that the term phenomenology refers only to the *rules* that will be found operating in any perspective—scientific, religious, aesthetic, practical, etc.—whereby certain areas of experience are regarded with a neutral attitude, i.e., are made non-relevant to the problem in hand, while others are accorded the accent of affirmation and just so, i.e., the accent of relevant matters of fact.

In other words, according to Garfinkel, phenomenology is not an approach, whether old or new, that magically puts the researcher in closer touch with their data. Rather, phenomenology is a way of referring to the fact that any intelligible enterprise has rules—or constitutive practices—background assumptions—in and through which its intelligible social order is constituted and recognized by its participant members.

Seen in this way, phenomenology turns out not to be a particular method or approach. Rather, "every philosophy," Garfinkel says (116), "every theory, every attitude toward the world has its relevant phenomenology. Every perspective includes its *rules* on which the irreducible character of data-experiences is based." It is these rules—public and social rules—which the scientist needs to keep in view.[29] These rules are not to be found in the logic of individual experience. Nor are they to be found in abstract theories, the phenomenological approach, or the logic of language. "Every perspective," Garfinkel argues, "provides the rules whereby the difference is made between that which appears with its theoretical sense and that which appears with its sense of a datum, whether it be the theoretic or data sense of the 'outer world' or of the world of 'inner experience.'" And, he maintains (117) that "[t]his holds for the businessman as well as the infant; the scientist as well as the theologian."

---

29. In his early writings Garfinkel consistently referred to the constitutive order features as social things and practices as rules. Debates over the status of rules and the possibility of following them ensued during the 1950s. In response Garfinkel refined his own understanding and began talking about members' methods et cetera. It is still useful, however, to think of Garfinkel as intending a modified form of constitutive rule.

One of the ways of looking at the world that obscures this insight from view is to see it as populated by whole persons. This is a theme Garfinkel elaborated in the 1948 manuscript and returns to repeatedly over the course of his career (1988, 2002). He argues that in any given instance—or situation—we relate to persons not as whole biological beings, but rather as particular identified selves. We never interact with, or as, whole persons, and objects are never seen or apprehended by whole persons—only by identified actors engaged in particular local orders.

When we theorize as if this were not the case, whether we theorize from a phenomenological perspective or some other, we create an unnecessary confusion. In 1948 Garfinkel argued that apparent problems like "role conflict"(that receive a great deal of attention) are in fact the effect of theoretical approaches that focus on the whole person, and not problems in actual situations. In 1952 he will say that the conceptual abstractions involved in information theory lead in a similar way to the creation of false problems. A confusion is created between objects, perceptions and persons. Garfinkel argues (117) that "[o]ne may see this if the terms 'scientist' and 'practical man' are used to designate ways of attending to a world rather than to designate concrete persons." The "scientist," he points out, will see one thing—the "practical man" another. There is no conflict, because the things they see live in different worlds like "apples and oranges" in the old saying. But, the differences in what they see are such as to prevent their talking about the "same" world, which is consequential and must be taken into account.

Those attempting to use phenomenology to address problems of information and social order, according to Garfinkel, generally make this mistake of focusing on the individual whole person, individual perception and individual projects, instead of focusing on the rules or practices, by and through which, perceptions are rendered mutually available. They focus on the actor—the actor's projects and goals and their relation to social "systems" of projects and goals—rather than on the "rules" or "ways" that actors have—their methods for "thingifying" objects that others engaged in the same practice share and which are what enable them to constitute and share a world of objects in common.

Furthermore, they usually do this from the point of view of the scientist, who cannot take the actor's view. Prominent forms of phenomenology, according to Garfinkel, even require a referee—an objective observer—and here he refers in particular to the approaches of Talcott Parsons and Alfred Schutz. The mistake in both of their cases is that there can be no objective observer if all objects are perceived only by identified actors within constitutive ways of looking. "Thus," according to Garfinkel (120, emphasis added):

[T]here is no salvation in this direction. We prefer the view that the actor is left with the light he has; he never has more or less. The important thing and the thing that stands without a standard with which to judge ironically *is that he keeps going.* Thus the nature of his factual knowledge must somehow be accounted for by considering what characteristics of his experience permit this continuity of activity.

Garfinkel turns neatly from the idea that how one looks at something is important—phenomenology—to the idea that the focus of looking must be on what allows continuity of practice—on the fact that people keep going, an approach that requires a participant's view and not an onlooker's, or observer's.

Continuity of Practice versus Objective Standards

This focus on the continuity of practice is central to the argument of the manuscript. The question of just how the actor does manage to go on is extremely important—and remains a hallmark of Garfinkel's approach throughout his later work. Although the positions of Alan Turing and Garfinkel are quite different in most respects, especially insofar as Turing inspired individualist and cognitivist approaches to information that have been heavily criticized by Garfinkel and his followers, this move by Garfinkel to focus on the continuity of practice is broadly analogous to Turing's focus on the computing mathematician in lieu of mathematics in abstraction. The difference between Turing and Garfinkel is essentially that Turing located the doing—the continuity of practice—in the individual "computer" whereas Garfinkel locates it in the shared social order they jointly achieve.

This is at the same time a small difference and a huge one. Turing discovered that a focus on continuity solved huge problems in math—and this was a great breakthrough. By focusing on the continuity of problem solving on the part of a computing individual Turing was able to show that doing a problem in math has a continuity in the doing of it that in abstract mathematical terms appeared impossible. It may not be possible to formulate abstractly "how" or even "that" a problem can be solved in mathematics—but Turing showed that the computing mathematician can nevertheless do the mathematics "step-by-step."[30]

---

30. The difference here, that will lead to their inspiring very different theories of information, is that Turing focuses on the individual whereas Garfinkel focuses on the continuity of shared and mutually coordinated practice. One could argue that mathematics is a shared practice and that Turing's arguments should not have led to individualist and cognitivist approaches. Nevertheless they did.

But, Turing's approach reinforced the idea that continuity was located in the individual and their cognitive structure. Given the complexity of modern information systems this is no longer a helpful approach. Without making the mistake of focusing on the individual and individual cognition, Garfinkel takes up the focus on continuity arguing that while theoretical approaches to the problem of information, communication and social order, that require "objective" standards make continuity seem impossible and ambiguity appear insurmountable, the essential thing is that the person *goes* on—that they *can* go on—that they know *how* to go on—and that there are methods or practices for doing this that are known in common to members of any given practice. Furthermore, since they can go on—and do so publicly—it must be possible to figure out how they are doing this.

Since there *are* no "objective" standards, and yet there is continuity, objective standards must not be necessary—and, therefore, Garfinkel argues, it has been a fundamental mistake to look for them (or to assume them as a requirement). The key to social order—intelligibility—and hence to information, by a process of elimination, must be in the practices with which people are able to go on. It is these which Garfinkel proposes we should study. It is the ways in which persons can go on that explain how they have a world in common with others and how they transform that world into mutually available "things" and objects—oriented objects. This possibility, he argues, can be explained in no other way. Abstract and objective explanations miss the point.

This argument has great practical implications, considering the amount of time, energy, and money being put into designing systems that will allow people to work better and more efficiently. If the designers do not know what makes it possible for the worker to go on—and they usually don't—their improvements will likely remove elements essential to the work (Rawls 2008). Studies by EM show that such improvements often meet with resistance from workers and that when the source of this resistance is defined as the worker's problem in being "backward," tradition bound, or just resistant to change— as it often is—important opportunities are lost (e.g., Luff and Heath 2002). The practical insights into what is required for the continuity of work at high-tech worksites generated by such studies explain why ethnographies of the workplace (aka workplace studies) are becoming an industry standard. Focusing on how people do their work and what they need to get it done is not only important for improving business, it is essential to the problem of order and sensemaking in all situations, including dangerous and crisis situations.

Constitutive Orders—The Social Constitution of Objects

Garfinkel's focus on what people actually do—how they make use of constitutive orders at the worksite to achieve mutual intelligibility, rather than focusing on the logic of words, or formal rules—has a parallel in Wittgenstein's (1945) argument that it was the philosophical approach to language—treating meaning as a matter of words referring to things (the "Augustinian picture theory of language")—that originally and mistakenly made the problem of meaning appear to be unsolvable. It also has a parallel in John Rawls's argument that a focus on summary, or basic rules has been responsible for obscuring the importance and prevalence of constitutive practice with regard to questions of morality and justice.

If we stop thinking that words have meaning through reference to things or ideas and focus instead on the idea of language games in which meaning is achieved through "use," it is Wittgenstein's argument that the apparent impossibility of explaining meaning disappears.

Garfinkel gives his own Wittgensteinian twist to information. For Garfinkel it is not only words but objects that are "thingified" through use. Any referential relationship between the two would need to come after this social process—in each case. "We know the thing information," Garfinkel maintains (113), "through usage. We're looking for the ideas that are immanent to the concept of information in use." The problem has been in treating information, like meaning, in abstraction—as a thing in itself. That approach requires a correspondence—or referential relationship—between individual ideas and social representations that simply doesn't exist. Seen in its context of use, however, as Garfinkel proposes, the issues with regard to information look very different. Use orders are constitutive orders—constitutive of the objects that live in them—and constituted by members of a shared practice.

This involves a constitutive approach to all objects. Objects are always seen in social contexts by identified selves. They are never seen in "objective" contexts by transcendent selves. Therefore, theories of objects and information that depend on the idea of transcendent objects as they would be perceived by such whole transcendental persons are problematic. An object is one thing seen in one context of social practice and quite another seen within a different context of constitutive practice.[31]

---

31. Context is usually taken to mean "perspective," cultural perspective, or even personal perspective. But, it is being used here in Garfinkel's sense—a context of shared constitutive practice, whose members, as participants, are all "using" the same constitutive context—and therefore taking the same "perspective" if we want to use that term.

Objects not so constituted would belong to individuals alone—and it would therefore not be possible to communicate intelligibly, or to share information, about them.

One example of an "object" that lives completely and entirely within a practice might be familiar to readers acquainted with John Rawls's classic paper "Two Concepts of Rules" (1955). There Rawls argues that a runner can only be said to have "stolen second base" if they are playing the game of baseball. They may perform all of the same actions—but if they are not playing baseball they cannot meaningfully be said to have "stolen second." There is another way of "stealing second base," but that way does not live within the game. Rather, it lives in practices that organize our understanding of what it is to take another's property without authorization. One can pick it up and remove it from the field. Without the practice of property ownership, however, this way of "stealing" second is not possible either. These two ways of stealing second are very different social objects—each constituted by a different practice.

The example illustrates what Rawls meant by "constitutive rules" in drawing his classic distinction between summary rules and constitutive rules (incidentally also formulated in the early 1950s—and also while he was teaching at Princeton). There are important similarities between Rawls's distinction and Garfinkel's argument.[32] The distinction between summary rules and constitutive rules differentiates between approaches which treat order as the aggregated result of many decisions by individuals pursuing projects over time—the classic normative approach—and approaches that assume that persons often work within constitutive frameworks to create the order properties and objects which constitute the world in which they live. Rawls expressed concern that most scholars take a summary rule approach—thereby obscuring constitutive rules. He suggested that constitutive practices require more attention than they had heretofore been given.

Baseball is one such constitutive framework of practice—but as Garfinkel has demonstrated—so are ordinary conversations and mundane worksite activities. The big difference between Garfinkel and Rawls is that ordinary conversation and interaction—which rely on implicit and taken-for-granted orders of expectation, rather than on more formal rules of play, turn out to rely even more heavily on constitutive practices for their orderly character than games—which have explicit rules—and are usually treated as having a strategic and rational character. Thus, Garfinkel's argument for the importance

---

32. There will shortly be a special issue of the *Journal of Classical Sociology* devoted to the implications of this distinction between summary rules and constitutive rules for sociology and for the understanding of Garfinkel's position in particular.

of constitutive practice strengthens and lends support to Rawls's supposition that significant social processes depend on constitutive orders.

Implications of Two Kinds of Rules/Orders for Social Science

There is a big difference between a social science which assumes that order is based on constitutive rules/orders and a social science that assumes that orders are the aggregate effect of individual orientations toward norms that can only be formulated as summary rules—or norms—after the fact. The implications of Garfinkel's argument are as serious and promising for social science as Rawls's have been for moral and political philosophy.

Traditional social science generally pictures a whole individual person pursuing a norm or goal, and then measures what happens, and attempts to formulate rules that would predict, or explain, the result. These are referred to as "norms." They are summary rules. No particular instance is expected to display order in its own right—because the idea that the orders could be constitutive has not been considered. It is only in the aggregate and after the fact that summary rules are applied. Garfinkel has argued that, in proceeding in this way, social science has ironically obscured its main object—social order—which, being constitutive, cannot be seen after the fact and cannot be formulated in terms of summary rules.

Rawls argued that because summary rules are retrospective it is a mistake to use them to try to formulate constitutive principles—and that, in doing so, philosophers have obscured essential questions of justice.

Garfinkel has made a similar criticism of social science approaches based on summary rules that measure the "normal curve" of aggregated actions and ignore their underlying constitutive properties. Summary rules can be useful in some cases, for plotting tendencies in the absence of constitutive practice. If you want to know—for instance—about traffic flow to the beach—specifically, when there should be additional officers on duty at intersections—it would be helpful to know that on hot days more people are likely to go to the beach. Measures could be taken, and predictions could be made based on the aggregate data.

However, as Garfinkel has pointed out, most intelligible actions are related to some constitutive practice and thus have intrinsic order properties. For instance, there are other aspects of traffic, such as "traffic waves," that have constitutive characteristics—and which therefore cannot be predicted using summary rules. People slow down because they are required by the constitutive requirements of driving to attend to others while driving—and, in particular, to monitor others' competence and compliance with constitutive expectations. This need for attention can lead to traffic waves on the opposite side of the road, and in lanes that are not otherwise effected by an accident or other traffic "problem." The cliché that people are "ghouls" who enjoy "rubbernecking" is likely the result of taking a summary rule view of a constitutive action. Such patterns have their own constitutive logic—and cannot be explained by physics, individual characteristics, or norms.

That orders of social interaction (interaction orders) have a constitutive character was the point of Garfinkel's famous and much misunderstood "Trust" paper (1963). Because the order properties, and hence the meaning and recognizability of "things," depend on constitutive rules, it is necessary for all participants to understand that they are engaged in the same practice and for all to be competent and able to demonstrate competence in this regard in order for mutually recognizable objects and meanings to be apprehended.

Where expectations of constitutive rules are operative, using a summary rule approach is highly misleading. Summary rules have a strong tendency to render constitutive rules invisible with important consequences for the understanding of human social and moral relations.

Rawls argues that some social behavior is always of the constitutive rule type—although he is not clear how much. Garfinkel expands the scope of the argument maintaining that to a significant extent information and communication, and indeed most social orders, depend heavily on constitutive practices. In this sense, whenever and wherever a social order is constitutive, it is a mistake to treat it as a matter of prediction—or summary rule. The tendency to do so has rendered constitutive orders of practice both theoretically and empirically invisible.

Garfinkel Supports and Extends Classical Theoretical Questions

What Garfinkel offers as a theory of information is consistent with Durkheim's "self-regulating" practices, Rawls's constitutive practices and Wittgenstein's meaning as "use." But it is only in Garfinkel's case that the argument is sufficiently empirically grounded to afford a detailed understanding of how such constitutive practices work. Even in the context of games, it is much more complex than a non-empirical view assumes. Garfinkel treats information as involving constitutive orders that are mutually oriented in concerted ways. They are therefore, shared orders *sui generis*—before they are anything else— and, as such, require being studied as orders and in respect to their sequentially ordered properties—rather than as individual actions, or objects—either singly or in the aggregate.

As a theory of information, Garfinkel's argument provides a way of relating current technical issues and debates to classical arguments—such as Durkheim's claim that differentiated societies would develop self-regulating practices (to replace shared beliefs and values)—and, thus, to the general theoretical questions of modernity and globalization. (See the discussion of the issue in *Enquete* 2007.) For Garfinkel, ultimately, constitutive order = meaning (and oriented objects) and therefore, constitutive orders = information, which is possible only against a background of constitutive expectation.

In a postmodern world of global communities and information transfer, in which people with nothing in common must, nevertheless, use the same technologies and access the same information systems, an approach that focuses on the constitutive practices in and through which such intelligibilities are mutually constructed will become increasingly necessary as a replacement for theories that require shared beliefs and values—or matching cognitive schemas. These no longer exist—they are not only not necessary—but are not possible, or even desirable, in a diverse global community.[33]

Garfinkel has from the beginning been engaged in a deep theoretical/empirical project with implications for the way we see meaning and objects, information and social order, and the moral commitments on which their order and mutual coherence depend.

SECTION THREE: Detailed Analysis of Memo #3

General Sketch of What the Memo Attempts

Garfinkel's memo #3 consists of fifteen major parts—preceded by a short two-paragraph introduction. *Part I* takes up classic information theory, represented by short summaries of five major theories. *Part II* presents a list of properties that information should have. *Part III* considers six questions that Garfinkel says are essential to information. In *Part IV* he discusses what he calls the

---

33. It was Durkheim who first argued that justice requires a transition from belief to practice. When I have made this argument several times people have become very upset and accused me of trying to destroy everything they believe in. It is what Durkheim argued. I think the emotion with which people cling to divisive belief-based systems and theories proves Durkheim's point. (See Rawls 2003, 2007.)

"Object in General"—and in this part he presents an equation for information. I consider this equation to be of particular importance.

The parts from five to eight really function as subsections of *Part IV.* They consider how we are to talk about information—the object—so conceived. *Part V,* with eleven subsections, discusses the "Imbedded Possibility of Experience." *Part VI* consists of a series of definitions of terms. *Part VII* builds from the definition of terms in section six to a working definition of information itself. *Part VIII* then goes on to consider various kinds of information.

Then *part IX* begins a series of parts that consider the factors that condition information. The tenth through thirteenth parts function as subsections of *part IX. Part IX* itself presents the general issue. *Part X* discusses factors that condition information (A)—factors of the order of possibilities, ten factors are discussed. *Part XI* discusses (B) role factors that condition information. *Part XII* considers a third set (C)—factors of communicative work that condition information. *Part XIII* introduces (D)—net-work factors that condition information. This latter is interesting to consider with regard to the later development of network theory.

Part XIV was intended as a summary of the theory—but there is a note to the effect that this part was never written. And, lastly, *Part XV* lists ninety-two problems and theorems that follow from the argument.

Introductory Paragraphs

The first few lines of the memo, refer to something that happened in the prior seminar, the "mischief" as Garfinkel refers to it, that he says the last seminar performed on his definition of information. This mischief occurred during the discussion of his theory of communication (Memo #2)—and apparently prompted Garfinkel to write the third memo in which he focuses directly and at length on the problem of distinguishing information from other things—including communicative meaning—and saying what it is about information that makes it a social thing and not something standing outside of social arrangements.

It is unfortunately not clear from the manuscript how Garfinkel's theory of communication was found wanting by the seminar and from comparisons between memos #1 and #2 and the 1948 manuscript it does not appear that he changed it significantly. What he does do is to elaborate the theory of communication in ways that clarify the relationship between communication, interaction and information. It may simply be that his "definition," as he calls it, of information seemed originally too close to his theory of communication—and that he needed to seriously take on information theory. Thus, his theory of communication remains the same, whereas his theory of information begins to take independent shape. As Memo #3 begins by distinguishing meaning and communication from information, it may have been as simple as that.

The memo then turns in part one to summaries of various theories of information: Claude E. Shannon, Norbert Weiner, E. Deutsch, Bateson and Ruesch, and von Neumann and Morgenstern. Both the choice of persons to consider and the order of presentation are significant.

Part I: Summaries of the Five Information Theories

In this first part, Garfinkel proceeds by presenting an analysis of five information theories, that of Shannon, Miller, Weiner, Deutsch, Bateson and Ruesch, and von Neumann and Morgenstern, in that order. Both the order of presentation and the choice of persons are significant. Several, including Deutsch and Bateson, actually came to Princeton during the project and/or seminar and participants in the seminar were going to hear their presentations. Summaries of these theories would have been chosen, therefore, because their authors were participants, and not only because their ideas were the most relevant. Other theories summarized (von Neumann and Morgenstern) were being worked out at Princeton at the time.

The order of the summaries is also important. While Garfinkel gives only short summaries in the introductory section he notes at the beginning of the summary of Weiner that the critique is cumulative—with Shannon setting up for the rest. He uses Shannon to set up many issues and then develops specific points in the other summaries. Because of this he spends much more time on the summary of Shannon than on the others.

With each summary Garfinkel introduces one or two ideas that he will then add something to with the next. There is a process of refinement and a movement from pure information theory—so to speak—to a more social treatment of information as he proceeds through the summaries, each one adding an aspect of the social, with von Neumann and Morgenstern representing the most thoroughly "organized" or structured treatment of information considered by Garfinkel (albeit a logical or rational structure and not, strictly speaking, a social one—in Garfinkel's sense).

It is important to note that there is no real critique accompanying the presentation of the summaries—which can be confusing. This is typical of Garfinkel's treatment of other authors. It does not mean that Garfinkel accepts everything about the theory being summarized. What he tends to do is pick just what he wants to use and ignore the rest—which he sometimes refers to as a purposeful misreading. The summaries pick out for the seminar what it is about the theory in question that is relevant to the argument that Garfinkel wants to make. Because the discussions build on one another, Garfinkel is essentially borrowing from Shannon to set up the framework and then taking something from each of the subsequent theories. He is not criticizing them. Nor is he accepting their positions. What he does is to introduce some aspect of each position that moves him closer to a social conception of information.

It is probably also the case that students in the seminar had limited familiarity with the information theories in question and that the summaries were also intended as a minimal review, necessary to develop a position that both makes use of and challenges them. It is the selection of one part or parts of each theory that evidences Garfinkel's critical view at this point.

Information and Ordered Contingencies of the Unexpected

Garfinkel opens the discussion of information theory with a consideration of Claude E. Shannon. This is the longest discussion—and a number of points are made before he considers other theories.

Garfinkel points out that Shannon's information theory makes a distinction between information and knowledge—which is important and he will keep it. This is a technical problem—he says—and the distinction is necessary for engineers to deal technically with information.

Shannon also makes a distinction between meaning and information—and Garfinkel will keep this distinction too. Messages do have meaning—but that is irrelevant to the engineering problem.

Another distinction between knowledge, meaning and information that Garfinkel uses Shannon to clarify is that if choices are limited then there is less information. Why? Because information is what is unexpected. It lives in the comparison between what could have happened and what did happen. If what happened is predictable—or constrained—then there is less information.

If we think about the implications of this for the type of society that would be compatible with information—or the type of formal organization (which is one of Garfinkel's chief concerns as an assistant to Moore on the Organizational Behavior Project)—we can see that only a very flexible type of society would be able to gear itself around information—that is, around the unexpected. The information society needs to be one in which the unexpected becomes the center of order—the unexpected is an essential constitutive aspect of that order—and the ordering of society must be geared toward both managing and benefiting from the unexpected.

This is very unlike—almost the opposite—of the way society is usually modeled theoretically. Garfinkel is concerned about this lack of fit between popular, or conventional, theoretical models and the actual conditions for information. The crisis that occurred in modern social theory as contingencies multiplied is predicted by Garfinkel's approach. He argues that understanding information requires a very different way of thinking about the society that can support the required contingencies.[34] The information society, by contrast with traditional belief based societies, must be an open one in that the contingencies of information—anomalies—provide the center of its order, rather than a consistent set of shared beliefs. Therefore, it cannot be modeled in generalities. Theories that try to do so will fall into paradoxes—as postmodernism demonstrated. Constancy in an information society should only be found in the details of ordered contingencies.

Not only are generalities in theoretical models of order a problem, but, the way information theorists treat contingencies is also a problem. Contingencies are not elements of disorder, or chaos, but should be seen as contributing to order. According to Garfinkel the business of managing the unexpected does not work the way the information theorists think—just by contingencies driving things. What has to happen—he will argue—is that constitutive orders (social orders of practice) must be able to provide a stable constitutive framework for keeping people focused in the way they must be on both ordered contingencies and on anomalies, in order to be able to make something mutually intelligible out of an increasingly unpredictable order. It is not just chaos, Garfinkel argues. It is an ordered set of constitutive practices—an order of "use"—that provides an order against which contingencies and anomalies can be meaningfully perceived and managed.

I would also make the historical point that as contingencies increase—a form of order develops that thrives on contingencies—but is at the same time a device whereby people can reduce those contingencies to order—moment by moment—by working together—using a shared practice to do it. This was the essence of Durkheim's argument in *The Division of Labor* (1893), although it has not been read that way (Rawls 2001, 2007). Popular theories that portray modern society as a "risk" society—focusing on the unpredictability of modern society (and not just on the increase in environmental and physical risks)

---

34. In traditional societies the unexpected is always a problem and requires being neutralized and brought under the scope of traditional beliefs and practices.

do not take this possibility into account. They see uncertainty as something people have to accept—not as a resource for creating certainty. By contrast, Garfinkel treats contingency as a resource out of which stability and solidarity can be created.

Information Is Situated

Garfinkel notes Shannon's reference to the "situation as a whole"—and not the message—as being what information is. This is where the models come from—and how models of social order and game theory come to frame the problem of information. It is not possible to address the issue of information without involving social order. Information is what is unexpected against a background of the expected—and the expected has inevitable social contours. Theorists try to model the expected—so as to create a framework within which the unexpected can be recognized—and they usually create abstract models that posit qualities of perfection and reason that real people engaged in situated action never have.

The irony here, that Garfinkel is trying to point out—is that what the theorists are trying to figure out how to do—people working together in situated interactions have already done. Therefore, he argues, the "real" answers to the engineering question can best be gotten from a study of those constitutive orders that naturally develop to manage and order contingencies. Abstract models do not help. What they do is obscure the contingencies that should be the focus. What is required, Garfinkel argues, is an approach that preserves those order properties of contingencies that constitute order in highly technical circumstances of work and information. Because models by definition lose these contingencies, they prevent their examination.

Not just formal structural models, but any rationalized models of action—even individual rational models such as game theory presupposes—will obscure the necessary contingencies—a point Garfinkel will emphasize in discussing von Neumann and Morgenstern. Furthermore, using overly mathematical models that don't take constitutive orders into account has obscured the importance of things like redundancy. This problem he begins to develop in his discussion of Shannon, and it will run through the others.

Redundancy

The problem of redundancy comes up first on pages 2–3 in connection with Shannon's discussion of entropy. The idea is that information that is repeated is redundant and therefore not information. Because, if it is already known, it would be like knowledge and not information, and there is no information in what is already known. Information is something that is different, unexpected. It is the anomaly. That is what makes it information.[35]

If limiting choices limits information—because information is what is unexpected—then maximizing information also requires freedom of choice in addition to a lack of redundancy.

The way the engineers see the problem is that they need to make the system more "free" so that information does not have to be repeated. In other words—insofar as grammar requires people to repeat bits of information to complete a sentence—people are not free to convey information. Grammar increases the predictability of language (which is the point of grammar) but, in doing so, decreases information. Because what cannot be otherwise is not information. Only the unexpected—somewhat free—can be information—the freer it is the higher the information content.[36]

But, as Garfinkel points out (and elaborates later, as well as in the two earlier memos), things that are repeated are not necessarily redundant. This is because of an essential *indexicality* of terms. The "same" words can mean very different things in different sequential positions. Sequential positioning is an essential part of any message—anything can mean anything—he says, depending on where it is placed. Furthermore, because repeating is itself a necessary part of many social relationships and signifies things about the relationship between participants (e.g., an army private saying "yes sir" each next time), repeating always says something new (i.e., we *still* stand in the same relationship). Garfinkel describes subordinates being required to repeat—and their doing, or not doing so, being information for their supervisors—each next time. He also describes superiors being required to repeat, and here it is an issue of both clarification and power.[37]

Thus, while the engineer's objective has—from the beginning—been to streamline language, making it both more logical and more free (less redundant), if Garfinkel is right, it is the indexicality of language, and the subsequent requirement that actors mutually orient toward sequentially ordering speech in order to get the sense of indexical talk, that conveys information and makes communication possible. If we assume that information works something like

35. This ties back into Garfinkel's argument that anomalies are what allows us to get a glimpse of the order in things. The order is carefully made—but the work of ordering is—must be—invisible and taken for granted. The occurrence of anomalies makes the work visible.

36. It has been my argument that grammar has simplified into a sort of creole as cultures have diversified and sequential orders have taken over in the development of modern languages.

37. There are echoes in this discussion of the repeat/repair discussions that Sacks and Schegloff develop later in which a repeat conveys critical information.

language—as information theorists do—then treating communication as an exchange of logically ordered non-contingent symbols—their approach—really leads to less freedom and hence *less information*. Garfinkel's approach to language as ordered sequences of indexicals introduces possibilities and freedoms that traditional theories of language eliminate. This is one of many instances where Garfinkel's later work with Harvey Sacks on language—and the subsequent development of CA—is a natural outgrowth of his theories of communication and information.

On these pages Garfinkel also begins to develop his criticism of theories of formal organization that want to improve the flexibility and information capacity of organizations by using a formal "top-down" model. Such formal social/organizational models, he points out, have the same weakness that theories that treat language as a formal and logical symbol system have. These theories can succeed only insofar as formal organizations are actually organized in the way the model supposes. In other words, designing a social system to be better able to handle information requires understanding how social systems actually do handle information—which in turn requires understanding the interrelationship (or interdependency) between information and social orders (ordered social practices).

Models of formal top-down organization are also at odds with the idea of maximizing uncertainty. Unless there is uncertainty there is no information. Information is highest when the probabilities of all outcomes are equal. That is, no outcome can be expected and anything is as possible as anything else. Then anything that happens next—compared to all the things that were equally likely to have happened—gives the greatest total amount of information. Formal models of order do not allow for this.

This brings to mind another aspect of Durkheim's argument that self-regulating practices will necessarily develop in modern situations in which contingencies have multiplied (1893, Book III, Chapter One).[38] In addition to arguing that self-regulating practices will not work if they are regulated or predetermined, he says that there must also be an equal opportunity to participate, or the social order cannot self-regulate (1893, Book III, Chapter Two). This suggests the argument that in a social situation (or society) in which

---

38. Durkheim's argument in this regard is much misunderstood. The rendition of the argument that has dominated the past half-century is well represented by Wilbert Moore's discussion of what he calls "Durkheim's Dilemma" (1951: 638–39). The idea is that Durkheim argued that modern societies are only viable when a context of shared belief remains strong. This is in fact the position that he criticized—and the opposite of what he argued. How this became the accepted version of Durkheim is a problem that I am currently working on. Nevertheless,

rights to participate are pre-allocated and what people can say on any given occasion is highly constrained—the possibilities for information are also lower (as are the possibilities for change and "progress"). It also suggests that formal "top-down" organizations will inhibit change (an argument that Durkheim was making—but which has been interpreted as its own opposite).

To sustain an environment in which information is a high probability—or has a high probability of occurring—Shannon maintains that the probability of all messages must be equal. But, if we take Garfinkel's point that the "same" message is actually different messages at different points in the order—then redundancy of grammatical forms is not the problem it was thought to be. Message recognition, however, *is* a problem. Because now the "same" message is not the "same" message. Disambiguating messages, in Garfinkel's view, requires complex sequentially ordering—not formal logical ordering.

It is easy to see why logical symbol systems would be preferred: They are theoretically much neater. But, they involve a referential theory of meaning or signification and a top-down model of order and organization—that does not hold up—and which actual communication does not depend on. Furthermore, formal logical orders—the very things to which information theorists have turned to solve their problems—constrain possibilities in ways that also reduce information and prohibit change.

Information Requires Equality of Probability

Garfinkel continues this thread of argument through his discussion of G. A. Miller. The amount of information is directly related to the number of possibilities. The information is lower when the number of possibilities is lower, because the information comes not from what is done—but from a comparison of what is done with what could have been done.

Engineers see it mathematically as having to do with equal probability of messages (without seeing the ambiguity of "same" message—or the problems

---

it needs to be pointed out that what Durkheim did argue is that it would become impossible to maintain shared beliefs in a society in which people from different backgrounds were able to move around freely and communicate. Such freedom was an ideal for a modern industrial society according to Durkheim (Book III, Chapter Two) therefore, it was necessary for a new form of order to develop. This, he said, would be a form of order based on self-regulating practices. He used scientific bench practices as his primary example. Treating self-regulation as if it applied to beliefs and norms has given the contemporary forms of functionalism that modeled themselves on the false interpretation of Durkheim a conservatism that Durkheim's own functionalism did not have. A self-regulating system of practice that is completely and entirely separate from belief is not conservative—and it is a lot like Garfinkel's argument with regard to the self-regulating aspects of members' methods.

with the idea of reference). Therefore, any "messages" that reoccur because of the statistical regularities required by language are treated as unfree, or unequal, and therefore as reducing the probability of information.

Garfinkel's point, by contrast, is that since the "same" message (sign) at different sequential points, is really a different message—and different messages can actually be the same—this kind of redundancy does not reduce the equality of probabilities and, therefore, does not reduce the possibility of information.

What is required is a way of telling whether and when the "same" message is really the "same" message.

There must be limits to the number of possibilities—because too many possibilities cannot be processed. But reducing the possibilities for each next turn or utterance limits information. Sets of priorities, or preferences that are sensitive to basic interactional imperatives, are more flexible and can unfold in many ways.[39]

If an answer is preferred after a question, then the probabilities are limited. But, the possibilities are not limited. An answer does not have to be given. And, there is information in anything said that is not preferred. If what comes next is not an answer, then that in itself is information. This is essentially how CA analysis works: looking for the regularities against which "missing" items have significance. Looking for the "work" that orders of preference—and violating them—can be doing.[40]

Orders of preference limit probabilities to a manageable level. Without some limiting of probabilities nothing can be expected—nothing can be an anomaly—nothing can be understood—and there can be no information. Unless there is some order of expectation there is no information, because if everything is equally probable there can be no anomaly. Having an anomaly requires that something that is expected does not occur. That is why anomalies prove there are orders. What information theory requires for maximum information is the optimum balance between freedom and an order of expectation.

Having a system of priorities with regard to sequences of talk does not over-determine the system of speech. Whenever more possibilities are needed

---

39. This is probably one of the reasons that Garfinkel worries about the prevalence of an overly formal use of CA. If it is treated as a formal order it loses the ability to capture the endless reordering of contingencies that actually makes up the constitutive order of daily work.

40. The "Turntaking" paper (Sacks, Schegloff, and Jefferson 1974) is a good source for a discussion of preference orders—as are also Sacks's lectures (1996).

in order to exploit some larger need for "information" people use deviations from the priorities—or create new priorities altogether and thus create more information. Even ambiguity can be information, because the receiver does not have to be able to process the message for the difference between it and what could have been said to be calculated. Preferences for repair work on this principle: In other words, ambiguities can be offered as occasions for repair (Schegloff).

Putting more information on a computer chip, by contrast, or increasing its capacity, means increasing the number of places that the encoder can discriminate between. Information is just the difference between positions. So, increasing the number of possible positions increases the capacity for information (storing).

While this may be true for storing information on computer chips, I think Garfinkel will be saying that it won't work as a theory of communication—where the *way* in which messages are discriminated between must also be attended to (and where endless multiplication of non-redundant possibilities is not a good thing—indexicals working much more efficiently), and, finally, where *what* makes something an anomaly is essential to the constitutive order of the system.

The Regularity and Irregularity of Patterns

At the beginning of his discussion of Norbert Weiner, Garfinkel notes that there is a direction to the summaries—moving from the notion of information as relevant to engineering through its application to the problem of human communication.

Weiner's contribution—as Garfinkel treats it—has to do with the fact that the regularity and irregularity of a pattern—which has an obvious social dimension—is necessary for an intelligent discussion of randomness—of something like "noise." Garfinkel (107) argues that information thus must be in some way the measure of the regularity of a pattern. Therefore, there must be some pattern. This relates directly to Garfinkel's argument that meaning not only requires order—but that it *is* order. But, information—as opposed to meaning—is an *improbable quality* of order. Nevertheless, nothing can be improbable without order as a background—so redundancy is also required.

In other words, randomness doesn't even make sense as an idea without regularity. Garfinkel has many times over the years offered the example of "leaf blowers" in his Southern California neighborhood to illustrate the argument that noise is a social object that cannot be measured with machinery.

That is, the regularity of the noise pattern is constituted largely by the social background against which it is heard. When citizens complain about the noise, town officials can't measure the irritation level of the noise in decibels to the satisfaction of the citizenry. This is because a leaf blower on a Sunday morning is noise heard against a background of Sunday morning silence— something "heard" that cannot be measured in decibels. A leaf blower heard at noon on a weekday sounds very different against the background of weekday noise. But, town officials try to measure it with the same instrument in order to determine whether or not the person using the leaf blower is making too much noise (violating a local noise ordinance), which does not measure what people are hearing.[41]

Information Is Relationships Not Things

Garfinkel builds on this idea in considering the work of E. Deutsch, beginning to develop the idea that information does not transmit events—but a patterned relationship between events. The "thing" is not the information. Information is the relationship between the thing and other possibilities. This also necessarily invokes a more social approach because relationships are *between* things. They are not actual things. Therefore, they are either interactive or conceptual; socially patterned relationships between events.

The social is exactly what information is on this account. Furthermore, social "things" exist as things only in and through their relationship to a whole fabric of social relationships in and through which they are constituted—just like information. Something must remain constant across these events that are not the thing—but still somehow information about the thing. The constant is the pattern. This is another way that the social begins to get into information theory—in addition to theories of language.

In contrasting the new information sciences with the 19th century conservation sciences—in the discussion of Deutsch on page six—could Garfinkel have in mind something like the difference between modern communication (as a self-regulating constitutive order) and symbolic communication systems?

---

41. I suspect something like this may be going on when people complain about cell phones in restaurants as well. They have no problem listening to—or rather tuning out—the conversations of diners at other tables. But, a person on a cell phone, even when they are careful to speak quietly, may be harder to tune out because their words cannot be heard against the background of a conversation—the other half is missing—creating an anomaly to which persons have difficulty disattending—and are therefore bothered by.

A symbolic communication system would conserve and preprogram, rather than being free. Meaning in such a system would be less a patterned relationship between parts and more something assigned to each next symbol in a way that remains constant: an allegorical, metaphorical, and semantic system. As such it would be static and limit possibilities.

In a communication system that increases the possibilities for information there would still be symbols—but they would less and less carry meaning in the old static/symbolic way and would more and more be used as indexicals. That is, they would increasingly be placed sequentially in ways such that meaning is increasingly a function of placement, and of the relationship between words as membership categorization devices and utterances as turns, rather than symbolism. This would mean that words are in this way more and more getting their meaning from the contrast between just how they are used on any next occasion and the ways they could have been used (consistent with information theory)—and the patterned order between those uses and possible uses, and the uses and possible uses of the other bits (gestures, pauses, timing, etc.) that order a given conversational sequence (Rawls 2004).

Language—information—and the order of the society in which symbols are related—is no longer either mechanical or ideal—in Durkheim's sense. It has become a self-regulating order of constitutive practice. It is the relationship, not the symbols per se, that carry meaning and information.

Perceiver and World Simultaneously Constituted

Garfinkel notes that Bateson and Ruesch move even farther into a social domain. In their view the perceiver and the world are simultaneously constituted. Information, according to their theoretical perspective, only exists as and when perceived against a background of patterned expectations by a perceiver.

The perceiver is equally constituted at the point of experience by the experiences and the patterns that organize them. On this view there is no transcendental observer and no transcendent object.

This seems quite close to Garfinkel's own position on embodied action which also insists on imbedding both object and perceiver in developing sequential orders on which their existence as such depends: an argument that Garfinkel will pick up again in discussing "oriented actors" and in the section on "imbedded objects."

The difference is that in treating words and logical relations between words—even imbedded in social contexts of action—as the basic apparatus of the meaning system—Bateson and Ruesch become encumbered with limitations that adhere to semantic systems, but are not a problem for a reflexively and sequentially constituted relationship between indexicals.

Game Theory and the Rational Individual

While the first four theories all posit an individual signal sender and receiver and in that sense—like game theory—take an inherently individual approach to the social, they do not require the actor to be completely rational.

The irony is that while von Neumann and Morgenstern take another step *toward* the social—conceiving of the patterns that make information distinguishable, as rules in an elaborate game—at the same time their approach depends on a rational model of the actor and social situation that are impossible in actuality: a step *away* from the social. In order for the actor to keep track of what is expected and what is not—and to compare the possibilities for what could happen with what does happen in the way that game theory requires—Garfinkel points out that the actor would need to have both perfect reason and perfect information.

Garfinkel is very critical of this requirement, drawing an analogy between his consideration of information and his consideration of game theory. For a player in their model, he says (109) information "is tantamount to the total state of the game …" Here the requirement, developing over the course of the earlier theories, that social order be taken into account in any consideration of information, becomes in the hands of von Neumann and Morgenstern the requirement that each individual player have perfect knowledge of the total state of the game, a condition that is not only impossible, but which limits information.

On the one hand, game theory appears to constitute a thoroughly social way of approaching the problem of information. And, as a consequence, the work of von Neumann and Morgenstern on game theory has been very influential and often treated as a model for a social theory of rational choice.

But, as Garfinkel will point out, game theory and rational choice do not describe a workable social order; in fact, they model social order in impossible and limiting ways. As it became clear that information had a social dimension—instead of turning to the social to see how information was actually handled—theorists, ironically, tried increasingly to deal with it in terms of rational and mathematical models. This trend continues.

The criticisms of game theory and the model of the rational actor that Garfinkel begins in this manuscript continue for years. They inhabit the argument of his "Trust" paper (several versions of which were written between 1954 and 1963) and motivate many years of experiments with games and their background expectancies. It is Garfinkel's point that game theory makes assumptions about the individual actor, and the organization of society, that are completely at odds with what actually occurs.

Because in the "Trust" paper, and in his studies of games, Garfinkel felt so strongly that he was offering an important alternative to game theory—that game theory was fundamentally wrong—he was very unhappy to have his arguments about constitutive practices treated as game theory—and his constitutive rules treated as formal rules, which they were by many people. For years Garfinkel gave lectures on rules and eventually stopped using the word, in the hope that he could correct this misperception. Unhappily, the misperception persists along with many others.

For Garfinkel the challenge is to specify how real people—who never have perfect information—and who are never perfectly rational—make mutually intelligible sense. Clearly people are capable of handling enormous quantities of information. But, they do so in ways that are never much like the models.

Garfinkel argues that the focus should be on what people need to achieve in interaction in order to create and maintain patterned orders against which information can be discriminated. The needs for social bonding, attention and so on, that actors have, make demands on the actual constitutive orders that develop. The constitutive orders people use will need to fulfill these social needs while also providing ways of discriminating between messages sequentially, and in other social ways—such that what the engineers treat as the "same" message—and therefore as redundant—is actually not redundant and also carries information.

Part II: Some Desired Properties of the Thing Called "Information"

In the second part of Memo #3 Garfinkel lists various characteristics that "the thing called 'information'" should exhibit. This list is really a prelude to the discussion of six theoretical questions in part III—and is given a fuller explanation there. It also serves as something of an outline for the remaining parts of the manuscript. Nevertheless, the list is never specifically addressed. Given the seminar context, the list may have functioned as a set of talking points and been given verbal elaboration.

When I first saw the list I read it as a fantasy catalogue of ideal characteristics—and also as something of a tongue-in-cheek nod to various conventional requirements. But, after working on the manuscript for some time and discussing it with students in my own seminar,[42] I realized that if information as it is defined in theory is to work in the ways that information actually works in practice, it would indeed need to have all of these characteristics—however impossible that might seem. In fact, I now believe that is Garfinkel's overall position and why and how he believes that sociology can be a science.

The idea is that in everyday interaction people have access to something that has all of these properties. If a theory of information is to be adequate, it must at least be capable of what ordinary people can do in everyday life. And, it will only be adequate in the ordinary way if it works in just the same way.

The way I now understand this part—Garfinkel is listing the characteristics information actually has in everyday human practice. It seems like an ideal list because according to formal models people should not be able to do all of these things—but they can. If a theory of information is to be useful for engineers and the purveyors, exchangers, and managers of information—and also measure up to what ordinary people can already do—then it would have to have *at least these characteristics*. The job is to discover how ordinary people do this and then build a theory of information on the characteristics of the actual practice.

This insistence also helps to clarify the ways in which Garfinkel is not a theorist. He is not a theorist because formalizing anything theoretically and moving away from everyday life loses capacities that people actually have. At the same time, unlike most formal theorists, he believes that these things can be really done—and that a sufficiently empirically based "theory" of information—that does not abstract from—or formalize—the way things actually work—will be capable of explaining how.

The first characteristic Garfinkel requires of "the thing called 'information'" is that it be actual and physical—rather than merely conceptual. This accords with his emphasis on the empirical as a grounding for theory—rather than conceptual abstraction. Not only should information be physical, but it should be "capable of spatial and temporal patterning." It needs to be physically transmissible from one place to another—and remain invariant across variations of signaling. It must be measurable—or have an amount. But, it also needs to be amenable to sequential ordering.

In addition to these various empirical—or physical—characteristics, information must be capable of having varying degrees of certainty—of being

42. I would like to thank those students in my spring 2006 senior seminar for taking the time to read and discuss this difficult document, with particular indebtedness to Kyle Bedell and Jessica Larsen.

doubted. This again distinguishes information from conceptual abstractions—which just are. Concepts remain the same, they don't change—and remain certain if they were certain—or uncertain if they were not.

Because information involves signals, words, messages, and so on, and can be doubted—it is different from—and yet necessarily stands in some relationship with other symbol systems. Therefore, Garfinkel requires of "the thing we call 'information'" that it "stand in some clear and determinate relationship with notions of signal, message, error.... " And, this in turn requires information to stand in some clear relationship with a theory of communication—which is where he started in Memos #1 and #2.

The contemporary interest in information—motivated to begin with by war strategy and later by profit interests—required it to be something that could be owned and managed. Otherwise, possession of it would be no advantage. Therefore, information must be something that can be stored, owned, lost, and found. It must be capable of being priced. It must be transformable—and possible to speak of as differentially distributed across a population. If everybody has it—then it is not new—not information. It must also be possible to speak of it as having a private or a public, or an anonymous, or an identified character, and so on.

Several of the characteristics Garfinkel lists relate to completeness of information. And, I think here he is being sensitive to a fundamental contradiction in the conventional theories of information. A rational actor with complete information is assumed—and yet information is the unknown—the new—the anomaly. In actual practice, actors never have complete information—and yet are capable of handling and recognizing information. In order to overcome this contradiction, information must be capable of being incomplete, or lost, or changed. It must be capable of being either clear or ambiguous. With regard to Garfinkel's critique of game theory, it must be possible to "permit the category of ignorance" into the conception of information without limiting the information.

The idea that information can be lost is an important one. Garfinkel will argue, in this and other manuscripts, that most theories proceed in a circular fashion. They define the situation in such a way that they cannot lose their phenomenon and therefore also cannot help but find that they were right. According to Garfinkel, this sort of tautology characterizes most of what goes by the name of science and makes it impossible to "discover" anything. Garfinkel, by contrast, emphasizes the idea that a discovering science must be able to "lose" its phenomena. Unless a "science" can lose its phenomena, it is a tautology. (See Garfinkel 2002, chapter nine.)

So, in order for a theory of information to be adequate, to be a real science, dealing with an actual thing—information—it must be the case that information can be lost. It is the instances of losing it that prove that it is "really" there—so to speak—that it is not a tautology—just information by definition.

In order for anything to be intelligible to more than one person, in Garfinkel's view, it must display an order—and that order must be social—and created by those actors who are engaged in a situation together and committed to a shared practice. There must be stable and shared background expectations in order for an order to be achieved and displayed. But participants must be able to alter those expectations—to change the rules, so to speak—or make up new ones to fit new situations or contingencies. Later, Garfinkel will refer to this as "ad hocing." It solves the problem of the incompleteness of rules and also increases equality of probability. There are always tacit assumptions—but the ability to make up new ones as needed—increases flexibility.

Ordinary persons must also be able to acquire information in ordinary situations. And, they must be able to acquire it even if they do not come close to the model of the rational man—because they never do.

At two extremes, information must be capable of randomness, in the middle of being somewhat predictable, or at the other extreme of "being so completely determined as to have the quality of certainty." In other words, certainty is not a necessary characteristic of information any more than completeness is. Information can be uncertain; it must be capable of being "free" and of being doubted.

Finally, it must be possible to treat information independently of the perceiver, but, also for its objective status to require information about the perceiver. This last is one of the most controversial features of the argument that information is inherently social—and, at the same time, one of the most important. It is often mistaken for a "subjective" argument. It is not. It *specifies the conditions for objectivity in terms of a relationship between actor and object in a context of practice.* The actor's viewpoint is not "subjective," nor is their perspective independent from practice. Every participant in a practice—in being oriented to the practice—is an identified actor. Their viewpoint is therefore a public and social viewpoint.

There is no information without an order generated by actors orienting toward rules—or constitutive practices—that they use to produce that order. Information can only be perceived against such orders. On the other hand, information is not just created by the human perceiver, not just emergent as some argue. Practices have histories, and changes occur in the stable context of those histories. It is the ability of human communicators to make common intelligible sense of what is there—to use shared practices for doing this, and to see anomalies against a background of order—that constitutes the social.

But, there is also something concrete "out there" that resists human construction. The physical features of information—or anomaly—are in some sense independent of how they are perceived—even though they can only be experienced *as* perceived and against a background of expectations. While objects may be concrete, however, it is social patterning that gives things and information meaningful and public form.

Part III: Conditions within Which a Definition of Information Will Be Sought: Six Basic Questions

Following the list of features information should have, Garfinkel opens his argument by considering six questions that he argues must be considered by any theory of order/information/meaning. While he has differentiated meaning from information (in the summaries of information theory)—both depend on order. Therefore, the sociological questions of order are the same. Not only are the sociological questions the same—but because it is the actual order practices in contingent details that need to be known these questions cannot be passed off onto philosophy—where they would be handled in abstraction. The order questions are essentially sociological questions that can only be answered with the details of social orders of constitutive practices.

These fundamental analytic problems Garfinkel elaborates in terms of six questions: 1) the nature of language; 2) the nature of purpose in human action; 3) the nature of the attitude for apprehending the irreducible datum; 4) the nature of rationality; 5) the nature of the object that the actor treats; and 6) the individual as a source of social change.

(1) The Nature of Language

The big question most people ask with regard to the nature of language, according to Garfinkel, is how words are related to things. He says that one can either assume a nominalist or referential theory (correspondence theory), in which the sign is a tag for the thing, or, one can assume that language (the language games, or constitutive practices that constitute it) is constitutive of the objects that it designates (coherence theory). Garfinkel chooses the latter.

After discarding referential theories—in discussing his constitutive theory of language, Garfinkel introduces the idea of language as action: "Another solution," he says (114), "and the one we prefer is that of regarding language as constitutive of the objects it designates. Thus we prefer not to make a separation between linguistic functions and action, but rather will hold that linguistic functions are actions."[43]

Treating linguistic functions as actions opens them to sociological analysis in original ways. Also, although he makes no explicit allusion to Wittgenstein, Garfinkel makes a parallel move when at the beginning of part III he says (113) that we know the thing information through "use" and will search for whatever "it" is he says—through "use." We are—he says—"looking for the ideas that are immanent to the concept of information in use." According to Garfinkel "the ground rules for the search" involve decisions on the six questions.

Garfinkel then describes the ways in which the kind of sociology he proposes fits into this idea of language—and the communicant—and the communicative net—as constituting the objects it designates. As he says (114), "we are faced with the problem of the multitude of ways in which language 'thingifies' various possibilities of experience. ... "

Language, in this sense, would have to do with information because it has to do with (1) objects, which are thingified through language (and constitutive of social orders); and (2) anomalies (a thing being different from itself—or unexpected). Both have to do with the patterns of relationship between "things"; things already being social constructs and the patterns of relationship between them then also being thoroughly social—although they can be described materially and empirically (because they also exist and are not just conceptual relationships—but embodied relationships in space and time).

Given the importance of language to Garfinkel's position, the break between Garfinkel and the development of CA after the death of Harvey Sacks is unfortunate—because CA is in so many ways working out problems and possibilities that Garfinkel discussed—but without his working relationship with Sacks, the connection became unclear. Thus, CA tends to proceed without benefit of the overall implications for a theory of social order, communication, or information—and without the strong connections to EM that only come from a firm grounding in Garfinkel's ideas.

(2) The Nature of Purpose in Human Action

Most theories approach human conduct, or action, as though it has a purposive character—people having a project or goal—and that purpose or goal giving

---

43. The idea of linguistic functions as actions in 1952 is rather original. John Searle will not write the book *Speech Acts* until 1968. Searle worked with Goffman who had read the information manuscript—so it may have had an indirect influence on Searle. Searle had also read J. Rawls 1955 on constitutive roles. The argument also predates J. L. Austin's

form to what they see and hear. These theories usually posit an individual actor and ultimately assume (in a summary rule way) that it is purpose (individual purpose shaped by social norms) that imparts an order to human activity. Purpose, as a theoretical constant, has been refined in various ways. Some influential theories assume that the relationship between means and ends defines action. Sometimes that relation is posited as rational—other times as normative. Action is in this sense irreducibly defined by the relationship between means and ends in which individual purposes, and some version of individual reason and cognition, in conjunction with social norms, play a defining role.

The error in both cases, on Garfinkel's view, is that constitutive practices would be rendered invisible by this approach in instances where they are in fact definitional. Purpose is only measurable in the aggregate.[44] Thus, trends that are the result of local orders of action are treated as organizing and ordering those local orders when they do no such thing.[45] Garfinkel argues that constitutive practices are operational everywhere—even when there are also norms and purposes. If Garfinkel is right about how widespread constitutive practices are—then the problem would effect almost every study that involved social organization in any way.

Finally, Garfinkel proposes that where there *are* purposes at work in social orders—the purposes themselves, and the quality of purpose or non-purpose, still depend on a background of constitutive order. For Garfinkel, even being

---

How to Do Things with Words—although the work was being done at about the same time. Wittgenstein's influence on ordinary language philosophy was strong at Princeton while Garfinkel was there. Norman Malcolm had been there from 1940–42 and had forged a connection between Princeton and Cambridge where Malcolm had studied with Wittengenstein. After the war James Urmson followed Malcolm to Princeton and was visting associate professor in 1950–52. Rogers Albritton, another rising American Wittgensteinian, did his graduate work at Princeton and was a graduate teaching assistant between 1951–54. What influence any of this had on Garfinkel is unknown—but the ideas were in the air so to speak. (See the special issue of *The Journal of Classical Sociology* on the influences of J. Rawls 1955, an EM studies of order.)

44. This is an argument that Garfinkel worked out directly with reference to Parsons in 1988. Part of this argument also appeared in 2002—and is referenced as the "Parsons's Plenum" argument.

45. Constitutive practices generate trends, but those trends cannot be used to enact the practices. For instance, players in the game of baseball generate statistics. Announcers, in analyzing the play endlessly refer to these statistics. Nevertheless, at any moment of the play these statistics cannot be used to generate the constitutive order of the game. If one used the statistics as "norms" and treated the players as geared toward producing just those statistics one would be wrong. The players are geared toward winning, and toward working together as a team in order to do so in the context of the "game." Players like good statistics—but are not playing to generate statistics. The analogy with using demographics as a proxy for social order should be obvious.

able to see goals and means, and to hold them in common so that they can be mutually acted upon, depends on shared practices in and through which means and ends are constituted as intelligible social objects.[46] Therefore, norms do not come either from individual persons and their projects as transcendent, objective and defining matters, or from "society."

Furthermore, if goals and means must be thingified in order to be acted with and upon, then they cannot be what is organizing action in the first place.

(3) The Attitude for Apprehending the Irreducible Datum

Garfinkel argues that no datum is irreducible; all depend on constitutive practices. Apprehending the irreducible datum—the problem of phenomenology—therefore necessarily involves constitutive rules for constituting objects within practices. There are no objects without practices. Faced in a practice with the "actual datum" we have methods for "going on" that put us into a world in common with others who share the practices involved.

Adopting Garfinkel's approach to practices (member's methods) solves certain paradoxes in information and social theory. If one takes a traditional approach that posits an objective observer and irreducible objects, then the observer acts as a referee and the information the receiver can get is limited by the observer. According to Garfinkel (119):

> If one actor sends a message to another, the amount of information that the receiver gets from the message is limited by the observer as a matter of method-ological principle by the extent to which the receiver operates upon the message according to the canons of rational endeavor. Everything he receives and makes sense of outside of this is in the observer's view ignorance, error, or myth.

It seems an obvious point that applying the canons of reason equally to all actions—and ignoring the situated aspects of the engaged actor's interests and competencies—rules out information that belongs to constitutive practices. But other theories have not seen the point—generally treating reason as superior to the contingencies of situated events.

As Garfinkel points out, applying the criteria of reason rules out a great deal and leaves the so-called rational actor looking like a cultural dope.[47] According to Garfinkel (119):

---

46. It could be argued, based on *Economy and Society* ([1921] 1968, pp. 8–20), that Weber was sensitive to these nuances—but he has not generally been interpreted as such.

47. One of the things we see in this memo and in the 1948 manuscript is that "cultural dope" means several things—not just one. It refers to the creation of an empty dummy that must be

To the extent that we subscribe to the Parsonian actor's definition of the situation, known to the observer as we have seen through a neo-Kantian phenomenological attitude, the observer can have information in the world only after he has discounted the actor's situation of action in light of the observer's "wider knowledge" and wiser procedures of information gathering and interpretation.

Garfinkel argues that a focus on actual procedures is required to restore the relationship between information and practice (reason). Such a focus reveals the actor to be accomplished—no longer a cultural dope. New possibilities for information are revealed by examining the actor's orientation toward sequential positioning as they gear into the world.[48]

Furthermore, a focus on member's methods is able to distinguish coherence, where the approach that assumed an irreducible datum and an objective observer found only incompleteness. It is able to reveal information, where the summary rule/normative approach could not find information. Reason is no longer complete information and perfect logic—it is now competence, attention and commitment to sets of shared constitutive practices: all of which increase the possibilities for information.

Because contemporary information systems prefer the most information possible—the approach that increases information and reduces the problem of incompleteness should be preferred. Garfinkel's approach does this.

(4) The Nature of Rationality

Adopting a focus on actual practices changes what rationality can be. It changes from pure reason and complete information to competence to enact particular sets of practices and to be mutually engaged and committed in so doing. According to Garfinkel if the researcher takes a thoroughly empirical approach—focused on constitutive practice—this "radical empiricism cuts [them] off from the use of the rational man as a device for assessing the information that the experiencer has" (119).

---

filled. It references the presumption that reason is the criteria, which leaves a culturally skilled actor looking dopey. It can also mean positing culture in such a way (as norms) that a skilled actor appears to be a dope. Finally, it can mean that it is being culturally and/or normatively oriented that makes an actor appear to be a dope—as over against a purely rational individual. The individual is viewed as the source of error in a logical rational world—rather than as the creator and maintainer of both reason and logic. Assuming that things and meanings have an independent existence makes the work that actors do to create objects and intelligibilities look dopey.

48. Methodological questions are easy to answer. What method is required? One that preserves the nuances of positioning and timing in all of its possible socially relevant aspects.

The "rational man" posited by classic information theories can never be found in the world. Therefore, that model is incompatible with an empirical approach to practices. The ways in which actual actors are rational must be drawn from empirical research and not abstract models.

> [T]he make-up of the rational man *even as a mere construction*—and it can be demonstrated that if we follow Schutz, this is the best we can ever hope for as far as the use of the rational man in our endeavors is concerned—must, if we are to avoid discovering in the world that which we have put there ourselves—must be drawn from our investigations of how men, isolated and yet simultaneously in an odd communion, go about the business of constructing, testing, maintaining, altering, validating, questioning, and defining the orders that in various degrees and in various ways match each other in contents and organization. (119)

Real persons—as oriented actors, selves—have great competence and the ability to reason. What this means is lost by the application of a radical model.

Assuming a rational man, on the other hand, results in creating a model of the actor who is a dummy—and whose own experiences count for nothing. It is the observer (or the model) who decides everything in rational man theory. The observer's reason is always complete, while the actor's reason is always incomplete (because the model requires perfect knowledge of the whole model—which only the observer has).

Focusing on constitutive practices, by contrast, treats the actor as competent and their information as sufficient to any situated action that works. If they were not competent—and their information were not sufficient—then they would not be able to produce mutually intelligible practice. Garfinkel (2002) will later refer to this as "the praxeological validity of instructed action." The actor must be competent to both produce and recognize practices in order to make any mutually intelligible sense. They must be morally competent as well, because they must both trust the competence and commitment of others and be trusted in return: a gift exchange at a highly detailed sophisticated sequential level of interaction.

(5) The Nature of the Object That the Actor Treats

Garfinkel's ([1948]2006) discussion of objects—which he refers to as "oriented objects" is very relevant to the issue of objects—or "bounded objects"—as it has been taken up in the context of current studies of science and information. He will take this question up in several extended sections of the manuscript. Here, he attempts only an initial sketch. Garfinkel poses the question how to "conceive the relationship between the theories we make about concrete objects and the concrete objects" (125).

As he did with language, Garfinkel proposes a distinction between a correspondence theory and a coherence theory of objects. A correspondence theory treats concreteness as a property of the object in the outer world, and requires that a difference be posited between the perceived object and the outer object. Information in the case of a correspondence theory would then require a correspondence between perception and object. It is achieving the required correspondence that will cause problems for this theory.

The actor's interest in the object, and the object's reality—in the context of a correspondence theory—would have nothing to do with each other. What Garfinkel has to say about this (125–26) is close to what Whitehead said in 1929 in his theory of misplaced concreteness.[49] Given a correspondence theory of the object—the object can only be conceptual in Whitehead's sense. The idea that the individual has of the object is treated as belonging to the object in its own right. That the object appears as "real" is, for Whitehead, a quality that the perceiver mistakenly puts into reality. Adherents of the correspondence theory, Garfinkel says, treat it as a "miracle" of sorts that there is a sufficient correspondence between the two sets of objects (idea and reality) to make practical action with things possible—and they do not inquire further into this miracle.

For Garfinkel, on the other hand, this alleged miracle—like the alleged miracle of intelligibility—is exactly what needs to be looked into. Science doesn't allow miracles as explanations—he says, and nor should social science.

On a coherence theory of the object by contrast—which is the one Garfinkel proposes—"concreteness depends on the nature of the scheme of apprehension" (126–27), and not on a correspondence between a perception (or a concept) and an object. Garfinkel's coherence approach respects Whitehead's critique—but moves beyond it. It is no longer concepts—which are either individual or ideal—that give concreteness to reality. Rather, for Garfinkel it is *constitutive schemes*—which are social and shared—that give such concreteness. This makes "reality" a constituted object, but, one which all members of a practice will share equally.

---

49. Whitehead argued that concepts define the limits of objects and make us think of objects as having qualities—including reality—that are in fact only qualities of the concepts that we attribute to them. We perceive objects as real and concrete when really we are not perceiving the object—but only our idea of it.

In the context of this theory the correspondence between objects and theories, or ideas, must be created and managed by actors together in shared, mutually oriented ways. In actual practice this process is taken for granted, but as a matter of theory and research it should not be taken for granted. This approach solves the problem of the relationship between objects and perception. According to Garfinkel (128) "The leading premise of the 'coherence' theory of reality is that the perceived object of the 'outer world' is the concrete object, and that the two terms mean precisely the same thing." Since they are mutually constituted, their relationship is not a problem. Rather, what remains to be explained is how this is done. The object perceived according to a shared practice, according to Garfinkel (128, emphasis added), is the real object: "Rather than there being a world of real objects cut this way and that, the cake *is constituted in the very act of cutting.* No cutting, no cake, there being no reality that is approximated since the world is just as it appears; there is nothing behind it."

Given a coherence theory of reality, it is a mistake to take the idealist position that concepts are the limit of reality—the limit of what can be known. In the context of a coherence theory the limit of reality lies in the shared practices in and through which participants mutually constitute the taken-for-granted reality of things: or, "cut the cake," as Garfinkel puts it. Given that mutually enacting shared practices constitutes a visible/hearable social process—that must be seen and heard by participants in order to work—it can also be seen and heard by researchers. Consequently, as I have argued (Rawls 2002), treating concepts and not practices as the limit of reality constitutes a fallacy in the other direction, a fallacy of misplaced abstraction. This fallacy is consequential, as it prevents the sort of research on practices that would reveal just those sequential orders of practice that Garfinkel (128) argues are at the core of all mutual coherence.

> The nature of the observed event as well as the relevance of the event to others (found in statements of fact) is possible through the operation of a set of related standards, these standards being the things that provide the categories of reality and irreality, of relevance and irrelevance, of actuality and fantasy.

In Garfinkel's view it is only in and through their imbedding in achieved social orders of practice that objects and information come to have concreteness and relevance. "*The schema of specifications in fact is precisely the object itself,*" he says (128).

Thus, "we are left," according to Garfinkel (130), "with two large consequences for addressing the task of describing a communicant's information:

(1) each world has an order of information peculiar to it; and (2) the order of information is a function of the mode of attending to it." The earlier leaf-blower example would do as an illustration here as well.

(6) The Individual as a Source of Social Change

Garfinkel has often been accused of being conservative—the presumption being that because he focuses on describing things as they are—his approach has nothing to say about change—the way things should or could be. In this section Garfinkel makes the point that other theories of information, which focus on the individual, or on semantic meaning, end up having a problem explaining change. If perfect information or total conformity is necessary—as those theories assume—then where is change going to come from? What is needed, Garfinkel argues, is a theory of the individual as a situated participant in situated interaction. This, he argues, is the only way of adequately providing for change.

In 1952 there is no adequate theory or model of the individual as a situated actor working within the constraints of constitutive rules to render the reality of objects, situations, meanings and selves. Yet, only on the basis of an interactional model of self and communication—he argues—can change be explained. Although I would maintain that no adequate model yet exists, the work of Garfinkel, Goffman and Sacks has brought us much closer to what is required.

It is Garfinkel's argument that it is only by focusing on the person as an oriented actor and not as an individual, and only by focusing on shared practices, which he will refer to later in the memo as the "e" operator (134–35), that the problem of where change comes from can be adequately addressed. This challenges both the conventional interpretation of Garfinkel's position as "micro," or individualistic, and the conventional assumption that Garfinkel's approach cannot explain change.

"Micro" sociology has been characterized as a focus on the individual and individual action—instead of on the "more" important social institutions that are assumed to organize social life. However, Garfinkel's emphasis on practice, schema, and mode of attention does not, as many critics have argued, mean that he focuses on individual modes of attention. He is not looking at individual action—he never has done—and he does not accept the premise that institutions are the primary organizer of social life.

In Garfinkel's view, insofar as the individual is acting as a social being they must be acting within a constitutive framework of practices that are shared by a set of members—participants—in a situated action. The identity of oriented actors in any given situation is given by those practices (batter, speaker, rude, embarrassed, competent, etc.) and not by their own personal characteristics—or generic institutional positions.

Goffman, who also worked out important aspects of the idea of an interactive self, is known to have read this manuscript, and he and Garfinkel discussed this issue often during the early years of their relationship (1954–64). The manuscript copy of Memo #3 came from Goffman's archive, and there is also a copy of the 1948 manuscript with his comments on it. Both Goffman and Garfinkel went on to work up a more adequate theory of the "individual" self as "actor" in the 1950s and 1960s (Rawls 2003). This actor, they argued, cannot be either an individual, or a whole person in the conventional sense. Rather, it is a "self" engaged in "facework," presenting a "face" that displays a commitment to situated practice—and the trust relations that practice requires.

There are lots of misunderstandings of what is meant by "actor"—not least of which attributing to the actor a strategic character. Therefore, it is important to point out that for both Garfinkel and Goffman the actor is bound to others through a "working commitment" to "background expectancies" that constitutes both their existence as actors and the situation in which they act—and thereby imparts a serious moral overtone—and prohibits actions that threaten the working consensus (Rawls 1984, 1987, 1989, 1990). "Actor" does not mean fake—or strategic—it means "oriented toward" the situated practice by an "identified self," identified each next time in a particular way: the particular identity specifying the relevancies of a practice.

Garfinkel refers to an "identified self" as an actor within a context of practice. Like the object, the actor is constituted in and through the practice. It is only as an actor—an identified self within a particular practice—that anyone constitutes meanings or thingifies objects. While playing baseball I thingify "runs" and myself as a "third baseman." These things have no "reality" otherwise. As Garfinkel says, they can only be "thingified" in and through practice.

It is important to see that Garfinkel rejects the idea of a whole person—their beliefs and projects—as constituting a model of the actor in question. All discussions of EM as a micro sociology assume the very model of the individual Garfinkel has rejected. Instead, Garfinkel treats the actor—the identified actor—as both constitutive of, and a constituted feature of, the situations and practices within which they act—the same as objects.

It is the identified actor who orients toward and thingifies objects and information. It is not the individual person who acts, and, therefore, not the individual person who acts in expected ways—and by the same token, not the individual person who makes change. It is only the identified self—the actor—who can make change.

The argument here is the same as it is for information. Information can only be new against a background of expectations. Individuals and individual purposes are not predictable enough to be expected (outside of perfect game theoretic conditions)—so they also cannot produce change. But, an identified self, in a context of shared practice, faces social expectations that *are* specific enough that changes do have meaning and can produce information: can be seen as "changes." Unless they can be seen as expected patterns they can't be changed—and there can be no change.

This plays a big twist on the way the question of change is usually posed. It is generally posited in terms of freedom and determinism—with regard to pursuing norms, goals, or socially or (biogenetically) determined ends. Garfinkel is arguing, by contrast, that people could be totally free in this sense and that freedom would not result in change if there is no recognizable pattern in the first place to change.

Thus, Garfinkel's focus on the identified actor has the unexpected effect of enhancing the possibilities for creativity. Perspectives based on the whole individual must be heavily refereed, and the individual person standardized into a dummy in order for even the most general patterns to appear. This dummy was made to carry society's values and routines around with it in order for their knowledge to be considered valid and they were required to conform to be understood.

Garfinkel's identified actor, by contrast, whose identity depends on the practices in which they are engaged—and who is bound by constitutive rules of practice—the actor who thingifies objects through those practices—also has the ability to make use of those practices in creative ways and has been doing so all along. The patterns of practice do not require perfection—and the unexpected constitutes information when it occurs in ordered sequences of action. This is a creative capacity that is not available in a society populated by standardized dummies.

Part IV: The Object in General

The question of how it is possible for objects to be mutually apprehended—or, how the "same" word is to have the "same" meaning for more than one person—has come to be a practical problem for information sciences. Explaining how "objects" can be distinguished (without falling into total relativity), if their boundaries are socially constituted, is a particular problem for a "science" that must deal with categorization, classification, and data sets that are defined by contingent and only locally relevant parameters.

The Constancy of Objects

Garfinkel offers an alternative to approaches that try to build constancy into either the objects, or their linguistic designators—and to the postmodern and pragmatist view that significant relativism cannot be avoided if such constancy cannot be achieved.

Instead of beginning with the pragmatist idea that individuals who are trying to effect joint projects with others must produce a pragmatic level of agreement, enough to get on with, or with the postmodern idea that societies in some general way institute the meaning of terms, or Luhmann's nihilistic acceptance of the fact that they can't, Garfinkel approaches the problem through constitutive practices. Like selves, he argues, objects do not exist as such until and unless some mutually oriented principle of selection is used to constitute something as an object—an oriented object. In specifying how it is that objects can be mutually constituted in stable ways, through practice, Garfinkel introduces an equation to represent this principle.

For Garfinkel, "objects" are, in fact, arrays of possibilities—and could be seen in many different ways. Even the boundaries of objects can vary—is the object a cigarette, or a pack—tobacco or cigarette papers—and differently oriented—smokes or carcinogens—legal or illegal? It is only through the use of a unifying principle that these "phenomenal fields" become coherent as particular objects. Garfinkel's information equation "e(Pn)," represents this unifying principle. If more than one person is to see the same object—to see just that object out of the whole array of possibilities—then, Garfinkel argues, they must all use the same principle of selection—the same "e." For Garfinkel, the possibility of mutuality—of mutually available objects—rests on ordered relations between the various possibilities. He says (133): "An object is viewed then as an array of possibilities of experience constituted through some "unifying" principle, some logical operator into an *order* of relationships to each other."

Ordered relationships between things—interaction—thus, stands at the heart of Garfinkel's theory of information. It is the requirements for mutually intelligible interaction, and not institutional values, or individual purposes, that set the criteria that must be satisfied.

The Information Equation

Garfinkel introduces an equation for information (135): "e(p_n), where 'e' is the operator, 'p' means a possibility of experience, 'n' means number, and the parentheses ( ) say that the aggregate of 'p's is a set of 'p's relevant to each other by virtue of the ordering operations represented in the 'e.'" This equation specifies that information stands in some ordered relationship to other things—an order of interaction. "The object" he says (133), "is experienced as an object, through an order of specifications; this *order of specifications* being all of what is meant by the term 'object.'"

First, Garfinkel says a number of things about what "e" is *not*. It is not a Platonic "form." It is not an essence in Husserl's sense or in a metaphysical sense. It has nothing to do with the "substance" of the object. It is not a name or a category—even though we use names for objects.

Garfinkel is not trying to say that objects have no substance, or that there are no ideas, or names. What he is saying is that what we "see" when we orient objects in common is not a function of whatever "substance" the object may have. That objects can be mutually identified, and that they can be named in the same way, is not a function of the use of a category or classification. Rather, the mutual availability of objects is a function of the ordering principle that constitutes the object as a mutually oriented object in a context of use. Only when participants use the same ordering principle do they have the same object in front of them.

Therefore, the ordering principle will be the key to mutual intelligibility and also to what as "scientists" we can take "objectivity" to be. "This," according to Garfinkel, "leaves us with the necessity of trying to make clear the nature of the ordering principle." It is the way in which the ordering principle, the "e," works that needs to be the focus of research.

While "e" has nothing to do with substance, and is not an essence in the metaphysical or phenomenological sense, Garfinkel says that "essence" will do as a term if we put aside various considerations, treating "e" instead as a principle of selection. "In this sense" he says (134), "we have the 'essence' of the object when we have specified with full clarity all of what an object consists of in its meanings. No reification, no object; no reification, no action." It is the process of reification that constitutes the object. The point is not to avoid reification, but to accept that reification is the process through which objects come to have reality.

Since reification cannot be avoided, it is essential to specify how reification is accomplished. According to Garfinkel (134) "The problem for the investigator who would describe the properties of the objects that the actor is treating is not that of separating those persons who reify from those who do not, but is that of describing the multitude of ways in which reification is accomplished."

The "e" is, then, a principle of reification. It is "a principle for grouping experiences," and, Garfinkel says (134), "in its absence there is neither specification nor grouping." Because it is a principle of selection it has no content. People "use" it to create the appearance of objects. What it does is to "instruct" participants on the selection processes that are in play in any given situated practice. In order to have objects in common they must use the same selection process to reify those objects.

It is Garfinkel's position that objects cannot even be seen or heard *as such* in the absence of the selection principle that corresponds to them. A person listening to Morse Code, for instance, would hear only noise if they did not know "about" Morse Code. As Garfinkel says, "For the case of empirical objects, the absence of the 'e' reduces the idealized signal to a signal that signifies only itself, i.e., to the meaningless experience." And they would only hear something that in a general sense might be Morse Code, unless they actually knew the code. If they knew the code—then instead of hearing "noise," or "Morse Code in general," they could apply the appropriate selection principle and hear particular sequences of letters and words.

Garfinkel's (2002) tutorials with summoning phones are another illustration of this point. A phone that is ringing for "you" is oriented toward differently than a phone that is ringing for someone else. It carries a different obligation—but it also *sounds* different. A ring that is expected, or which carries an obligation to answer, comes out of the silence that goes before the ring differently than a ring that is unexpected, or which carries no obligation. Garfinkel's point (134) is that "[i]n the absence of the 'e' for the analytic object, like Cinderella and the triangle in general, the object is lost in the cessation of activity; the picture fades from the screen."

He also says that the "e" has the characteristic of invariance. This point is relevant to the issue of boundary objects. The "e" operator, according to Garfinkel (134) "remains invariant with reference to the transformations of phenomenal appearances." The object can be many things according to which "e" operator is used. But, a given "e" operator will produce for many different people *the same object* under the same social circumstances of "use." Within practices that are stable and shared all members will thingify in the same way, and each time a phenomenal field is "thingified" in the same way it will appear as the same object—regardless of differences in the field (as long as those differences are not significant enough to confuse the relevance of the "e" operator).

The "e" is a relational operator—a principle that is used to relate things to each other. It selects phenomenal experiences from an array "relating them to each other in some determinate fashion." As a relational grouping principle, the "e" is a principle of interaction, grouping "things" in relation to one another in the context of shared practices. A phenomenal field of experience only appears as a coherent object against a context of other ordered possibilities. According to Garfinkel (134) "the name in 'preparing the world for treatment'—Mead's 'collapsed act'—is, as far as we can make out, the designator *not of the object but of the grouping principle* by which an array of possibilities are arranged to present together with the principle that relates them, the object."

"Membership Categorization Devices," developed later by Sacks and Garfinkel, one of the staple ideas of CA, are devices for categorizing "names" according to shared—but also local and varying—grouping principles. The grouping principle tells the hearer which of many meanings of a term should be selected for any given utterance. For instance, in Sacks's famous example (from his lectures), "The baby cried; the mommy picked it up," there are several ways in which the Membership Categorization Device, or pair,—"mommy/baby"—works to make the object classifications in the utterance mutually coherent.[50]

While, on the one hand, the "e" is used to create the possibility of worlds in common, the failure of the "e" is, on the other hand, the failure of a world. Garfinkel says (135); "The failure of the "e" operator implies at the point of its failure the disruption of a world, or, in more precise terms, implies the formal consequence of confusion." Because people are constructing worlds of objects together using a principle of selection—not using the same principle of selection causes the object construction to fail to be mutual. Worlds of mutual intelligibility just fall apart. According to Garfinkel (134–35), "Where one is oriented to a world of sensory encounter, the failure of an 'e' (which of course is not the same thing as 'not having a name for it') makes it impossible to idealize a signal; hence the experiencer experiences not the data of the world but experiences signals."

There are similarities between this principle and Goffman's discussion of the failure of a self. It is not just that a self may fail—but a whole world of mutual relations can crash. Thus, the presentation of self—and the interaction order that supports it—needs to be treated with great care, because the failure of a self is also the failure of a world and, as such, threatens the existence of all other selves in that world.

Thus, there are moral implications of the "e," not only because it requires mutual commitment and trust but also because its failure effects every

---

50. "Baby" can be a term of endearment. "The baby" could be someone else's baby. The "it" could be something other than the baby. "Picked it up" can mean speeded it up, and so on. These are just a few of the ambiguities that could be heard—but which competent speakers would ordinarily not hear—because they are using the taken for granted selection principle "mommy/baby" to hear these as a related pair and to select the meanings that work with them as a pair. Using such a pair acts as a selection principle—in addition to other selection principles that may be imbedded in the local order of practice in question (regarding the order of turns, etc.).

participant in the "world" of situated possibilities which depends on that particular "e." Although the trust argument is not fully articulated until later (Garfinkel 1963)—a preliminary discussion of trust appears in this introduction, not surprisingly, in conjunction with this discussion.

For Garfinkel, a "thing" is defined by its relationship to other things in a sequence of ordered things—within a constitutive practice. This involves ordered sequences, reciprocity with regard to practice, and trust in the mutual commitment to producing those recognizably orderly patterns without which there are no mutually available objects, or meanings, and all becomes meaningless confusion. It also makes displays of trust, attention, and competence essential to the interactional process.

The coherence of worlds depends on participants' coherent use of the "e" operator. The principle of selection and the object are equivalent. In providing for the coherence of a world of experience, for how to thingify objects, Garfinkel says, each thingified object is "conceived as a schema of possibilities of experience." All participants are dependent on the competence, and good intentions of the others, for the production of a mutually available world of objects and meanings.

Part V: The "Imbedded" Possibility of Experience

In this part Garfinkel challenges both the individualism of utilitarian—or rational choice—theory, and the primacy of ontology with regard to objects. If the object is a schema of possibilities of experience, then there is no such thing as an object in isolation. Neither would any individual in isolation experience any meaningful or mutually available object—they can only do so as an identified self. Garfinkel contrasts the popular idea that the individual and events stand alone with the sociological idea of imbeddedness. Only the sociological approach will be able to specify the possibility of experience.

His point is also that ways of approaching the reality and continuity of objects and events that place their faith in a catalogue of definitional features—or "objective" observation—take for granted the very sociological process of reifying, or constituting, objects that they should be examining. Thus, their objects are not objective at all. The observer and the exhaustive process of definition have to do with ideal objects: objects as posited by utilitarian theory. They treat the object as a function of individual perception—which it is not.

Garfinkel articulates a familiar idea usually associated with pragmatism: multiple worlds. But, because Garfinkel does not begin with the individual, his worlds are multiple for a very different reason. It is not that every individual experience constitutes a different world—as it is for William James. Rather, for Garfinkel there are multiple worlds because each context of constitutive practice, each "e," constitutes a different world. The number of such different worlds should not be a problem either—that is, should not interfere with communication between people—because each world is shared by a social public of oriented actors that belongs specifically to it—and whenever people communicate they do so from within the same shared world of practice.

Also, in contrast with pragmatism, for which each world is subjective, each one of the worlds Garfinkel is talking about is an *objective* world—because it is shared meaningfully with others. According to Garfinkel, "a world experienced subjectively is a world experienced without meaning." Thus, in contrast to pragmatism and its multiple "subjective" worlds, Garfinkel posits multiple "objective" worlds.

Garfinkel challenges all theories that begin with the individual. He also challenges all theories that assume that objectivity is a quality of the observer, the object, or of reason. Anything that is experienced in isolation and not in its imbedded relationship with other things—that is, in imbedded social relationships—is a meaningless experience. Things appear only in "an interpersonally valid and validated order."[51]

Objects are real for Garfinkel not on the grounds of their ontological structure but in their constitution as unities of meaning. Whereas in the theory of communication Garfinkel offered the equation meaning = order, now in the theory of information he argues also that order = reality. The continuity of experience rests on a world that is constituted and maintained through mutual attention to the "e" operator.

Arguing this leads Garfinkel to consider the social conditions that condition the imbedded possibility of meaning. He offers a list of conditions each of which he discusses, and then asks what the various criteria are that order the objectivity of experience. There are eleven subsections:

a. The Criterion of Continuity of Experience: Continuity refers to the invariant character of the relationships between parts of an experience or between sequences of experience. They are experienced coherently as *continuous*—and this quality of experience is shared with other members of the experience. Continuity requires more than one thing—and it requires some things to change against a background of constancy. If everything changes there is no continuity.

---

51. This formulation is a lot like the later "praxeological validity of instructed action." Can they do it together recognizably? If so, then it is.

Garfinkel (138) considers a hypothetical conversation as an example of what happens when the grounds of continuity shift too much.

b. The Criterion of Consistency of Experience: Garfinkel uses a cigarette example (also in the 1948 manuscript) to illustrate consistency. He says "[It] stands as a real thing on the basis of the way in which the sensory materials have been idealized." The visual image and the perceived package are not equivalent in their meanings. There are various possibilities relevant to meaning that Garfinkel says cluster around a visual image. Garfinkel asks (139) "with reference to what rules of procedures its order of existence is to be confirmed?" He treats as relevant, only those possibilities that form "a constitutive element of the appearance of the thing." Appearance would include its meaning and its reality.

The phenomenology of Helmut Kuhn is mentioned in the context of a discussion of inner horizons and "serial potentialities."

c. The Criterion of Compatibility of Experiences: In addition to an inner horizon, the object also has an outer horizon. It is not an isolated object—no objects in Garfinkel's view are isolated—all exist in contexts of constitutive practice. In its relationship to other objects there is anticipation—and an expectation of "what goes with what."

d. The Criterion of Temporal Continuity: There is a sequence of perceptions in which the present perception is just one link in an unfolding temporal horizon. Each apprehension of an object, Garfinkel says (141) connects to a past, a future—and a present: "The absolutely new is inconceivable. Strangeness exists only with familiarity." The temporal horizon is not like a time line. Rather—each experience (objective experience—meaning social and shared) has its own temporal horizon in a situated practice: "[T]o perceive an object," he says (141), "means to locate it in a system of expectations."

e. The Criterion of "Clarity" of Experience: The criterion of clarity requires that the "style" of an experience be recognizably distinct from other competing or conflicting experiences. For instance, in Garfinkel's example, a referee cannot shake his head "no" without creating confusion if his head also shakes in a similar way for medical reasons.[52]

A Working Classification of Possibilities. An object is always determined by a constitutive order. But there are various ways in which this can be done.

---

52. In my commentary I have followed the set-up of Garfinkel's manuscript even where it departs from expectations of outlining. Switching from letters to headers here is one of many inconsistent and unexplained changes in Memo #3. But, it has been left as in the original manuscript.

Primary and Secondary Possibilities. Primary possibilities are used to test whether an object is one of a particular sort. Not all of these are usually necessary. The length of time typically available during interaction constrains the size of the list of primary possibilities. Secondary possibilities, he says (143), are "integral to the object constituted as a unity of meaning but not tested." Although they have to do with objects, these categories are interpretive not ontological. For Garfinkel the reality of objects is not ontological.

The et cetera assumption (143)—"that as things were in the past they are now"—also appears here. This is a very different seeming version of et cetera than the one articulated by Garfinkel later—and seems to be drawn from Schutz.

Crucial and Equal-Moment Possibilities. The "crucial" specifier is of the essence of a thing. Equal moment possibilities—Garfinkel gives as the batting average. Either an object is objective—and has crucial (constitutive) identifiers—or it is equal moment—and falls under the possibilities of logic and summary rule. Nothing can be both, at least not at the same time. Furthermore, the implications of being one or the other are quite different. The specifiers in some sense specify the same object. But, it is not really the same object, because objects are given by the constitutive modes of their apprehension.

Relevant and Non-Relevant Possibilities. "[I]t is a peculiarity of the action frame," Garfinkel says (144), that "a given moment or sequence of moments of activity ... involves the treatment of the object according to terms that are relevant to the actor's interpretive scheme at hand in a Here and Now." Trying to list out the specifications of objects or categories is a task for the theorist—for someone trying to create an exhaustive ontological catalogue—which is not relevant to the treatment of objects in imbedded sequences of objects. The actor does not need this. The observer has a different procedure from the imbedded actor. The observer treats the specifications as having "statistical relevance." The actor treats them as having "constitutive" relevance.

Fulfillable Possibilities: A fulfillable possibility is one that has the possibility of closure through being fulfilled. This means that it has the character of comparability—it can be compared to the state of affairs that would constitute its being fulfilled. An expectation is open and fulfillable. An anticipation may or may not be. In this context Garfinkel discusses some critical terms: retention, protention and durée (e.g., anticipation is protention within a course of activity governed by a teleological principle). A fulfillable possibility that has not been fulfilled is an open possibility.

Open and Problematical Possibilities. On this point Garfinkel makes a reference to Schutz and no more is said. It seems that the seminar members would be reading and discussing this point, so Garfinkel does not elaborate it here. This is unfortunate, because there is not enough to determine what Garfinkel might have said about it—or what it has to do with the overall argument.

Part VI: Some Preliminary Terms

The prior parts of the memo have presented the "object" as a schema of possibilities of experience. Later parts, 9 through 15, will consider properties of the ways in which these possibilities are ordered as conditions for the possibility of information. This interim part, and the next two—7 and 8—offer some definitions of terms: signal, sign, expression, message, and communication, and so on. Garfinkel's theory of communication also makes its appearance in this part.

Signal—sensory stimuli which are by definition meaningless.

Sign or mark—a stimulus experienced as an indicator of something else.

Expression—Some things have meaning that refers through their representations "beyond itself." Representation, signification, and reference.

According to Garfinkel (150), signs have no intrinsic relationship to the objects they represent. "The sign or expressional character of an experience," he says, "is dependent on the 'rules' by which signals and meanings are 'matched.' These rules include not only the usual sense of grammar, but matters of temporal order, context of meanings, . . . the rules that prescribe what kind of interest one is to take in a set of signals." In a state of confusion we experience signals instead of signs or expressions.

Some meanings, Garfinkel says, have to do with the person speaking and some do not. Some words are ambiguous, and some carry many meanings without ambiguity (a characteristic he will later call indexicality). These qualities make things like secrecy possible—and are one reason why rationalizing "organizational structure" causes problems.[53]

In considering the relevance of these distinctions to information and formal organizational work—Garfinkel begins by considering the ways in which the rationalizing of organizational structure involves "depersonalizing"

---

53. Garfinkel (152) refers to Moore on this point.

communicative work. This brings him to say that the work-related instrumental features of talk that are useful to the workers are at odds with the quest for objectivity and depersonalization.

So, it's another theoretical point. In trying to make language objective and depersonalize organization in order to promote easy succession of leaders, what happens is that workers lose the details—including the words—that they need to get their work done.

Message—"a spatially and/or temporally patterned set of signals," whose pattern is imposed by the observer.

Communication—"a spatially and/or temporally patterned set of signals," whose pattern "is the patterning of the communicant." Thus, for the observer communication is empirically problematic. This all assumes arguments from the first part of the 1948 manuscript.

Communicative work—The process and the work of orienting toward that work.

The rest of this part—which consists of a series of definitions (tactics, strategy, plan, design)—is elaborated more fully in the 1948 manuscript (Garfinkel 2006) and I will not go into it in more detail here.

Part VII: A Working Definition of Information

After giving definitions of the other terms, Garfinkel works out a definition of information. In doing so he focuses on the game of Kriegsspiel, which is a version of chess in which the players cannot see one another's boards (see Appendix 4). One reason for this focus, he says, is that while playing Kriegsspiel, the players discuss information. Therefore, it offers a natural example of how information is talked about. Because players are deprived of information about one another's play, their talk is about how to get information from the play—from the grunts, hesitations, and so on (much like poker). Garfinkel says that "wherever there are messages, there is the possibility of information." Furthermore, information during the course of an ongoing practice is cumulative—and continuity can be lost if every possible source of information is not attended to.

In this part, Garfinkel gives an interesting and detailed description of the various ways in which a player in Kriegsspiel can get information. It resembles later EM descriptions of practices in details (such as Doug McBeth's "basketball notes"). One of Garfinkel's points is that information is not just passively experienced—it is judged (158). This will be a big point in later parts (11 through 13), where he argues that the fact of experience is a given—what is in question is how experience comes to have mutually recognizable shape. Objects, he says, are not just given to experience. The process of applying constitutive rules to experience and making judgments is what constitutes objects.

After being judged—which is how information is created—it also needs to be stored. According to Garfinkel (158):

> Instead of conceiving of the coincidence of meaning and the thing meant as a little package that gets tied together and filed away in the recesses of memory, "put on the drum," to be drawn out again when the need arises, I would prefer … to regard information as something not recalled but re-created out of the resources of the available order of possibilities of experience, available sensory materials, actions, etc. Thus preferred usage would be to talk of a communicant as knowledgeable rather than talking of his knowledge.

Garfinkel makes a plea for helpful discussion from the seminar on this point. He is trying to resolve a dilemma—between information as a momentary product of experience and information as an a-temporal sum of things experienced. The idea of information as a judgment according to criteria, and not just an experience is important. Garfinkel (159) treats "memory," which is an information storage process, "as a describable set of operations by which a previous meaningful experience is reproduced or re-presented." What should concern us as a research question, he says, is what "conditions of social structure" will "give us probabilities of a certain kind of re-creation."

Part VIII: Kinds of Information

A number of different kinds of information are discussed in this part. But the primary considerations have to do with perfect versus imperfect information, and the equality of the distribution of information. The latter raises questions of the validity and appropriateness of statistical approaches, in addition to considering the effect of distribution issues on information itself.

Perfect and Imperfect Information

The issue of perfect and imperfect information involves the argument of von Neumann and Morgenstern, and what they meant by perfect information. In their version of game theory the communicant's definition of the situation must be related to the rest of the communicative-net. In perfect information, what Garfinkel calls the *preliminarity* and *anteriority* of moves are the same (161). The player with perfect information knows the outcome of all choices (which would seem to decrease information). Information is imperfect whenever there are outcomes that the player does not know about (which would seem to increase information).

Garfinkel points out that imperfect information is a much more prevalent characteristic of communicative nets than game theory allows for. Some communicative nets—such as Kriegsspiel—are set up in such a way that information will be imperfect by design. In other communicative orders it is the communicant who does not know things that the setup of the net does, in fact, allow for.

The stability of a communicative net, according to Garfinkel (161–62) can also be achieved with various "devices that overcome the requirement of perfect information and uniformity of definition." Systems of occupational specialization, he says, have this characteristic. Worksite practices develop indexical details that can only be mastered each next time through close attention. Harvey Sacks's (1996) discussion of the utility of indexicality for ensuring listening and hearing requirements is related to this issue (Rawls 1989, 1990). A communicative net can increase the available information—turn-by-turn, by increasing indexicality such that understanding can only be achieved by close attention to turns. Imperfect information may thus be a requirement for achieving and maintaining mutual intelligibility, trust, and reciprocity in a number of important communicative nets.

Relative Equality of Distributed Information

There is a "relationship between what two or more communicants in a net know and do not know *between* them," Garfinkel says (162). The point is that what people know in common is much less than what they know individually. Every new person who enters a net increases this disparity. The "total ignorance in a system," according to Garfinkel (162), is the information that communicants have but do not share. The more that people do not share what they know, the more total ignorance there will be in a system.

Garfinkel uses some Venn diagrams to illustrate this and it is interesting that he refers to them as a very new way of diagramming orders.[54]

The point Garfinkel is making relates to his argument in the research proposals on predicting the effects of leadership turnover (see Appendix 4): that adding new people to a net creates a problem when personnel are switched

---

54. Venn diagrams were invented in 1881 by John Venn, a mathematician working on set theory. In referring to Venn diagrams as new, Garfinkel is probably referring to connections between Boolean algebra (which he references often in conversation) and Venn diagrams developed by Marshall Stone in 1936. Stone also worked with von Neumann in the 1930s.

during the course of a task. Every time a new person is added to a net there will be things they do *not* know and things they *do* know that are *not shared* with the others (relevant to the task)—and this adds ignorance to the net.

To the extent that knowing how to do a set of practices constitutes information—knowing the practices would give the information—and this can be learned over time. But, to the extent that information is cumulative—as it is in Kriegsspiel—that there are histories and et cetera—it will not matter how well a newcomer masters practices, if they come in part way through the sequence, they are missing the essential history of moves. This is most likely to be the case, according to Garfinkel, when personnel changes occur over the course of a single event. People who come in after the end of the event can learn the features of the event through narrative accounts. People who come in at the beginning will have most of the necessary history. But, personnel changes in the middle, or near the end of an event may leave participants unable to orient objects adequately. This may create so much "total ignorance" and confusion in the net that objects cannot be coherently oriented.

Equality and distribution of information raise different issues. Over time, as people communicate, any system will tend toward a state of equality of information (and this would also decrease total ignorance). Either perfect equality, or perfect inequality, will decrease the probability of innovation. Thus, innovation requires constant input from outside the net—input producing constant inequality and increasing total ignorance in the net. Introducing new personnel into the net can achieve this.

Therefore, personnel change is a good thing because it promotes innovation. But, it is a bad thing if it produces too much total ignorance. Garfinkel will argue that this effect can be controlled by changing personnel at or near the beginning of a task. This is consistent with Garfinkel's developing position—in focusing on tasks at the worksite and what they require—instead of considering information in the abstract.

Complete and Incomplete Information

When states of incomplete information occur—which is frequent, Garfinkel says (166) what is most interesting is that communicants do not experience incomplete information. "The usual response is that everything that was *needed* to be known was known." What we are interested in here, he says (165–66), are "the devices whereby continuous action is maintained in the face of what appears for a fully rational communicant to be an insufficiently specified situation."

Police decision making is discussed in Memo #3 in conjunction with incomplete information—and, in fact, several of Garfinkel's early students, including Egon Bittner, Aaron Cicourel, David Sudnow, and Don Zimmerman, went on to study the police.[55] The police constantly have to make decisions in the face of incomplete information—they never have anything like complete information—and Garfinkel points out that it is part of their ideology that they are able to do so. Garfinkel suggests this problem for possible inclusion in the document to be sent to the Ford Foundation.

The Probable Character of Information from Randomness to Certainty

The probable character of information is effected by alterations at any one of a number of points: in the signal field, the coupling system, interpretive devices, and the communicant's attitude or role. This includes all the communicative devices and everything about the reciprocity system that gives information. Probable character has to do with the clarity and style of a message. Clarity and style matter because when messages are not clear, or, as Garfinkel says (167) where "no separation can be made in a signal field between the noise character of a message and the informing character of a message," there is confusion.[56]

Primary, Secondary, and Inferential Information

Garfinkel made a distinction between primary and secondary information in Memo #2. He refers to that distinction again in Memo #3. Communicants need to know how they are being heard—and whether they are being understood. One way they get this information is by evaluating the responses of the other in relation to what has been said. This is "secondary information," which according to Garfinkel (168), refers to "any information that a communicant finds in a message by which he knows how his communicative efforts are being generated and received." What Garfinkel discusses in Memo #2 are the effects of not having sufficient secondary information. And he refers to experiments with depriving communicants of secondary information—which he will continue later; the medical student interviews (1967) providing one notable example.

---

55. Early collaborative work between Garfinkel and Harvey Sacks also focused on policing. It was a case of figuring out how they made judgments in environments of incomplete information.

56. Although Garfinkel uses the word "message" he might not mean message here. Earlier he said that message was an observer's term—and here he is clearly using it to refer to the communicant's problem.

Inferential information is another type Garfinkel introduces here that is different from primary and secondary information. Inferences are made based on bits of primary and secondary information—or on judgments (information is a judgment). Primary and secondary information are each based on judgments according to constitutive rules. According to Garfinkel inferential information increases as relations become more communal. And as relationships rationalize, inferential information decreases relative to direct (and secondary) information. This is because the ability to make mutually intelligible inferences depends on having a high degree of congruence on primary and secondary information—and that in turn requires the constitutive features of a communicative net—which rationalizing a system interferes with.

According to Garfinkel (170) "The way in which a person draws inferences from a message may be used as an empirical measure of the normative integration of a group." This suggests that workers—at a worksite—can come to share a net to such a degree that they are able to function as a traditional communal solidarity for purposes of drawing inferences from information. It is different—of course—because the basis of the order is in this case not shared belief, but rather shared practice. The degree of integration however, makes a similar level of inference possible (something that Durkheim's [1893] argument with regard to practice also suggests).

A rationalized system, by contrast, forces workers back on judgments about primary and secondary information without sufficient overlapping competence in the net to allow for drawing mutually intelligible inferences.

Eidetic and Material Information

"The distinction is between information that bears upon the question for the communicant of what the world means (eidetic information) as compared with information that bears on the question of what the world consists of in fact (material information)."

Eidetic information about what the world means has no probable character. Either it is certain or it is meaningless. Only material information about what the world consists of has a probable character. Every message that has one kind of information has the other. They are theoretical categories and not epistemological ones.

The difference consists in the factors that condition the possibility of experiencing error. Any event that is governed by any rule, other than a rule of chance, has a moral requiredness. If events have a requiredness, according to Garfinkel (172), it "is always a moral requiredness."

Part IX: Factors That Condition Information

This part begins a series of parts on factors that condition information. In this first part of the series there is a general discussion. Then parts X through XIII each consider a particular sort of factor: factors of the order of possiblities, role factors, factors of communicative work, and net-work factors. Properly speaking, parts IX through XIII elaborate subsections of a single issue—factors that condition information. But, although it would be easier to follow if it were set up as an outline with subsections, the document has been left the way it was written.

In part VIII, one of the things Garfinkel considered was perfect and imperfect information. Here he considers factors that would condition not only the perfection and imperfection of information—but the factors that set up the conditions for the communicative net itself. Garfinkel poses the question (174): "[I]f we assume a discrepancy of x-value between what a communicant knows and what a referee knows about a course of outcomes, how will this discrepancy be altered toward greater or lesser discrepancy as we manipulate the communicant's image of himself to reinforce the image or to make it unstable?" Timing, status hierarchy, and relative equality of distribution all effect secondary information and efficiency.

The remaining parts of the memo have to do Garfinkel says (175) with "sketching in … the factors that condition the properties of information." Four sets of factors are considered in the next three parts: 1) factors of possibilities, 2) role or attitudinal factors, 3) factors of communicative work, and 4) net factors.

Part X: (A) Factors of the Order of Possibilities

In this part two types of factors are discussed; factors of allocation between two domains that are considered exhaustive and "criteria of the organization of imbeddedness." Ten factors in all are discussed.

Constancy and Variability

This is a very long section. Here Garfinkel uses tic-tac-toe to illustrate a discussion of two sets of rules and gets into issues that look like an early version of the "Trust" paper. In fact, this whole section outlines what will come out later as the lectures on rules and the trust papers.

The basic rules, Garfinkel says, serve as standards of play against which the "strange" move can be recognized. The basic rules are invariant. Variations on these (like picking up second base and running off with it as a player approaches) are not proper play. The rules of preferred play, by contrast, are characterized by their variable character. It is these against which variations and innovations are made. The domains of constancy and variability are meant to stand in for the distinction between basic and preferential rules.

Garfinkel points out that if all of the rules were basic rules—and we abided by them—then outcomes would be completely known and no variability of outcome would be possible. It is the rules of preferred play that introduce the possibility of contingency, and hence of information and change.

The need for innovation and the need to conserve information stand in some conflict with one another. Garfinkel invokes Weiner in considering "information loss." Information cannot increase between two points—it can only be lost. Routinizing minimizes the probability of confusion and loss of information during transmission. But, according to Garfinkel (179–80), routinization also has the downside of reducing communicative efficiency.

In addition to routinization, another set of devices is needed for managing incongruity. Garfinkel expects every communicative net for non-trivial tasks to have two such sets of devices: one to maintain routine aspects of the net, and the other to control incongruity.

In discussing his model of a game as consisting of both basic and preferred rules—Garfinkel (182) refers to Hobbes—as a precursor of modern rational choice theory. According to Garfinkel, if the two types of rules were conceived of as two separate poles, the Hobbesian theory of rationality would treat the pole of "the rules of preferred play" as the "state of a completely rational pursuit of self-interest"—in other words, as the "pole of the war of each against all." What is wrong with Hobbes's view, from Garfinkel's perspective, is that it assumed that preferred play can take place in the absence of basic rules. Garfinkel argues that no meaningful action at all is possible except against a background of constancy—against a background of constitutive background expectations (although it is not clear that these are only contained within the basic rules of play—and Garfinkel will later modify his view to include this insight).

For Garfinkel (182), in contrast to Hobbes, "the state of all preferential rules is a state of the complete extinction of activity." That is, without constancy in the constitutive background expectations there is a state of confusion. Messages in such a state are experienced as meaningless—and he says (182) that he will call this "a state of anomie or randomness." One important implication of this argument—since the basic rules are a social order—is that no information is possible except against the constancy provided by a background of invariant social expectations.

A state of anomie is the same thing as a state in which messages are experienced as "noise."

Garfinkel ends this discussion on a postmodern note: "[A]ssume that some 'amount' of noise is always present" (184). We can assume that much action and many devices will be oriented toward minimizing the amount of meaninglessness and maintaining "interpersonally valid definitions of the situation." But "our communicant will be conceived to be always in some measure confused."

The Criteria of Organization

Garfinkel proposes some difficulties at the end of this section—with proposing a "determinate description of the order of objects" or "the problem of stating the defining dimensions of a definition of the situation"—and offers some "constructions" to attempt to deal with the problem. These constructions are *The Criteria of Organization* (185), *Continuity* (185), *Consistency* (186), *Compatibility* (186), *Temporal Continuity* (186), and *Clarity* (187). After an extended discussion of each of these, however, Garfinkel concludes (188) that the difficulties are only conceptual and that what they really mean is that "when we abandon concrete descriptions we must be prepared to talk nonsense." This is why Garfinkel uses concrete descriptions for everything. He even talks that way.

Part XI: Factors That Condition Information: (B) Role Factors

We start with the assumption, Garfinkel says, that we have an actor who experiences. It is not the fact of experience but the organization of experience that needs to be explained (189): "how one experience succeeds another, the organized character of experience" and its mutually available character. In this part Garfinkel specifies the conditions of the experiencing actor's "'make-up' under which the order of possibilities of experience is determined in its possible properties of organization." He will do so by elaborating six constructs: form of epoche, form of sociality, mode of attention to life, form of spontaneity, mode of time consciousness, and mode of giveness of the self. The six, he says, are taken from Schutz (although I doubt Garfinkel uses them in anything like the way Schutz intended), and, he also says that experience may show that there are more than these six.

It is the way in which an actor attends, or orients, an order that matters. But in this part Garfinkel confuses the issue by talking about what is "determinative of meaning for the observer" (189), and whenever he talks about the observer you have to be worried about what he means because he does not believe that the observer's observations/conclusions are valid within the constitutive domain of action. Here he ends up saying that the observer "plays the game of theorizing" and their constructs "have nothing to say about the world" (190).

Role Constructs Defined

The argument with regard to role is worked out in great detail in the 1948 manuscript, and in Garfinkel's PhD thesis, and he alludes to this here. He says (190) that he is restricting himself to bare definitions in this part because "to do more would require a revised duplication of the better part of some 120 pages in my [PhD] thesis, and I do not feel up to the task."

Form of Epoche: "The communicant assumes a set of procedural rules whereby a class or classes of possibilities are removed from operations of judgment."

Form of Sociality: A set of attitudinal relationships. Like any object, he says (191), the other person "is an order of specifications of conduct."

In their course: Sequences that are experienced in their course by an "I." Mead's distinction between the "I" and the "me" is intended, according to Garfinkel—as is James's stream of consciousness, both of which can only be "seen" in the past tense—but is lived in. In order for two people to stand in any relationship with one another over time there must be an invariant way they reciprocally reproduce their roles and relationships in time. According to Garfinkel (191), "[T]here stands in the stream of experience an invariant interpretive scheme designative of a thou or a me": a reciprocity of definitions of the situation. It is essential for all parties to be imbedded in the flow because "there are times when the 'thou' changes directly with the flow," as in two strangers meeting and trying to place each other. Anyone not fully imbedded in the incourseness of ongoing processes would get lost.

Mode of Giveness of the Self: The past is a set of memories, selected from—and made relevant to each other—by an oriented actor, an "attitudinal me." There are public and private standards of treatment. The public standards have consensual objectivity. The private standards are only individual. The actor acting according to public standards is "given as a person" according to Garfinkel, while "the actor treating the object-me according to private standards is said to be given as Individuum."

This part of Garfinkel's argument sounds like Durkheim's thesis on dualism (Rawls 2004). No one is ever only an Individuum or a person, he says. They are always both at the same time. As with Durkheim, the two stand in conflict with one another. In Garfinkel's terms, the process of socialization is the process through which "the communicant acquires a disparity between them." The individual animal learns to orient a world of social standards, meanings, and objects—that may stand in conflict with their own short term self-interests, but because they cannot be a "person" without these standards they do not stand in conflict with their long-term self interests in being and acting as a rational social being.

Mode of Attention to Life: The world is something that can be effected by the communicant and which, Garfinkel says (following Schutz) (192) "one must master through one's bodily intervention."

Mode of Time Consciousness: Time is constitutive of both objects and relationships between objects, according to Garfinkel. Three meanings of time are distinguished: (1) durée, (2) phenomenal, or inner time, and (3) standard or interpersonally standard time. *Standard time* is "socially validated schemes of temporal reference." This is the one that Garfinkel (193) says interests those in the natural attitude. *Phenomenal time,* because it is internal, can be reversed or even halted. And *durée* is "a succession of Nows," which, unlike phenomenal time, cannot be reversed. All objects constituted in durée are unique; "each Now," he says, "is an instance only of itself, hence the categories of sameness and difference do not apply."

Form of Spontaneity: There are two forms of spontaneity—activity undertaken for its own sake and activity that is motivated or goal oriented. But goal orientation is also treated by Garfinkel as oriented toward ordered sequences of events, and not goals as values or ideas.

The Constructs of Role and Their Relationships to Each Other

In this part Garfinkel makes a number of points with regard to how role is related to change: (1) the ability to organize experience in socially valid ways is not given at birth; (2) role can be changed, preventing the properties of organization from being relevant, and inducing confusion; (3) altering one set of specifications alters others; and, (4) there is change involved in the succession of roles over the course of a single day's experience.

Garfinkel then lists fifteen postulates; only two of which I will mention here, #5 which discusses anomie, and #11, which discusses ontology and ontological "leaps."

Postulate #5: "The road to anomie," Garfinkel says (196), "will be found in the destruction of the structures of the natural attitude and not in the destruction of the attitudes dependent on it." Although the statement is somewhat oblique—it takes a clear stand on the accepted version of Durkheim's dilemma espoused by Moore and Parsons—that without sufficient shared values social integration declines and anomie increases. From Garfinkel's perspective it is not shared beliefs and attitudes that are required for the integration of modern society but, rather, the reciprocal constitutive structure of the communicative net. The road to anomie, he says, is to be found in the destruction of the constitutive and reciprocal aspects of the communicative net that comprise the natural attitude, not in the weakening of shared beliefs and values that are dependent on it.

Postulate #11: Differences in attitudes create different worlds. They do not do so by degree either—but as a matter of a "leap." The accent of reality is placed elsewhere. This is only possible because—and here Garfinkel (197) alludes to Schutz—"[I]t is the meaning of our experiences and not the ontological structure of objects that constitutes reality." The attitude creates an order of objects. This sounds like Whitehead, but it will turn out to be different, because the constituting of objects is done empirically, by gearing into the world through shared practices, and not conceptually. Also, "attitude," as used by Garfinkel, does not denote a mental state—but, rather specifies a publicly identified self—or role.

The section ends with a discussion of role conflict that is covered in more detail in the 1948 manuscript.

Part XII: Factors That Condition Information: Factors of Communicative Work

In this part Garfinkel contrasts his approach to Parsons and Schils's (1951) structural functionalism. In their view the actor orients toward a situation of objects—and is considered qua actor to be an object in the situation. The question then is how the actor relates themselves to the available objects and why.

For Garfinkel, by contrast, the actor and the order of objects are both constituted by the constitutive aspects of the situation. In his view (201) "the actor and the structure of the object world are simultaneously constituted." Assuming either an independently real object world—or an independent actor—conflicts with this view.

Instead of asking why and how the actor relates themselves to objects—Garfinkel asks how mutually constituted objects and actors come to stand in the relationships in which they are found to stand in a communicative net. He treats communicative work as "operations by which various orders of transformation are effected upon the relationships between objects."

This way of viewing the relationship between actor, object and situation, has consequences for formal organization. Reorganizating relationships changes both the objects and the roles of actors. Changes in any one effects the others. Any organizational change will have this effect. Garfinkel (202, emphasis in original) offers a postulate that, in the natural attitude, *"those operations have the greatest probability of occurrence which involve the minimum amount of reorganization of the socially validated realities depicted in the order."* Changes lead to the least disorganization and confusion when they adhere to this postulate.

Garfinkel offers a review of the literature concerning people who find themselves in extreme situations (especially prisons and prison camps) to support this postulate. When things change too much in a short time, people continue to fall back on their previous background expectations to process information and objects. There is insufficient constancy in the new domain to allow them to adapt. The information that is clearly available to the outside observer, thus, is not available and cannot be seen from an insider's view—and changes from an old net to a new one, under conditions of extreme indeterminacy, are slow and difficult. Changes, he says, under extreme conditions are easiest to mutually orient when those who will need to change their constitutive orientations participate in the decision to change.[57] This also, he says (203) underlines the "importance of the timing of communicative work in the net as it is relevant to the assumptions of the reciprocity of perspectives of the natural attitude for the problem of social change." This is a problem that he suggests they include in the report to the Ford Foundation.

Part XIII: Net-work Factors

As Garfinkel acknowledges toward the end of part XIII, it is not really a discussion of net-work factors. What the part does do, however, in my view, is to supply the theory that is missing from part XIV, and it does so through explicit discussions of Parsons and structural and functional aspects of organization.

Garfinkel opens this part with a paragraph that demonstrates his reluctance to adopt a theory of organization. He says (204) that the perceived need to do so made him feel like "Norman Maier's rats felt when they were being goosed off their perches but were unable to choose where to jump." He found relief in the idea that instead of a theory he could elaborate a list of "ideas that seemed

---

57. As Garfinkel has pointed out in many lectures over the years, Nazi prison camps traded on this ability to cause confusion as a way of controlling the prisoners.

to be immanent in the 'conception' of organization." Even producing such a list, however, might be a mistake, and Garfinkel (205) alleges that "maybe my trauma on the perch knocked me loose from my good sense." In fact, in producing the list, and in summing up, Garfinkel does produce a theory of organization, albeit of his own very unique kind.

The list includes the following: (1)The idea of the communicant, (2) the idea of numbers of communicants, (3) the idea of communicative work, (4) the idea of communicative territory, (5) the idea of communicative timing, (6) the idea of social relationships, (7) the idea of a normative order (institutions), and (8) the idea of communicative paths.

In the last discussion of communicative paths, Garfinkel considers various representations of interaction that were current among social theorists in his day—simple representations of interaction that involved two heads and arrows between them. The fact that interaction has been represented in this way, through simple metaphor, he takes as evidence that it has previously not been considered a problematic idea.

Then he says (207) that "with the recent popularity of the ideas of communications engineering it [interaction] has come under examination as a problem in its own right."

After elaborating each of the eight items on the list, Garfinkel considers how they all implicate each other. He decided "that any related set of theoretical specifications of these ideas, considered as constructions, would be referred to as an organization." So, having said that he will not offer a theory of organization—he now proposes that the interrelationships between the items on his list do constitute a theory of organization. An organization, in his view, is "a set of interpretive rules" rather than "a concrete entity."

These are important paragraphs.

According to Garfinkel (208), "It remains then for the actual operations of observation to settle the question of whether the restricted frame of possibilities that the terms of the organization propose can be realized."

System means, for Garfinkel (208) "[T]he system-like character of events will be found in any type of significance for each other that the observer assigns to a set of events." "Events of conduct" are related to each other within a net.

Self-regulation, means, (209):

> For a communicative system, the possibility that it is a self-regulating one would lead us to ask how the temporal patterns of communicative exchanges—measured for example in frequency of message exchanges between communicants—are related to formal regulations that govern frequency, how the distances over

which these messages must travel are related to the timing of messages as well as to the extent of subscription to the regulations, how there will be found at a relevant time certain numbers of persons that are by regulation required to have an "up-to-the-minute" definition of the overall state of the net-work, etc., etc., until we would finally get back to the characteristics of the timing patterns.

Garfinkel (209) then moves on to talk about the "structural and functional prerequisites of a self-regulating communicative net." He says that he will be using these terms differently than either Parsons or Levy. A theoretical discussion follows.

First, Garfinkel (209–10) considers the structural problems. Although most theorists talk as though structures act, he points out that "a system does not allocate job functions." On the contrary, he says, "there are persons who are regarded by others in particular ways, who make demands, issue orders …" The "system" is a construct—not an actor. "The notion of the system is found in the fact that the observer can describe these events as they stand in typical orderings to each other.… "

Then there are the functional problems. These, like the structural problems, are observers' problems and not communicants' problems. He treats these as the "problems of motivation, of control." These, Garfinkel says (210), "have to do with communicative work and are inserted as operators by the use of which the notion of A as a function of B can be handled in the specific senses in which the specifications of A stand as operational consequences of the specifications of B." This is obviously a very different notion of functions.

Garfinkel then discusses the three functions—motivational functions, coordinative functions, and control functions—in more detail. Information he says (210) can *motivate* changes. Coordinative functions have to do with maintaining a shared definition of the situation—of commitment to the same set of constitutive practices. Control functions have to do with "the regulation and resolution of incongruity."

Every communication serves all three functions simultaneously. It must do so if mutual intelligibility is to be maintained—a point that Garfinkel says (211) he made at greater length in Memo #2.

He concludes part XIII with a discussion of primary and secondary feed-back loops (212). This part is difficult—but important with regard to discussions of secondary information and reflexivity. Garfinkel explores several characteristics of feed-back loops: time between transmissions, time delay, and loss of information during transmission. He also says that there are first, second, and third order loops (212). There are circular and linear routings. He will link these to all the other properties of the paths. What he is doing here is linking together everything in one grand network of interrelated paths.

"The paths," he says (213), "are also immediately relevant to the properties of information in many ways." Things that happen to information are functions of these paths. The ways in which communicants assess the meaning of messages are conditioned by these paths.

Part XIV: Summary of the Theory (Omitted)

I am not sure why Garfinkel retained this empty section. That in itself is interesting and in the interests of changing nothing I have left it as it is. The theory is essentially elaborated in part XIII. But leaving this section empty suggests that no theory has been given. It is consistent with Garfinkel's position that what is missing is also information.

Part XV: Problems and Theorems

Here Garfinkel lists ninety-two theorems. Probably a chapter could be written about each one of these—but I hesitate to attempt this here. Instead, I advise the reader to treat each theorem the way they would treat one of Wittgenstein's paragraphs—as loosely related to one another—and, together, as making up something of a whole. The form of presentation is also another expression of Garfinkel's reluctance to formulate theoretically and in abstraction the order properties that he treats as primarily empirical and constitutive matters of fact/order.

SECTION FOUR: Discussion of the Appendices

Relation of Garfinkel's Theory of Information to Other Manuscripts

Already by 1948, in the manuscript published as *Seeing Sociologically* (2006), Garfinkel's focus on communication and interaction as the key to questions of social order was well developed. In that manuscript his focus on the anomaly as the way taken for granted orders can be made visible was also apparent. Garfinkel's insights with regard to the importance of anomalies came initially from Gurwitsch and the idea of "gestalts," which he had studied between 1939 and 1942 at North Carolina. When he arrived at Princeton in 1951, and began dealing with information theory, Garfinkel once again encountered a field in which the anomaly figured prominently.

This is somewhat ironic. Of all the sociologists who could have gone to Princeton to work on this project—Garfinkel is probably the only one at that time who already had a deep appreciation of the importance of the anomaly and who had already worked out a theory of communication and constitutive order that revolved around the idea that anomalies can only appear against a background of patterned order—an essential idea for information theory as well. Without a background of order, he argued, there is only noise—no anomaly, and no information.

This unique conjunction of Gestalt theory and interactionism would enable Garfinkel to see quickly a new way of conceiving the constitutive orders that are necessary to provide the background expectancies which explain the possibility of information—without resorting to overdetermined schemas like game theory or the rational man, or to cognitivist schemas in which information just maps onto perceptions—or even worse onto brain states.

Garfinkel summarized the relevant elements of his 1948 argument in the first two memos that he produced for the Princeton seminar.

The First and Second Memos and the Research Proposals

The manuscript "Notes Toward a Sociological Theory of Information" was produced as Memo #3 for the seminar on April 17, of 1952. Memos #1 (undated) and #2 (October 4, 1951) were titled "A Statement of the Problem of Communicative Strategies in Self-Maintaining Systems of Activity" and "Some Problematical Areas in the Study of Communicative Work," respectively. Garfinkel also wrote two short research proposals describing research projects which explicitly reference Memo #3: The first is titled "Predicting the Effects of Time and Rate of Supervisory Success upon Group Performance," and the second is titled "Initial Proposal for Some Studies of the Determinants of the Effectiveness of the Communicative Work of Leaders." Lastly, there is Garfinkel's study of Bastrop, Texas, and his accompanying letter to Moore dated June 24, 1942.

Memo #1: "A Statement of the Problem of Communicative Strategies in Self-Maintaining Systems of Activity" (Appendix 1)

Memo #1 summarizes ground covered in *Seeing Sociologically* (2006). There, Garfinkel discusses the problem of action and the scientific observer. He contrasts the positions of Parsons and Schutz—again, in summary form—and alludes to other papers where these issues will be elaborated (including his PhD thesis—which he was just completing at the time—and a later document titled "Parsons's Primer"—which he taught at UCLA). What this first memo does is to establish a relationship between the pre-dissertation work on communication and interaction, the dissertation work that tries to establish a new model for sociological work through a comparison of Parsons and Schutz, and the work on information and formal organizations that Garfinkel is engaged in at Princeton—and which occupies memo #3.

What these memos did for students in the seminar would have been to get them ready to take on the issues discussed in Memo #3, and, also to prepare them as sociologists to understand the complicated information and game theories that they would hear from conference participants such as Bateson and Deutsch.

The discussion of the scientific observer (228–29) considers the difference between a scientific observer—and a science based on scientific observation—and a science based on the participant's or communicant's perspective. It is essentially the same as his discussion in 1948—but in several respects it is clearer. The scientific observer defines a world of possible objects according to the basic and procedural rules of science. Because of this, the observer has no access to the objects that participants in the situation construct for themselves using the basic and procedural rules of situated constitutive action. The "empirical" constructs of the scientific observer, therefore, do not describe the world in which actors act: "[T]hey *are* the world," Garfinkel says (229), in their own right. This raises the question of what "empirical" would mean in a science that took the participant's perspective and looked for the ways in which reality is socially constructed according to constitutive expectations—rather than making up a world that belongs only to the science.

Garfinkel introduces (234) the "concept of communication" with the admonition that to "make this concept capable of bearing up under thorough going criticism" would require "an excursion into the various meanings of 'Time' as a structure that is constitutive of experience." In *Seeing Sociologically* Garfinkel engaged in an elaborate and detailed discussion of time (see also Rawls 2005). But in this summary document he says he will "leave it to the discussion of this paper."

Garfinkel revisits what he means by an actor—that an actor treats symbols and objects—and that objects are therefore social in character, requiring time. Constitutive action is accomplished sequentially; that is, it has an essential time factor. Objects oriented in this sense are the reality; for Garfinkel, there is no other. Therefore, a theory of information—or objects—will have to take these features of the actor and communication into account as they sequentially create the mutual intelligibility of objects.

He also introduces the notion of communicative tactics.

Garfinkel gives a definition of communication that is similar to his definition of information in Memo #3. He says (240) that "[a]ny alteration of the expressional field, i.e. the difference between two states of the expressional field separated by any arbitrary interval of standard time will be known as a communication or a message." Therefore, what communication refers to are "alterations of an expressional field." The inputs are pressing in from all sides and something needs to be done with them to order them—for them to be mutually intelligible.

In differentiating his position from von Neumann and Morgenstern, Garfinkel (241) makes an early version of an argument that Lucy Suchman went on to make famous. Von Neumann and Morgenstern are talking about plans (when they say strategy), but this is not what Garfinkel means by strategy. Their idea of strategy requires a full rule set and complete information. By contrast, what Garfinkel means by strategy is that the actor tries for certain immediate or long-term effects: but without a complete plan, complete information, or the ability to predict outcomes confidently. These are actions within a situated context of constitutive order.

Garfinkel announces at this point that he plans to study various naturally occurring contexts in which plans and strategies are important so as to work this out better. He mentions trial protocols as one of a list of situations to study, and we know that he went to work on the jury project when he left Princeton in the spring of 1953. So, we can see here—in his projection of that sort of study—where it might fit into the overall development of his work.

The very important idea of "self-maintaining" orders is introduced near the end of Memo #1 (245):

> The problem of stating analytically the conditions under which a system is self-maintaining is the problem of stating those conditions of a communicative system which determine a flow of tactics which in serving the effects of correcting for error and regulating discrepance maintain the conditions that determine the flow of tactics that in serving the effects maintain the conditions etc., etc.

The idea of self-maintaining orders was introduced by Durkheim in *The Division of Labor* (1893) and then picked up by Parsons, becoming a staple idea of structural functionalism. Garfinkel's approach is quite different—a point that he elaborates in more detail in Memo #3. On the conventional view, self-regulation involves something of a balancing act between systems goals and individual self-interests. But, that model retains the idea of top-down orders and action directed by individual interests. What Garfinkel argues, by contrast, is that practices actually are self-regulating—that in them it is not conflict that results when interests are not balanced but instant confusion. Since constitutive practices are the ideal case it is ironic that they get treated as trivial and contingent by philosophy and economics alike.

At the very end of the memo (245–47), Garfinkel again lists topics for investigation. The third involves formal organizations and interaction and interaction effects between the two.

Memo #2: "Some Problematical Areas in the Study of Communicative Work" (Appendix 2)

There are two sorts of problems in the area of communicative work where Garfinkel's position clashes with information theory that are addressed by this memo: redundancy and efficiency.

In opening with a consideration of Role and the orientation of the actor in communication, Garfinkel considers the many ways in which the actor is looking for feedback to confirm their definition of the situation. Responses are appraised for whether they validate "the way in which the communicator" structures, or assumes the situation to be structured (249). Because he proposes that there is a need for constant feedback the issue of redundancy has a very different character for Garfinkel.

People repeat themselves. They say the same thing again and again: "Yes sir—no sir." But because each next utterance in Garfinkel's examples has the character of a social obligation, each next repeat carries information. In the case of "sir" this is information about how how we stand in a hierarchical relationship. But it works for ordinary communication, too. For instance, if a person greets you—it means something new each next time: We still stand in a relationship that involves the expectation of a greeting. If a greeting is missing, it means something. Silence, Garfinkel says, can also be information.

When these aspects of language are considered by information theorists, however, they miss the point and treat redundancy as "noise"—not carrying information. Therefore the aim is usually to reduce redundancy.

One of the functions of repetitions, Garfinkel says (251), "is that of inciting the return of information." "Rationally inefficient" repetitions may also serve to identify persons as accepted members of a group. They may constitute "ritual nonsense" against which the part that is not nonsense can be highlighted. Thus, "nonsense" may turn out to be essential to information.

Garfinkel (252–53) then discusses the possible negative results when management, ignoring the social functions of redundancy/repeating—try to rationalize office procedures and eliminate it. This tends to produce a deprivation of just those kinds of confirming information that communicants need to create and sustain a world of mutually intelligibly objects together. The kinds of deprivation produced and the problems caused are sketched in here. They are dealt with at much greater length in Memo #3.

Bateson is mentioned in a discussion of time (255–56) in which Garfinkel considers the problem of the situation and the actor being mutually constituted—a position he shared with Bateson. Bateson, he says, has sent a letter in conjunction with the paper he is preparing for the seminar that focuses on something Garfinkel refers to as the "grammar of time" and seems to involve the problem that cultural difference in time orientations will produce.

The discussion then returns to the problem of deprivation (257), where we find an important precursor to the "Trust" paper. That mutual intelligibility is possible to the extent that people have grasped "a definition of the communicative net that they can assume is common to others." Trust and routine come up again (260) in relation to the amount of "nonsense" normally to be found in any given communicative system (a point related to the discussion of routine in Memo #3).

What plant managers want is more efficient communication. But, to the extent that redundancy and other inefficiencies work to establish meaning, it will turn out that increasing rationality, or efficiency of communication, at the expense of reducing necessary redundancy, may lead to greater ambiguity of communication.

Garfinkel refers to these as operations of deprivation. And he is including here the rationalization of the grounds of communication (such as would occur when a plant manager attempts to streamline or control communication between employees) as a deprivation. These would be done to improve organization—but would actually produce deprivation.

The discussion of deprivation (258) involves secondary information (also discussed in part VIII of Memo #3). Rationalizing or messing with the requirements for communication make it difficult to achieve understanding/order. Here Garfinkel discusses the medical interview that he will write about later in *Studies in Ethnomethodology*.

Garfinkel (259–60) produces a list of nine deprivations of secondary information. There is another list of eleven deprivations at the end (13). All of these deprivations can be seen in large-scale organizations—although one would have to elaborate on how this is the case with some of them. In conjunction with the discussion of deprivations (260–64) Garfinkel introduces problems with oriented objects, Adelbert Ames and visual illusions (262), and visual and other spaces. These have to do with both information and formal organizations, as they will come up in Memo #3 in parts VI–XV.

The Two Research Proposals

(1) Initial Proposal for Some Studies of the Determinants of the Effectiveness of the Communicative Work of Leaders (Appendix 3)

This first proposal deals with the question of what makes for effective leadership. Garfinkel (1) opens his argument with the observation that traditional approaches to the leadership question tend to assume a "viable system of activity and ask what contributes to its viability." It follows from this assumption that "the structural properties that appear to determine viability are then treated as conditional of the leadership effectiveness."

By contrast Garfinkel insists (1) that "order is not to be assumed or settled." It is an ongoing achievement—and the work of achieving it, he says (1) "requires accounting for in terms of the very activities of the system whose patterned properties are otherwise regarded as 'equilibrated.'" Equilibrium, which conventional theorists propose a well balanced system maintains on its own—Garfinkel treats as the carefully managed effect of a great deal of ongoing carefully coordinated work of various kinds in an "operative net." He refers to Memo #3 for a definition of communicative or operative net.

Learning about the ways in which trouble can be introduced into a net will shed some light on what self-regulation of a task net—or equilibration—means for that net. Garfinkel (266) says that "by learning specifically how one may make trouble, and addressing the devices whereby these troubles are prevented from arising," one learns the process of self-regulation.

He refers to this process as "equilibrium"—and self-regulation—ideas that come from both Durkheim and Parsons—and leadership is then proposed as having to do with the reciprocities in the net that create equilibrium—from the inside out—not what we usually think of as leadership.

Garfinkel (266) assumes a set of persons "whose activities are mutually oriented and who must act in concert." Work that does not need to be mutually coordinated would display different order properties. Building on the idea that problems are caused when the task set is not shared—Garfinkel will use anomalies to locate the ways in which problems can be produced in the task set. Doing so will concretely illuminate the leadership question.

If we understand leadership in this way, we need to reconsider what kinds of problems will negatively impact on leadership. Garfinkel (267) attempts to construct a model that will propose "the manipulations that can be performed upon a communicative net to undercut leadership effectiveness" and then to say why these problems occur in some organizations and not in others.

Garfinkel says that he will use Parsons's definition of leader. But, in elaborating his use of this definition it becomes clear that he has altered it. First, he (267) interprets "is responsible for," in Parsons' definition, to require a particular form of "me" orientation toward a social world. And, there is an interesting discussion here of various me orientations of actors. Second, he locates "blame" in the reciprocity obligations that hold between various "me" identified actors. The order of "reciprocally intertwined relevancies and social types" sets the parameters for blame. This is relevant to later work on accountability and conversational preference orders—which show actors working to satisfy the accountable requirements for responsibility within a turn such that blame never materializes.

This is interesting—both in terms of Garfinkel's development of the idea of the oriented actor—and for pushing his trust argument toward a theory of morality. What he is talking about here is morality in terms of a particular orientation—"is responsible for"—toward a specific shared communicative net.

For Garfinkel (267) the definition of leadership involves the idea that "every constitutive order provides a distribution of rights to control the actions of others through casual review of the other's actions relative to the probability of action in concert." A person can claim to be a leader if others in the communicative net honor such a claim.

Having gotten this far—and positioned himself as using Parson's definition of a leader—Garfinkel (269) then goes on to say that this communicative production of "a leader" *has nothing to do with the definition of a leader.* What he means, I think, is that the varieties of communicative work that persons with the right to claim to be leaders can engage in remain to be *found out*—it does not follow from the definition. It will also be the case that the varieties of communicative work that leaders can and should engage in will vary from task set to task set and between communicative nets.

Garfinkel (269) also wants to challenge the idea of leadership effectiveness that assumes effectiveness can be measured by "matching some outcome against a standard found outside the system"—another representational approach. He will opt again for a coherence approach, proposing by contrast that leadership means "the difference one person's communicative work makes for another's definition of a situation."

Garfinkel also gives a definition of influence or power here—as the ability to manipulate the other's definition of the situation—that also appears in the 1948 manuscript. Here he equates the same influential character with leadership effectiveness as well as with power. In a footnote on motivation (n5), he discusses the motivation issue in a way that is also related to the issue of the ability to influence the other person's "grounds for action"—relative to leadership.

So, what are the troubles—or anomalies—that will show us what leadership is? Garfinkel proposes that given this theory of order it is possible to rationally order the principles for doing evil.

In considering the ways in which trouble can be caused, Garfinkel begins with a discussion of secondary information. Because communicants always require secondary information in order to make sense—it is possible to create trouble in a communicative net by interfering with either the transmission, or the reliability, of secondary information. There is a similarity between what Garfinkel means by "secondary information" and Goffman's consideration of the importance of the information the other "gives off" unintentionally. But, Garfinkel's treatment here is much more systematic—sequential and time sensitive and covers intentional deprivation of secondary information.

Being deprived of secondary information will make participants in the net uneasy and prevent them from making sense. They will work hard to get the secondary information so as to restore meaning to the net. But, if they cannot they may also develop a lack of trust that makes participation in the net meaningless and work impossible.

Garfinkel again (272) lists a number of ways of restricting secondary information in a communicative net, many of which he later followed up with research. Giving back contradictory or random information, time delays, increasing message density, increasing redundancy, giving secondary information that is either insufficient, too much, or unrelated to the original message and randomizing the sequencing of responses (many of these also appear in Memos #1 and #3).

Garfinkel's (271) discussion of the need for secondary information in order to know how one is being heard—"How do you *read* me? How do *you* read me?"—makes an appearance both in the 1948 manuscript and in Memo #1. Here we find it in a developing context of argument and it seems clearer. Some of the conversational devices elaborated in the 1948 manuscripts also seem to find a context here—which suggests that some of this may have been written before 1948—as part of an early study of the military during the war.

Garfinkel's focus on what causes trouble also explains why the conversational devices he considers there are almost entirely strategic, because what he is considering are ways of causing trouble (that reflect on leadership) in a communicative net.

He is not arguing that social order is a process of strategic action. Quite the contrary. It is strategic actions of various sorts that destabilize the mutual coordination of communicative nets and make it impossible for participants in the net to get the information they need to go on with.

Simply put, in order to cause trouble, he says (271), we can "[operate] on secondary information while at the same time making it necessary for [a participant] to coordinate [their] own communicative work with others."

For centrally directed systems the likelihood of deprivation is greater, he says, where there is a; 1) large population; 2) low probability of honoring status differences; 3) status rules are ambiguous; 4) secondary feedback loops are greater; 5) fast growth; 6) technical preferences conflict with institutional prescriptions; 7) messages are sensitive to small time variations; 8) power coalitions are more powerful than the constitutive rules of the net; 9) individual advantage effects information exchange; 10) the system maintains relative equality of distributed information; 11) division of labor multiplies incumbents rather than specialties (resulting in more people at worksite and/or higher turnover); 12) power and responsibility are incommensurate.

Wilbert Moore (1946) maintained that accountability is a necessary accompaniment of power. But Moore argued for this in abstract and logical terms—following from the ideas of leadership, morality, democracy, and power. Garfinkel's argument supports some of the same conclusions. But, rather than drawing his requirements for leadership from a definition of terms, or an abstract understanding of democratic ideas—Garfinkel argues instead that accountability—and other types of secondary information, are necessary because a communicative net, that is, an organization and an organizational task group—cannot be effectively maintained without it.

The need for secondary information imposes both moral and organizational requirements on leaders and the formal organization itself—that they cannot violate without damaging the task nets that, as organizations, they depend on.

Secondary information and moral accountability are first and foremost required because they have essentially to do with constitutive features of the communicative-net. It does not matter what political theory a person adheres to, the moral requirements of leadership and task-nets are essentially the same. And, they look surprisingly like the requirements posited by liberal moral philosophy—an idea that Garfinkel will develop further in the "Trust" paper (1963).

(2) Predicting the Effects of Time and Rate of Supervisory Succession Upon Group Performance (Appendix 4)

In this second proposal Garfinkel lays out the problem as follows.[58] Because of constant turnover, getting a new person to be able to quickly fill a job—in a highly organized worksite environment—is a high priority. It is also a high priority if innovation requires turnover such that keeping the same personnel is a less effective option. Furthermore, organizations experience a great deal of disruption in some cases and very little in others. Instead of treating this as a structural issue, or as depending on the qualities of leadership involved, Garfinkel suggests that reasons for the variation in effects can be found in the requirements of the net, and asks "what can be done organizationally to a task-group in order to minimize the adverse effects of succession?" Being able to achieve unproblematic turnover of personnel would be a high priority for the military—but also for any flexible and fast moving peace-time business.

The question that needs to be addressed, Garfinkel says, is why some task groups seem to be more quickly able to make the substitution of new personnel, while others have serious and abiding problems. The conventional approach is to try to tighten the parameters defining the job and to standardize tasks—a kind of top down control—to solve this transition problem.

Garfinkel will suggest another approach, focusing on how the task group does its work, and on what the task group needs in order to complete the task. The proposals Garfinkel makes in this document—while broad in scope are notable for the following: (1) they focus on the importance of sequencing and temporally gearing into a present; (2) the idea of the "present relevant past"; (3) the idea of tasks as discrete bits of work that have their own developmental histories; (4) the idea that information is necessarily incomplete; (5) that competence for managing incomplete information is developed on the job and at the worksite; (6) therefore, overlap between personnel is essential to the succession; (7) that replacement during a task—any task—will present

---

58. Although Garfinkel did studies of the New Jersey State Prison and a mental institution during his year at Princeton, the examples in this proposal seem to come primarily from his military experience. He did several studies while he was in the military, one of the Gulfport hospital. But, the examples used may also represent a new study for the military—as he did several studies funded by the military during those years.

more of a problem than replacement after the task is complete—or before it begins; and, (8) that the later in a task the replacement takes place the worse the effects will be.

Garfinkel brings in the idea that task-sets must be learned on the job—they are not qualities of persons and cannot be adequately defined by rules or top down order. Furthermore, they have developing histories, and the coherence of each next thing done can depend on the things that preceded in the sequence. The competencies involved operate for the most part independently from formal rules, or institutional oversight. Furthermore, they require being positioned within the communicative net. Therefore, tightening the rules, or strengthening institutional accountability, will not make practices clearer to newcomers, or transitions easier.

Garfinkel is proposing that tasks are social orders in their own right, and that, as social orders, sequencing is an essential feature of how order constitutes mutual intelligibility within a task. Coming into a sequence late can render essential features of a task meaningless—just as coming into a conversation late can rob talk of coherence. Succession—change in personnel—should therefore, he argues, occur as near the beginning of a task as possible—or else wait until after it is finished. Understanding why this is necessary in order to facilitate formal organizational goals requires replacing a top down model of order with a task centered view of constitutive practices.

This model also enables Garfinkel to explain why some task groups have more difficulty than others. The differences are not related to the tasks, or to the leadership qualities of the group leader, or to the tightness of formal rules—as conventional studies suppose. Not focusing on the order properties has led to this mistaken focus on demographics. The differences have to do with how far into a project the succession/replacement has taken place.

In addition to building on Garfinkel's research on formal organizations, the proposed research plan is modeled on insights drawn from the game of Kriegsspiel, a form of chess—which is explained in an appendix to the proposal. This is an important explanation—as Garfinkel often refers to Kriegsspiel—but this is the only extended explanation I have seen of it. (Section 7 of Memo #3 discusses various ways players can get information in the game.) The explanation is not only valuable for what it says about the game—but it is revealing for what it is about the game that Garfinkel finds relevant to questions of social order—and just what those aspects of the game signify to him—that is—how they relate to various arguments that he makes.

The basic parallel he intends—I think—is that with Kriegsspiel—because information is incomplete—the only way a player can have any idea what is going on is to have followed every move so far. It is a game in which mutual attention to sequencing is maximized at every point—and failures to mutually attend sequences are self-correcting—you lose if you don't attend.

The player's idea of where the pieces are—and which moves could most profitably be made—will be entirely given by how accurately they have followed the developing series of moves.

What we can see in this proposal is a very early form of what Garfinkel will focus on later as "hybrid studies of work," with an emphasis on the importance of attending to sequential properties of order (Rawls 2008). We can easily see the relationship between this approach and Kriegsspiel. There is so much tacit knowledge being employed and so many decisions based on tacit assumptions—in a task based workgroup—that it is necessary to be in the midst of it step-by-step to get it. Too much is tacit and unspoken and too much has become the joint working knowledge of the working group at task site—such that each next decision is based on the developing series of worksite moves constituting "what they all know." It is a true collective in a self-regulating sense.

A newcomer can't know "what they all know," and it can't be found in formal rules or formal accounts. And as Garfinkel says in part VIII of Memo #3, the newcomer's lack of overlap with what the others know greatly increases the total ignorance of the group. The proposal is another early illustration of the difference between plans and formal rules versus situated and developing actions based on tacit competencies, and of the implications of this difference for understanding work in formal organizations.

Analysis of Garfinkel's Bastrop Notes and Letter to Moore (Appendix 5)

Early in 1942, after completing his M.A. thesis, Garfinkel traveled to Bastrop, Texas, to undertake a study of the effects of a "Boom" town environment on the town of Bastrop Texas for Wilbert Moore. A temporary camp had come to the area in the first year of the war—and plans were in place to build a permanent camp.

Moore was at this time preparing the manuscript for his classic work *Industrial Relations and the Social Order*. By 1944 Moore had completed the manuscript for his book, but wartime shortages held up publication until early 1946. The manuscript included several sections on boom towns and transient labor—although these don't mention specific research done by or for Moore. It seems interesting that the Bastrop study is not mentioned in the book—even though it certainly fits Moore's criteria of a town in a context of transient and "boom" conditions—a study of a town that had been in place for a long time under more or less stable conditions and then rapidly transformed as industry—in this case the army—moved in.

Of course, Garfinkel had not approached the town in this way—arguing instead that it has never really been "stable" in the way Moore supposed—a position consistent with Garfinkel's overall orientation to order. Therefore, Garfinkel could hardly evaluate "change" in the way Moore wanted.

Moore was interested in the destabilizing effects of such industrial incursions on towns—how they would change, secularize, and destabilize. Garfinkel was concerned that the idea that the town—or for that matter any order in the town—had once been "stable" was playing a problematic role in Moore's analysis.

Moore was also operating with a mistaken interpretation of Durkheim, which he refers to in his book as "Durkheim's dilemma." This interpretation attributes to Durkheim the idea that stability in modern society is only possible to the degree that people hold the same norms and values. In fact, Durkheim criticized this belief, and attributed the position to Comte. Nevertheless, it has become a sociological staple and it heavily informed Moore's expectation of the consequences of industrialization. Moore belonged to a school of research including the famous Yankee City study of Newburyport, Massachusetts. His research approach assumed an underlying functionalism, which meant that under "normal" circumstances a town would not change and that when new industries came abruptly into an area the changes they produced would destabilize a town.

Garfinkel in his report opens with a discussion of this first assumption. He says that he can't consider that the town had a stable history before the introduction of the camps—and he gives a short history of various changes the town has been through in order to support his point. It is a huge point of difference between the two—but Garfinkel produces it more or less as just another observation.

The thing is—if the town was never stable—and kept changing—due to both internal and external pressures—then Moore's argument that industry moving into the area will destabilize the town—cannot be made sense of. In order to argue that something has been destabilized—it must first be the case that there is a stability to destabilize.

Garfinkel's second point—that characteristics of interaction are more important for understanding the town than formal institutions and their beliefs and values—relates to Moore's misinterpretation of Durkheim. If shared beliefs and values—institutionalized beliefs and values—are necessary for social order—the position Moore and others attribute to Durkheim, then measuring institutions will measure the degree of stable integration of a town.[59]

But, Durkheim actually argued that what promotes stability in modern society is mutual commitment to a set of self-regulating practices. Given this position, and Garfinkel's further elaboration of it in terms of just what is required of people working together in a communicative net to sustain it— then the stability of modern society—is as Garfinkel proposes—best studied by looking at the communicative net and the secondary feedback people are giving one another about their mutual commitment to it—than by looking at the institutional features of a town.

Garfinkel did not find institutional stability in his study—and his apologetic note to Moore clearly underscores his awareness that he has not found what Moore would have hoped for. He did find stability in the communicative net—and in fact, this would suggest that Moore is wrong—in his overall approach to social order. I think it is characteristic of Garfinkel's approach that he does not criticize Moore directly, or say that he disagrees with his approach; rather, he writes that he is afraid that his way of seeing things differently will disappoint Moore.[60]

It is interesting to consider the relationship between Garfinkel and Moore. Moore was teaching at the Pennsylvania State College during the academic year 1940–1941. This would have been directly before Garfinkel undertook the Bastrop study for Moore. The book on industrial sociology developed out of a new course taught by Moore during that year.

There are several notable aspects of Moore's argument that seem to be echoed by rebuttals in Garfinkel's 1948 manuscript—and it is tempting to think that

---

59. Moore's (1946: 562) adoption of the Durkheim misunderstanding leads to his expecting various negative outcomes of industrialization. They may indeed happen because traditional belief based elements resist and react—but he misunderstands what Durkheim thinks this means. Moore characterized WWII Boom Towns as "previously stable industrial communities" that became "overgrown beehives of activities." In the opening lines of his Bastrop Report, Garfinkel challenges this fundamental supposition. The economy of such areas is in constant flux—and the "boom" was not only taken pretty much in stride—but as soon as the "boomers" left, everything seemed to go right back the way it was. Although, Garfinkel notes that someone should stay and study the changes that would take place when the new permanent army camp was in place. Maybe the permanence of the encampment would make a bigger difference.

60. It is important to understand certain character traits that underscore Garfinkel's relationship with mentors, students and the discipline. I would describe him as a very gentle genius. This description stands at odds with the many instances of his anger and cutting remarks. But like many very gentle men who have piercingly keen intellects and see farther than the rest of

in reading over Moore's work—during his work for him in 1942—Garfinkel began to formulate some of his counter-arguments.

For instance, Moore (1951: viii) references "a clearer exposition of motivational problems" and devoted a whole section of his book to "the question of motives." This corresponds to a major theme of Garfinkel's later manuscript 1948—in which his argument that the motivation question is misconceived is woven throughout.

The way Moore's book opens—with an extended statement of "impartial science"—also finds a rebuttal in the opening of Garfinkel's 1948 manuscript in particular and several times in the Princeton memos. Whereas Moore (1951: 4) says, "it will be useful from time to time to view the world from the standpoint of the laborer, the manager, or the public official . . ." Garfinkel opens the 1948 manuscript with the argument that action is only performed from the perspective of the engaged and identified actor. The scientific observer is not involved and therefore does not—cannot—have the perspective of the actor. This means, for Garfinkel, that the scientific observer can never see the actual facts of social order. Therefore, an "impartial scientific observer" would not be able to see what was going on. Moore (1951: 5) actually uses the words "The observer is not playing the same game." Garfinkel echoes this. The observer and actor are not playing the same game. But, the consequences of this for Garfinkel are very different from the consequences drawn from the same statement by Moore. For Moore it is a reason for the scientist to remain impartial. But, for Garfinkel it is a reason why the impartial observer can never have access to the order properties of the "game" because they are not playing it and cannot see how it unfolds as a joint project of reciprocated mutual work for participants. They are not attending its developing order sequentially.

Finally, we find in Moore the argument that many "roles" are played by the same concrete person—and thus he gets into discussions of role conflict. Garfinkel will quite elaborately develop the idea that whole concrete persons do not act and that roles do not conflict, in both the 1948 and the Princeton memos. Garfinkel maintains that since people inhabit more than one of these contexts—he needs to make it clear that the word "role" designates only "one aspect of the experiencing ego or systems of egos" and that they are experienced only one at a time. In this way he avoids the problem of "role conflict."

---

us—he finds himself constantly boxed in: unable to speak directly and say the penetrating things he wants to say and unable to criticize people directly. Such impotence in the face of conflict and criticism makes him angry and he lashes out—for lack of an ability to perform more constructive actions.

However, there is one important thing Moore argues—that does resonate with Garfinkel's later work. He emphasizes the social aspects of work and industry—even the technical aspects of work and machines. This, ironically, in spite of their differences—makes the work of the two broadly consonant in insisting that the social sits at the heart of industrial relations of all kinds.

To my mind, one of the most important statements that Garfinkel makes in his letter to Moore is that he does not consider information about the "institutions" in Bastrop to be either more important or more real—than observations about the activities of various people around town. He says that usually theorists argue that institutions are causal—the source of order and stability—and that information about them is necessary and sufficient for drawing conclusions about what is going on in a town.

For Garfinkel, by contrast, information about social institutions is only a background. He says that he learns more by seeing a poem on a wall of a men's room (titled "make Me a man"). Or, that if one of the respectable women came to the reading circle in a business suit it would tell him more about changes going on in the town than descriptions of—or formal measures of—the so-called "five institutions or the 16," as he rather flippantly writes to Moore.

The poem, he (282) says, "is an objective indication of institutionalized sentiments" and "the women's dress is relevant to the complex of the expressional virtue of competition for social leadership and acceptance." These are social facts related to the presentation of self and reciprocity in the net—to the way actors mutually orient a communicative net. If these "facts" changed, he says, that they would "point to a far-reaching shift in 'community organization'"; changes which, he (282) says, "might occur without necessarily being accompanied by the town's accoutrements of town streets and new store fronts." In other words, the communicative net can change without there being corresponding changes in the formal institutional looks of things. The reverse, however, is not possible.

This insistence on the relevance of single instances of what might look like "behavior" would likely be read by Moore, as it was by others, as an instance of Garfinkel apparently focusing on individuals—which is what he is accused of later. But, he is not focusing on individuals and he is not interested in behavior—individual or otherwise. What Garfinkel is arguing is that the orientation of actors toward interactional requirements—that are public and shared—tells him about the real social organization of the town—not about individuals. Furthermore, he argues that these facts about how people—identified selves—present themselves in town, tell more about the social organization of the town—than "facts" about streets and storefronts.

Garfinkel goes on to say that "for me a study of community organization meant a structural and functional analysis of a system of agents related to each other in time by interconnected modes of appraisal of the objects of their environment." This is what he refers to later as both a communicative net and a theory of organization or interconnected "net-work" paths. As with other statements of alignment with Parsons and others, notably Schutz—by "structural functional" here Garfinkel means something very much of his own design: "Interconnected modes of appraisal of the objects of their environment," very much a focus of his own and still evident later in the development of Ethnomethodology.

One other thing that is worthy of comment is Garfinkel's list of the social systems he found in Bastrop. I don't think that many other sociologists would have identified most of these as social systems. Each specifies a local order of ordered arrangements—in Garfinkel's terms a net. For instance, he lists, "merchant's community" and "worker's communities represented by trailer areas." For Garfinkel each of these specifies a different social system—within which there will be different identities and different social facts and value orientations. Unless each of these is specified in detail, he does not think that it is possible to say what is going on in the town.

Traditional studies—as he acknowledges—would focus instead on the "five institutions—or the 16." Garfinkel, by contrast, considers information about social institutions on this order to constitute only background. The real social systems consist of networks of people—oriented actors—the constitutive practices to which they are mutually committed—their relationships—and how they expect each other to behave, dress, and otherwise present themselves in specific contexts of action.

Garfinkel was only twenty-four years old when he did this study for Moore—just out of a master's program, heading for the army, and yet to begin working toward his PhD. He says on the first page of his letter to Moore that he is attempting to "use the conceptual apparatus developed in the writings of Talcott Parsons." Garfinkel had not yet gone to work with Parsons, but had admired his work since he first read *The Structure of Social Action* in 1937, and went to study with him at Harvard in 1947—as soon after the war as he could manage to get there.

Garfinkel: Memo #3
Organizational Behavior Project
April 17, 1952

Introduction

THE MISCHIEF THAT THE SEMINAR MEMBERS PERFORMED ON THE DEFINITION of information that I proposed at a previous meeting was enough to cause its discard.[1] With the loss of this central notion, the theory of communication that I had been so hopefully nursing was changed into something exhibiting the unity and appeal of a ball of snakes.

I tried getting another run on the problem by asking what properties in use the thing we called information had, as well as needed to have, if we were to cash in on the new developments in communications theory as well as preserve some continuity with sociological usage. The task of devising a suitable definition proved to be and still is formidable. The solution of sorts that I want to propose in this memo matches the task at least in this respect. Having just come out of a jungle, I can't promise you that in leading you in to show you what I've found that I won't lose the way for all of us.

---

1. [Editor's Note: This refers to Memos #1 and #2, which appear in the appendix to this book. They were handed out months apart and possibly to different audiences. Memos #1 and #2 cover some of the same ground as the overall theory of communication written in 1948 (published in 2006 under the title *Seeing Sociologically*), along with additional material.]

I

Various Conceptions of Information

THE CONCEPTIONS OF INFORMATION OF THE MEN CONSIDERED HERE HAVE IN common an exceedingly important feature: all treat information as an existent that is subject to clear, empirical, physical, and, in some cases, mathematical manipulations. The thing they designate by the term "information" is thus something quite different from the general philosophical notion of knowledge. I regard this as good, and in the theory I tried to borrow from each as much as I could.

1. Claude E. Shannon

In his essay *The Mathematical Theory of Communication*, Shannon, an electronics engineer with the Bell Telephone Company, elects as the fundamental problem of communication what Warren Weaver, Shannon's interpreter to those like myself who are ignorant of mathematics, refers to as the "technical" problem of communication (as compared with what Weaver designates as the "semantic" and the "effectiveness" problem).

The problem he is concerned with is that of reproducing at one point either exactly or approximately a message selected at another point. Shannon (1963, p. 3) writes:

> Frequently the messages have meaning; that is they refer to or are correlated according to some system with physical or conceptual entities. These semantic aspects of communication are irrelevant to the engineering problem. The significant aspect is that the actual message is *one selected from a set* of possible

messages. The system must be designed to operate for each possible selection, not just the one which will actually be chosen since this is unknown at the time of design.

If the number of messages in the set is finite, then this number or any mono-tonic function of this number can be regarded as a measure of the information produced when one message is chosen from the set, all choices being equally likely.

Weaver cautions that information, in Shannon's sense, must not be confused with meaning, and Shannon states explicitly that the semantic aspects of com-munication are irrelevant to the engineering aspects. Information in Shannon's usage refers not so much to what one does say as to what one could say.

It is a measure of one's freedom of choice when one selects a message.... The concept applies not to the individual messages (as the concept of meaning would) but rather to the situation as a whole. The amount of information is defined, in the simplest cases, to be measured by the logarithm of the number of available choices.

Where there is an information source that is producing a message by suc-cessively selecting discrete symbols (letters, words, notes, etc.), the probability of choice of the various symbols at one stage of the process may be such that this probability of choice is dependent upon the previous choices. Shannon shows that the information associated with this procedure turns out to be what is known in thermodynamics as entropy. Borrowing from Weaver to make this notion accessible to us, the term "entropy" is a measure of the degree of randomness or "shuffledness" in the situation.

Having calculated the entropy or information or freedom of choice of a certain information source, one can compare this to the maximum value this entropy could have, subject only to the condition that the source continue to use the same symbols. The ratio of the actual to the maximum entropy is called the relative entropy of its source. If the relative entropy of a source is, say, .8, this roughly means that this source is, in its choice of symbols to form a message, about 80 percent as free as it could possibly be with those same symbols. One minus the relative entropy is called the redundancy. This is the fraction of the structure of the message which is determined not by the free choice of the sender but rather by the statistical rules governing the use of the symbols in question. It is sensibly called redundancy for ... this fraction of the message is unnecessary (and hence repetitive or redundant) in the sense that if it were missing the message would still be essentially complete or at least could be completed.... Shannon estimates

the redundancy of English to be about 50 percent, so that about half the letters
or words we choose in writing or speaking are under our free choice and about
half ... are really controlled by the statistical structure of the language.

Weaver points out that the concept of information characterizes the statistical nature of the information source. This is done, he points out, to permit the
design of a system for which it is either not possible nor practicable to handle
everything perfectly. The system thus should be designed to handle well the
jobs it is likely to be asked to do and should resign itself to be less efficient for
the rare task.

This sort of consideration leads at once to the necessity of characterizing the
statistical nature of the whole ensemble of messages which a given kind of
source can and will produce. And information, as used in communication
theory, does just this.

Weaver finally notes some of the properties of Shannon's definition. He
writes:

Suppose we are choosing only between two possible messages, whose probabilities are p_1 for the first and p_2 equals $1-p_1$ for the other. The numerical
value of H, the symbol for information, has its largest value when the two
messages are equally probable, i.e., $p_1 = p_2 = 1/2$. That is, when one is completely free to choose between the two messages. When one message becomes
more probable than the other, the value of H decreases. And when one message is very probable such that p_1 is almost one and p_2 almost zero, the value
of H is almost zero. In the limiting case where one probability is unity and
the other zero, certainty and impossibility, H is zero. Thus, no uncertainty,
no freedom of choice, no information. If there are many rather than two
choices, then H is largest when the probabilities of the various choices are as
nearly equal as circumstances permit. Suppose though that one choice has a
probability near one so that all the other choices have probabilities near zero.
H calculates to have a very small value—and the information is said to be
low. If all choices are equally likely, the more choices there are, the larger the
amount of information.

2. G. A. Miller

Miller is interested in the psychology of speech and communication. In
his recent book *Language and Communication* (1951), he addresses himself

to the tasks of applying Shannon's definition of information to certain problems in human communication. Miller uses the term "information" to refer to the occurrence of one out of a set of alternative discriminative stimuli.

> A discriminative stimulus is a stimulus that is arbitrarily, symbolically, associated with some thing (or state or event or property) that enables the stimulated organism to discriminate this thing from other things. The content of the information concerns the range of possible alternatives that could occur.... The amount of information increases as a function of the number of alternatives.... If only two alternative stimuli can possibly occur, the occurrence of one carries relatively little information. But if there are 10,000 alternatives possible, the occurrence of one out of this large set carries considerable information.... The stimulus itself, the actual physical event that occurs, could be identical in two different situations, yet when it is one of two possibilities, it is less informative than when it is one of 10,000 possibilities. The amount of information a stimulus conveys cannot be determined from an examination of that stimulus alone; the amount of information depends upon the number of things that could have happened instead, but didn't.[2]

Like Shannon, Miller warns against confusing this concept of information with the popular usage of the term "meaning."

> Our definition does not say that the listener must be able to decode the message. The amount of information is the measure of the talker's freedom of choice when he selects a message. It is a measure, not of the particular message, but of a total situation.

Miller then asks how much information can be encoded in a speech wave and seeks a general quantitative measure of this amount. The task requires an estimate of the number of different alternative sound waves that can occur. The task is simplified by using the concepts of frequency, intensity, and spectra to specify any sound wave. He then takes the time interval of one second. By some ingenious analysis he arrives at a generalized answer to the question, stated as follows:

$$\text{Amount of information} = 2\,T\,W\,\log \frac{S + N}{N}$$

---

2. [Editor's Note: They might see this as a probable distribution of symbols—but for Garfinkel it is an order problem.]

Where T is the duration of the message, W is the width of the band of frequencies, S the maximum amplitude of the signal, and N the size of a discriminable difference in amplitude.

Or, as he says, in words: The amount of information in a speech wave is proportional to the duration of the speech, to the range of frequency components involved, and to the logarithm of the number of discriminable steps in amplitude. In order to increase the amount of information we must talk longer, or increase the range of frequencies in the speech spectrum, or make use of finer distinctions in intensity.

3. Norbert Wiener

The direction of elaboration of the notion of information from its engineering relevance for Shannon through the application to the problems of human communication gets differentiated further in Wiener's writings. In *The Human Use of Human Beings,* he says:

> The earlier work on the theory of information was vitiated by the fact that it ignored noise-levels and other quantities of a somewhat random nature. It was only when the idea of randomness was fully understood together with the applications of the related notions of probability that the question of the carrying capacity of a telegraph or telephone line could even be asked intelligently. When this question was asked it became clear that the problem of measuring the amount of information was of a piece with the related problem of the measurement of the regularity and irregularity of a pattern. It is quite clear that a haphazard sequence of symbols or a pattern which is purely haphazard can convey no information. Information thus must be in some way the measure of the regularity of a pattern and in particular of the sort of pattern known as time series. By time series I mean a pattern in which the parts are spread in time. This regularity is to a certain extent an abnormal thing. The irregular is always commoner than the regular. Therefore, whatever definition of information and its measure we shall introduce must be something which grows when the a priori probability of a pattern or a time series diminishes.

The message is a transmitted spatial or temporal pattern. It acquires its meaning by being a selection from a large number of possible patterns. The amount of meaning can be measured:

> It turns out that the less probable a message is, the more meaning it carries....

Entropy, says Wiener, represents the amount of disorder in a class of patterns. It is also closely associated with the notion of information and its measure, which is essentially a measure of order. Amount of information is a measure of the degree of order, which is peculiarly associated with those patterns which are distributed as messages in time. The notion of amount of information is essentially only that particular case of the notion of the amount of order which is applied to a time pattern. The general ideas of order and disorder are applicable to patterns of all types as well as to the special case of time series. They are applicable not to a particular pattern in isolation but rather to a set of patterns selected from a larger set in such a way that the smaller set possesses a measure of probability. The more probable the type of pattern the less order it contains, because order is essentially lack of randomness.

> If we appeal to the notion of logarithm … the usual measure of the degree of order of a set of patterns selected from a larger set is the negative logarithm of the probability of the smaller set when the probability of the larger set is taken to be one.

4. Karl Deutsch

In his article "Mechanism, Organism and Society" (1950), Deutsch proposes a definition of information that further extends the line of theorizing initiated by Shannon to bring it even further into the working domain of the sociologist. The critical part of his remarks for our purposes goes as follows:

> Communications engineering is unlike power engineering in that the latter transfers amounts of electric energy. Communications engineering transfers information. It does not transfer events but a patterned relationship between events.

Deutsch uses the example of the transmission of the spoken message. A message may be transmitted through a sequence of mechanical vibrations of a membrane, then through electrical impulses in a wire, then through electric processes in a radio transmitter, then through electric and mechanical processes in a receiver, then put on a recorded set of grooves, and, finally, played and made audible to a listener:

> What has been transferred through this chain of processes … is not matter … nor any significant amount of energy….

Rather it is *something* that remains unchanged, invariant, over this whole sequence of processes.

The same sequence applies to the sequence of processes from the distribution of light reflected from a rock to the distribution of chemical changes on a photographic film to the distribution of black and white dots in a printing surface or the distribution of electric "yes" or "no" impulses in ... television. What is transmitted here are neither light rays nor shadows, but information, the patterns of relationships between them.

He goes on to give this notion internal structure:

In the second group of examples we would describe the state of the rock in terms of the distribution of light and dark points on its surface. This would be a *state description* of the rock at a particular time. If we then describe the state of the film after exposure in terms of the distribution of the dark grains of silver deposited on it and of the remaining clear spaces we should get another state description. Each of the two state descriptions would have been taken from a quite different physical object—a rock and a film—but a large part of these two state descriptions would be identical whether we compared them point by point or in mathematical terms.... The extent of the physical possibility to transfer and reproduce these patterns corresponds to the extent that there is "*something*" unchanging in all the relevant state descriptions of the physical processes by which this transmission is carried on. That "something" is information—-those aspects of the state descriptions of each physical process which all these processes had in common.... These patterns of information can be measured in quantitative terms, described in mathematical language, analyzed by science, and transmitted or operated on a practical industrial scale.... [Information in this sense] can be transmitted, recorded, analyzed, and measured. Whatever we may call it, information, pattern, form, Gestalt, state description, distribution function, or negative entropy, it has become accessible to the treatment of science. It differs from the "matter" and "energy" of 19th century mechanical materialism in that it cannot be described adequately by their conservation laws. But it also differs ... from the "idea" or "idealistic" or metaphysical philosophies in that it is based on physical processes during every single moment of its existence, and that it can and must be dealt with by physical methods. It has material reality. It can be measured and counted. It exists and interacts with other processes in the world regardless of the whims of any particular observer....

5. Bateson and Ruesch

In their book *Communication: The Social Matrix of Psychiatry,* these authors extend the concept further to bring it well into the body of current sociological thinking, though at the cost of straining the bounds of current "equilibrium" theory. Their addition, as I make it out, consists in this: They conceive the perceiver and the world simultaneously constituted. They use the model of the actor as a signal receiver, transmitter, and transformer who treats a world constituted in some degree of organization in accordance with the make-up of the actor, a world that is constantly undergoing alteration, test, validation, etc. by the actions of the communicant that serve the actors as the instrumentalities for effecting such orders of consequences. Bateson and Ruesch then represent information as the outcomes or results of the perceptions and transmission of signals, i.e., codified signals.

> Negative entropy, value, and information are in fact alike insofar as the system to which these notions refer is the man plus environment, and insofar as, both in seeking information and in seeking values, the man is trying to establish an otherwise improbable congruence between ideas and events.

6. Von Neumann and Morgenstern

It can be shown, I think, that in the definitions considered so far, a wide variety of models of the actor can be used and are available within the requirement that he be depicted as a signal receiver and sender. The notion of information that Von Neumann and Morgenstern use in their book, *The Theory of Games and Economic Behavior,* entails the use of a radically rational actor. He never misses a message, he extracts from the message all the information it bears, he names things properly and in proper time, he never forgets, and he stores and recalls without distortion. Information for such a player is tantamount to the total state of the game as it is constituted at any moment by a complete and unqualified memory of the rules and recall of all moves in actual order that in principle he can have observed up till the moment of the next move.

11

Some Desired Properties of the Thing Called "Information"

The following list was devised by going over some of the more prominent ways that sociologists as well as others have treated "information." The
list is long but by no means complete. The trick is to find a definition that so
constitutes the thing we are after that these properties are retained.

In whatever way we define "information" it would be desirable above all
that the thing be conceived of as an existent and that it be capable of fairly
precise empirical description.[3]

Further, it should at every point be "coupled" to—to use a phrase that
Wiener employs—and be dependent for its existence upon physical as well
as behavioral processes. We require that a system of signals and a system of
information be capable of being not only coupled but *variably* coupled in the
sense that while this information would depend upon signal characteristics that
it not be given in one-to-one fashion with signal characteristics. We require
that it be possible to perform physical operations that will affect it while at the
same time logical operations like matching, counting, comparing, classifying,
measuring, be possible with it.

It should be capable of being doubted, believed, tested, and recalled. One
should be able to "invest" it with degrees of certainty. It should be capable of
being an object of the experiences of love, hate, respect, fear, judgment, and
so on.

---

3. [Editor's Note: This does not mean that it exists as information independently of being
perceived as such. But, rather that it has physical existence period—independently of being
perceived—it is not a concept or a "meaning."]

It needs to be capable of remaining invariant under variations of signaling characteristics. It needs to be capable of spatial and temporal patterning. One should be able to refer meaningfully to its "existing in amount" at least in the sense that in more than a metaphorical sense one could talk of a person having it while another person does not. We would like it to stand in some clear and determinate relationship to the notions of signal, message, error, randomness, order, memory, feed-back, communication, and communicative path, channel, and route though without sacrifice of sociological problems to engineering metaphors.

It needs to be transmissible from one physical spatial point to another. It must be transformable. It must be so defined that it makes sense to speak of its being differentially distributed within a social structure. It must be capable of being stored. It must allow of caretaker rights to it; of rights and costs of acquisition; of rights of use, control, and transfer. It must be capable of being lost, changed, bought and sold; it must be capable of being "priced."

It must make sense to talk of its clarity or ambiguity, of its uniqueness and typicality; of its private, public, personal, impersonal, anonymous or identified character. Usage must permit the category of ignorance, i.e., its presence or absence but without implying any notion of a finite total and without assigning motivational status to either information or ignorance. It must be capable of being used within the requirement of a sociologically conceived actor who is capable of autonomously altering as well as inventing or creating not only the rules of his own operation but this information as well. It needs to be capable of dissolving into randomness on the one hand, of having a probabilistic character, or at the other extreme of being so completely determined as to have the convincingness for the experiencer of apodicity.

It must be capable of acquisition through procedures other than and in addition to those of logico-empirical science. Further, the actor must be capable of acquiring it even though he fails in his make-up to approximate even closely the characteristics of the rational man.

It must somehow be found not only in the wide-awake attitudes of everyday life and be acquired through the senses, but must be found in the cloud-cuckoo worlds of dreams, fantasy, scientific theory, the theatre, children's play, etc. It must deal with tables, persons, motives, centaurs, laws, and ghosts.

It must make sense to speak of information about information. It must in an important sense require for its objective status a statement about the person as a perceiver and a world that is simultaneously constituted through the notion of the perceiver, yet it must be capable of being treated independently of the perceiver.

It must be capable of treatment not only with reference to the notion of purpose, i.e., its instrumental character, but with reference to usage for its own sake and without reference to the accomplishment of a purpose, i.e., its expressional character.

On top of all this the definition must be general enough in its designation to cover this ground, but specific enough and with enough internal structure to permit its immediate use in generating questions, theorems, concepts, measurements, and so on.

As the confidence men put it, the good sucker always wants the best of it.

III

The Conditions within Which
a Definition of Information
Will Be Sought

IF WE HAD NO PRECONCEPTIONS WHATEVER ABOUT THIS THING CALLED IN-
formation, things would be in a bad way with us. But we have some preconceptions: The properties that we want in the thing information settles that point.
We know the thing "information" through usage. We're looking for the ideas
that are immanent to the concept of information in use, and we seek to isolate
these ideas and arrange them in rational fashion.[4]

But knowing what we are after in the search still leaves us in the dark until we
decide upon some ground rules of the search. These ground rules are nothing
else than the decisions that decide between alternatively possible solutions to
some fundamental analytic problems that *any* theory of human communication, to the extent that the theory held to the ideals of rational consistency and
logical closure, would either explicitly or implicitly, but in any case as a matter
of formal necessity, be predicated on.

I'll consider a few of these problems, though these few I think are potent
enough so that varying decisions about them will differentiate one theory of
communication from another as far as the consequences for problem posing
and data interpretation are concerned. Most particularly, different decisions
on these problems yield different theories of information.

---

4. [Editor's Note: There is an important parallel with Wittgenstein's argument for meaning
as use here.]

The problems may be named as follows: (a) the nature of language; (b) the nature of purpose in human action; (c) the nature of the attitude for apprehending the irreducible datum; (d) the nature of rationality; (e) the nature of the object that the actor treats; and (f) the individual as a source of social change.

(a) The Nature of Language

One out of a large number of problems that are usually designated by the phrase "nature of language" concerns us. The problem that needs settling is how a theory of symbols and a theory of objects are to be related. One solution consists of doing what signaling engineers, for various reasons, are permitted to do: assume a nominalist theory of language where the word is a mere tag for our thoughts or the objects in the world. The task of relating the two systems is that of specifying the rules for matching symbolic and object systems with the view that the symbols are arbitrary designators of the object, it being the smell of the rose and not the smell of the word that makes a rose a rose. Another solution is that of conceiving the word as an abstraction from the fullness of the actual experienced event, a kind of schematic reproduction that by the very inevitability of its schematizing function is always in some measure false to the events it depicts. Another solution, and the one we prefer is that of regarding language as constitutive of the objects it designates. Thus we prefer not to make a separation between linguistic functions and action, but, rather, will hold that linguistic functions are actions.[5] We hope thereby to look to the conditions of the make-up of the communicant and the communicative net-work under which language does exhibit nominalist or copy properties. We are faced therefore with the problem of the multitude of ways in which language "thingifies" various possibilities of experience for our communicants, as well as looking to the conditions under which one type of thingifying rather than another occurs.

(b) The Nature of Purpose in Human Action

In various ways, though with the same effect, most of the currently available theories of human conduct assume the purposive character of conduct. There

---

5. [Editor's Note: Precursor of the idea of Speech Acts—but better and different.]

are some questions that arise in connection with this usage that are due to the failure to keep the empirical and analytic usage distinct. For example, one may speak of purposive activity and mean that the actor orients a future state of affairs as a projected end.[6] His actions then are treated as the means by which he alters a state of affairs so as to bring it into a form that approximates in some degree the "thing he has in mind." Frequently, however, this meaning of purposive activity is confounded with the sense that the observer conceives the actor as acting to maintain or restore a state of equilibrium, or to reduce or manage some painful state. In this case, even the grief work of a bereaved person is seen as purposive in the sense that the grief work effects the "reintegration" of the person into a configuration of stable personal relations with a group in which the beloved is now missing. Such mixed usage lumps together purpose in the sense of project oriented activity with purpose in the sense of the consequences of activity, project oriented or not. There are many such mixtures. We shall not linger over them since the questions they propose are interesting only as errors of theorizing.

Another usage, however, does not involve erroneous usage but is rather a matter of methodological decision. In this usage, purposive activity is assumed as a matter of principle on the methodological ground that to successfully conceive an action, any action, requires as a matter of general a priori law, the dimensions of ends and means.

The claim is that ends and means are "dependent contents" in the sense that an action is irreducibly defined by these two necessary conceptions. In this view, it is decided that an action is not thinkable without the two of them; that as one is taken away the whole conception of action fails. Ends and means can be likened to the dependent contents of the object, color-in-general, which requires, if it be conceivable, the specifications of hue and area.

Such a claim, however, is not to be honored by subscribing to some philosophical position, or some going theory in the field, but is rather to be subjected for the test of its authenticity to an examination of the actual structures of experience. In my experience I find that while many courses of experience are governed by a teleological principle, by no means is it the case that all of it is so governed even though one can assume a theory that would make it as the means-ends theories propose. While much communication, for example, is

---

6. [Editor's Note: Garfinkel uses the form of words "actor orients"—when "orients toward" would be the more usual form. But he uses it consistently and with regard to objects as well as actions and goals, and it indicates the mutual constitution of actor and object through interaction—the act of orienting.]

governed by an orientation to the accomplishment of an end, much is undertaken for its own sake, and particularly is this the case for ritually prescribed communicative relationships, for the communicative work of the arts as well as the communicative work that goes on between intimates. This is not to say, however, that it has no consequences. It does mean, though, that much of it goes on "as a matter of principle" so to speak, i.e., without regard to consequences, and without being regulated by any assessments of its effects.

So presented the argument, I realize, is a crude one, attacking as it does one claim by proposing a counter claim. I propose the dissent for the record and leave the claim for further discussion by the seminar members. The point is that the means-ends scheme is "merely" theoretically possible, and not apodictically necessary.

Some care is necessary, however. Rejecting the requiredness of the means-ends schema does not recommend the view that teleologically governed communication is dichotomous to non-teleologically governed communication and that any instance must fall into one, to the exclusion of showing characteristics that would put it in the other. I prefer to suspend judgment on the question of what the necessary dimensions are, even assuming that they are available to us in the manner of general a priori law.

I prefer to look instead to the actual structures of the communicative experiences that give it its experiential colorings of purpose and non-purpose.

(c) The Attitude for Apprehending the Irreducible Datum

Much talk has recently been going the rounds of social scientists about phenomenology. A prevailing accent in this conversation depicts phenomenology as a new philosophy of social-scientific method. Phenomenology is thereby frequently proposed as a touchstone by which one may get away from theoretical superfluities to the world of actual fact. What is not seen, by and large, is that the term phenomenology refers only to the rules that will be found operating in any perspective—scientific, religious, aesthetic, practical, etc.— whereby certain areas of experience are regarded with a neutral attitude, i.e., are made non-relevant to the problem in hand, while others are accorded the accent of affirmation and just so, i.e., the accent of relevant matters of fact. Every philosophy, every theory, every attitude toward the world has its relevant phenomenology. Every perspective includes its rules on which the irreducible character of data-experiences is based. Every perspective provides the rules whereby the difference is made between that which appears with its theoretical sense and that which appears with its sense of a datum, whether it be the theoretic or data sense of the "outer world" or of the world of "inner experience." This holds for [the] businessman as well as the infant; the scientist as well as the theologian. One may see this if the terms "scientist" and "practical man" are used to designate ways of attending to a world rather than to designate concrete persons.

There are many phenomenologies to choose from, or better, there are many phenomenological attitudes to choose from. There are also two leading contenders: (1) the so-called "neo-Kantian" phenomenology, which is prevalent in social science today and with this or that shading is found in the work of Cassirer, Lewin, Freud, Weber, and Parsons, and (2) the Husserlian phenomenology represented in the work of Schuetz.

The question that the choice decides may be asked as follows: If one allows the possibility that the world has a perspectival appearance to an actor, then in achieving a description of the world "from the point of view of the actor" how can the describer guarantee the anonymity of his description? That is, how can he guarantee that his description will vary independently with the occasions of his own social life?

For both Parsons and Schuetz an order is constituted simultaneously with the defining constructs of the actor. Both stress the importance of perspectival appearance. In achieving a description of the actor's world, Parsons'ss phenomenology requires that the observer suspend judgment on every thing but the possibility of a community between the actor and the observer. This possibility stands without question under the assumption of the invariant primal categories of understanding. Thus the truth is in all of us, if we act in accordance with logico-empirical procedures, these procedures being the guarantees of anonymity of results.

Put otherwise, adherence to these canons insures that the factual portraits will not reflect the occasions of our social life. The result that interests us for communication theory is an actor who orients a situation of objects that show this or that degree of prejudice, with the well-trained observer who follows the canons of logico-empirical method sitting as the arbiter of all disputes as to what the world consists of in fact. Thus, for a theory of information, the observer is the final arbiter over the question of whether or not and with what degree of coloration of ignorance, error, and myth, the actor has information about the world. Methodologically, the consequence of this theory of the actor's situation is that the observer must bring to the actor's assessment of the world a measure drawn from outside the actor's situation of action to decide between what it is that for an actor is actually theory, belief, hypothesis, fantasy, fact, etc. The measure is found in the notion of the rational man as he is given in an instance by the well trained observer. In this view, this rational man—and here is the point of large importance—does not stand as an arbitrary standard of comparison, but is treated as a methodologically necessary principle of the actor's action if he is to have information. If the observer as an instance of the rational man deviates from the ideal, the amount of his deviation is a measure of the extent of a community of myth that he shares with the subject he observes. But, the view holds, subject and observer can *together* enjoy a communality of rationally appraised world, automatically guaranteed as to its factual character by the supposition that the ideal rational man is miraculously unaltered and unalterable. He is in a word omniscient; he is in the world but unbound by time; the sole and only law-giver; the Judaic-Christian God who witnesses and can make sense of even the sparrow's fall, though, we are assured, at the appropriate "level of generalization."

Like Parsons, Schuetz proposes an order that is simultaneously constituted with the defining parameters of the actor, but unlike Parsons's phenomenology, the Schuetzian attitude begins its descriptive task by suspending everything that Parsons neutralizes *including* the possibility of a community between the actor and the observer. In suspending judgment on the solution of the primal categories, and with it the view that the method of understanding is methodologically unproblematical, it suspends judgment too on other solutions that have been proposed, as for example, the solution that proposes that the objects of the world are given directly through the senses, or the solution that the senses give mere appearance while only mind-study is real, or that it is objective Spirit that binds men in a community of knowledge.

The problem this attitude addresses is a simple one but potent: granted a world that actor and observer may know together, with whatever accents of doubt, hesitancy, certainty, typicality, uniqueness, publicity, privacy, orderliness, confusion, determinateness or indeterminateness, repetition or singularity, and with whatever accents of immanence or transcendence to thought. What are the conditions by way of the properties of experience and only of experience under which man as an experiencer experiences an order that shows these faces? Granted that there is knowledge that shows the peculiar and in many ways historically recent property of being invariant with reference to the social status of the knower—knowledge that is simultaneously "anonymous and communal" (to borrow a phrase from Thomas Mann). What is there propertywise in the structures of the attitudes that are constitutive of such an order of experience under which information shows such intriguing features? Clearly such a question cannot be convincingly answered by invoking philosophical doctrine. It requires in the very way it is posed that one seek an answer by addressing the nature of experiences themselves. If one allows the legitimacy of the question, its answer cannot be sought anywhere else.

But proposing such a radical empiricism cuts one off from the use of the rational man as a device for assessing the information that the experiencer has. Rather, the make-up of the rational man *even as a mere construction*—and it can be demonstrated that if we follow Schuetz, this is the best we can ever hope for as far as the use of the rational man in our endeavors is concerned—must, if we are to avoid discovering in the world that which we have put there ourselves—must be drawn from our investigations of how men, isolated and yet simultaneously in an odd communion, go about the business of constructing, testing, maintaining, altering, validating, questioning, defining the orders that in various degrees and in various ways match each other in contents and organization.

The consequence of adopting the Husserlian phenomenological attitude for a theory of information can best be shown by comparing the status of the thing called "information" under the two phenomenologies. To the extent that we subscribe to the Parsonian actor's definition of the situation, known to the observer as we have seen through a neo-Kantian phenomenological attitude, the observer can have information in the world only after he has discounted the actor's situation of action in light of the observer's "wider knowledge" and wiser procedures of information gathering and interpretation. If one actor sends a message to another, the amount of information that the receiver gets from the message is limited by the observer as a matter of methodological principle by the extent to which the receiver operates upon the message according to the canons of rational endeavor. Everything he receives and makes sense of outside of this is in the observer's view ignorance, error, or myth. Thus, despite the protestations of the actor that the Jews really have control of the country, as is evidenced in the newspaper reports of the current tax scandals, he is met by the observer with a quiet "Tush, *I* know better."

If matters did not go beyond the fact that the one maintained that the Jews were taking over while the other wagged his finger at him, we'd have no case of any theoretical or practical importance. But the case is otherwise. The observer not only wags his finger, but he maintains as well that unless the actor change his ways, that is, unless the actor revises his portrait to accord with the really factual state of affairs he stands a good chance of failing to realize his project. In fact, it is only by a random concatenation of events that he can realize his project, and then he will have been right but will adduce the wrong reasons. In the final analysis he will not have an accumulated body of empirically useful information, and will not know how to bring about the effect that for one reason or another he seeks. In effect, discrepancies from logico-empirical procedure reduce the instrumental efficacy of his knowledge. Or, following Hobbes, you can't be rational and lose. With reference to communication, the doctrine follows that if we rationally understood each other we'd have nothing to quarrel about. An interesting consequence of this view for structural-functional theory arises when one tries to find a place for the functions of ignorance in a social arrangement. Not only what a man knows but what he doesn't know has to be accounted for in rendering a logically complete description of the factors that condition the occurrence of a set of events of conduct. In short logical completeness requires that ignorance be accorded *motivational status.*

Now it is not a criticism to say that such a view requires a referee. But it is a criticism when we see that there is built into the motivation of the referee as a rational man the point that continuity of activity is possible with him to the extent that he both knows what he knows as well as what he does not know. Anything outside this is not only ignorance but from our point of view an ignorance that makes no difference as far as the pursuit of information is concerned, except for the referee's referee who alone can view with irony the referee's attempts to account for conduct on the basis of the information that he has. So we are back here to the use of a transcendental standard, though the peculiar thing is that this standard is not the Golden Book of knowledge, but is nothing more than the first referee's idealized procedures for learning about the world—i.e., his epistemological premises. Thus, there is no salvation in this direction. We prefer the view that the actor is left with the light that he has; he never has more nor less. The important thing and the thing that stands without a standard with which to judge ironically is that he keeps going. Thus the nature of his factual knowledge must somehow be accounted for by considering what characteristics of his experience permit this continuity of activity.

It is possible to circumvent this situation and to reintroduce irony. In fact, Moore and Tumin tried it, and to my mind, with mixed convincingness. First, hypostatize the social system. Instead of it being a set of rules for interpreting action, the social system is concretized as a thing in the world, most particularly a table of organization with its own operations whereby knowledge and ignorance are distributed among the slots. But then we have a fiat phenomenon in the form of a social system, defined as a system of patterned activities which stand entirely in atemporal fashion, in effect, a system treated as a phenomenon in the empirical world though it stands there in substance, i.e., by definition, and like anything that stands by definition, it remains constant through the variations of circumstance. Something remains the same throughout, and this something is the system. By obtaining a static system, this view gains what it is after and sorely needs, namely, a closed container, this being necessary in order to give ignorance convincing status as something that conditions the properties of action.

But here it seems to me that there is a fundamental error in that two meanings of ignorance are confounded. One sense of ignorance is that of what could be known but isn't. This involves, as we have seen, the referee who knows better, but that God-like figure is better forgotten as far as the tasks of sociological theory are concerned. In speaking of the differential distribution of information in a social system, in this sense, one refers to persons equally or unequally in possession of an overall amount in the system with what each does not know of what could be known being treated as a premise of the systematic consequences of his actions.

In the second sense of ignorance, it refers to the differential distribution of information among a set of actors. But here ignorance and information refer only to a matching operation that is performed between what the actors know. Comparing what A knows with what B knows is merely another way of talking about what A knows that B does not know, that is, what is not known *between* them. It makes no reference to a sum. Further, the information in the system and the ignorance in the system mean precisely the same thing: what it is that a set of actors do not know in common. Such matching operations to define the differential distribution of information in a system are nothing else than a way of saying in what degree and respects various actors's definitions of the situation are alike.

After all this, we shall elect the Husserlian phenomenology.

(d) The Nature of Rationality

Another decision concerns itself with the way in which the properties of experience that are often referred to as "rational" properties are to be handled. The problem is this: Which of the many properties that this term refers to should we "allow" the term to refer to? The problem is not that of choosing a designator. It is not that among a set of properties we must decide which we are going to label rational but rather it is that of deciding which of the set we must on experiential grounds lump together. Certain of these properties are experientially concurrent, so that though we may "allow" certain ones to go together, we must if we are to be true to experience "allow" all of those that experience shows do in fact belong together whether we would allow them or not. What are these properties, and what are the lumps of them? The following list is taken from Schuetz's article, "The Problem of Rationality in the Social World," *Economica*, vol. 10 (May 1943), pp. 137–140. In some places I have quoted directly; in others the notions are paraphrased.

The term rationality has equivocal meanings. (1) It has been used to mean "reasonable." That is, we act "reasonably" in the sense that we can apply to a new situation a recipe found in our store of experience that was tested in an analogous situation and which we suppose when applied to a current situation will be effective now as it was effective in the past.

(2) Rational action may mean acting deliberately. But the term, deliberately, has its own equivocations. (a) Routine action may be said to be deliberated insofar as it always relates back to the original act of deliberation which once preceded the building up of the formula which now serves as a standard. (b) The term may cover the insight into the applicability to a present situation of a recipe used successfully in the past. (c) It can mean the pure anticipation of the end, where this anticipation is the motive for setting the present act on going. (d) The term may mean a rehearsal in imagination of the various competing lines of action.

(3) Rational action is frequently intended to designate the fact or planned or projected action.

(4) Rational action frequently means predictable action.

(5) Rational is used sometimes to mean logical [and here too, it may be equivocal since logical can refer to logic in the sense of "pure grammar," i.e., the a priori general laws of thought, or it can refer to logic, or better logics, in the sense of the "merely" normative laws of thought, H.G.].

(6) Rational action may refer to the choice between two or more means toward the same ends or even the choice between two or more ends and the selection of the empirically appropriate means for the realization of an empirical end.

As far as the action that takes place within the attitudes of daily life (compared with the attitude of scientific theorizing of dreaming, of play, etc.), all of the above descriptions are applicable, though with this important structural qualification: There are three criteria that are utterly alien to the attitudes of daily life in the sense that these criteria can be met only by effecting such a structural alteration of the attitude of daily life that the objects in the world that the attitude orients become transformed in their organizational characteristics as unities of meaning. These criteria are that the means-ends relations be constructed in such a way that (1) they remain in full compatibility with the principles of formal scientific logic; (2) that all the elements be conceived in full clearness and distinctness, and (3) that they contain only scientifically verifiable assumptions which have to be in full compatibility with the whole of scientific knowledge.

This does not mean that rational choice does not exist within the sphere of everyday life. Indeed, it would be sufficient to interpret the terms clearness and distinctness in modified and restricted meaning, namely, as clearness and distinctness adequate to the requirements of the actor's practical interest.... What I wish to emphasize is that the ideal of rationality is not and cannot be a peculiar feature of everyday thought, nor can it therefore be a methodological principle of the interpretation of human acts in daily life.... Rational choice would be present if the actor had sufficient knowledge of the end to be realized as well as the different means apt to succeed. But this postulate implies (a) knowledge of the place of the end to be realized within the framework of the plans of the actor (which must be known by him, too), (b) knowledge of its interrelations with other ends and its compatibility or incompatibility with them, (c) knowledge of the desirable and undesirable consequences which may arise as by-products of the realization of the main end, (d) knowledge of the different chains of means which technically or even ontologically are suitable for the accomplishment of this end regardless of whether the actor has control of all or several of these elements, (e) knowledge of the interference of such means with other ends or other chains of means including all their secondary effects and incidental consequences, (f) knowledge of the accessibility of these means for the actor, picking out the means which are within his reach and which he can and may set going.

The aforementioned points do not by any means exhaust the complicated analysis that would be necessary in order to break down the concept of rational choice in action. The complications increase greatly when the action in question is a social one. In this case the following elements become additional determinants for the deliberation of the actor. First, the interpretation or misinterpretation of his own act by his fellow man. Second, the reaction by the other people and its motivation. Third, all the outlined elements of knowledge (a to f) which the actor rightly or wrongly attributes to his partners. Fourth, all the categories of familiarity and strangeness, of intimacy and anonymity, of personality and type which we have discovered in our inventory of the organization of the social world.

But where is this system of rational action to be found? We have already noted that the concept of rationality has its native place not at the level of everyday conceptions of the social world but at the theoretical level of the scientific observation of it, and it is here that it finds its field of methodological application.

It is found in the logical status, the elements, and the uses of the dummy or system of dummies which the scientist uses as a scheme for interpreting the events of conduct.

When we talk of rationality, then, we need to distinguish between rationality as a property of the activities of a person conceived of as a communicant, and the rationality of the actions of the observer using a model of the communicant. In the first case the term is merely a designation of the empirically problematical-characteristics of the person's communications that are of interest: Is it calculatedly pursued? How much of it is sustained by matters of bona-fide group membership? How much involves a plan that he is trying to accomplish? How much of his own communications as well as those of others does he find predictable? How does he form his concepts, use them, test them, revise, compare, judge, name, etc? How are all these relevant to each other? And so on. One could do here without the term rationality and never feel the lack of it.

The same questions can be addressed to the person employing a model of the communicant, i.e., the sociologist. Generally we expect, or rather assume, a different set of answers to these questions than we would expect of the person oriented to the accomplishment of practical purposes as compared with the observer oriented to the ordering of information for the sake of effecting the ordering itself. We assume the answers by assuming that such an observer acts with proper regard for the scientific canons of inquiry. However, even here the sociology of sociology might show much more to feel disenchanted about than we are inclined to believe is the case when we address each other as fellow scientists.

This much analysis is hopelessly insufficient to make, in a convincing way, the point that I want to make. Further argument will be found in Schuetz's conference paper, and in my paper, heavily based on his writings, "Notes on the Sociological Attitude."[7] The thing we are left with as problematical is this: that to the extent that we want to handle the rationalities of our communicants as our communicants are usually found, that is, to the extent that we want to build into the model of our actors their typical ways of handling messages so as to extract from them information that is relevant to them, to that extent we must address questions to the actor's ways of orienting and manipulating an order. Only under very special conditions does this order in its portrait and procedures of construction, of test and maintenance show the properties of rationality in the observer's sense. In the case of the signaling machine this is not so. Like the scientist, (at least in the ideal that the scientist unlike the person in daily life seeks to approximate), the machine extracts every bit of relevant

---

7. [Editor's Note: The 1948 manuscript (Garfinkel 2006) contains an early section that may be close to what is referred to here.]

information from the message; it never makes an error of logical procedure, it never forgets; it never distorts in recall; it never takes anything for granted; for its normatively best and most rational strategies of communication are always the same; its decisions are always based on evaluation of possible consequences and never on the basis of matters of principle, and so on.

(e) The Nature of the Object That the Actor Treats

The problem that is to be decided under this topic is this: How will we conceive the relationship between the theories that we make about concrete objects and the concrete objects? Whether we like it or not, we shall have to decide upon how we shall use the terms "real object" and "knowledge of the objective world." In that the sociologist is faced with the compound task of having to make theories about other person's theories (as accountable data), a task that involves him in almost every statement with the question of the meaning of the claim to objective knowledge, the decision is not one that he can or in practice does pass off as the proper concern of philosophers.

Many decisions are available, though we shall examine only two. (1) One decision, and the one most prevalent in social science today, is known as the "correspondence theory" of reality. (2) Another decision and the one we shall use may be called a "coherence theory" of reality.

We can say that a person entertains a correspondence theory of reality if it can be shown that the persons' theorizing about the world is predicated on the view that there is a difference between the perceived object of the "outer world" and the concrete object (e.g., exemplified in the metaphor of cutting the cake of the universe in diverse ways). Concreteness in this view is a property of the object and the object is real in the sense that the possibility of apprehending it is not dependent upon the many possible ways in which it may be apprehended. It is in this sense "actual." The fullness of the concrete object is marked off as different from the selective, schematic-like emphasis of a conceptual representation of the object. Hence the statement is found that a conceptual scheme can never exhaust the number of factual statements that can be made about the object.

The view holds further that the function of any conceptual scheme is to render some sort of approximation of what is in reality out there. The view is that through successive stages of improvement, the logico-empirical methods, based as they are on universal and unchanging primary categories of apprehension, gives to the properly qualified observer a view of the world of real objects that is such as to be independent of historical conditions as far as the accuracy of reproduction of the real things is concerned.

An analytical model is judged then not only with reference to its utility within the purposes of the observer but also with reference to the extent to which it renders an accurate reproduction of the reality that is out there. However, it should be noted that this test of accuracy does not consist of a comparison of what the observer says is out there with what is really out there as it is determined by criteria independent of those employed by the observer (a position that would make the tester akin to an interpreter of God's secret intent) but accuracy is an automatic result of acting with proper regard for the canons of logico-empirical inquiry.

That the objects that are reproduced correspond in their logical character to the logical design of the real world is taken literally as a miracle of a sort, and like all miracles is unproblematical with regard to how it is possible. Hence the lack of concern with the nonetheless legitimate question that arises within this view as to whether the world could go contrary to the laws of logic, and if so, under what conditions? The answer, at the limit of rationality, goes to the effect that it could but so far it has not, the "reason" being that the basic rules based as they are on the primary categories are not subject for their validity to the fluctuations of circumstance. A statement that is true for one place and time is true everywhere if it stems, to begin with, from the proper procedure. The truth is in all of us and we can see the world and see it whole, if we will do as the scientist does.

The correspondence theory makes a separation then between the real world and the subjective interpretation of the real world. The separation is such that there are on the one hand the concrete objects in all their fullness and on the other a conceptual representation of these objects which in abstracting certain features from them presents the scientist with a faded reproduction. The objects that an actor treats, whether he be layman or scientist, are these concrete objects though he treats them in terms of their features that are of interest to him. His interest in them and their reality are said to have nothing to do with each other, nor is his interest in them necessarily related to the objective character of the objects.

I'd like to indicate a criticism of this view, and then present the one we shall prefer.

There is an important difficulty in a correspondence view. Since the scientist as an actor treats the concrete object in terms of its selected features, which means that the object he is dealing with is a conceptualized object, and since it can be shown that no actor treats a concrete object at the descriptive level except in terms of an empirical system of constructions of some sort, the question then arises as to whether the notion of the concrete object is within this usage a useful, let alone a meaningfully clear conception.

I propose a preferred alternative to the view that concreteness is a property of the real object and hence is a function of the amount of sensory material that can be experienced. The preferred view runs that concreteness depends on the nature of the scheme of apprehension, so that the clearer the conception, the greater the possibility of concretizing the object through additional sensory materials. This of course would relativize all apprehending schemata as far as the question of objective knowledge is concerned. Holding to the first view risks the possibility that the scientist becomes a mute observer who can see the concrete object but cannot tell what it is. Nevertheless he very much needs to tell, for only in telling can he (a) avoid hypostatizing the system of empirical constructions, and (b) set up a body of observational rules whereby two independent observers can agree as to what has been seen without recourse to the scientifically invalid criterion of consensus. The latter problem is solved in our daily work by the pragmatic assumption that when all is said and done, the method of understanding works. But the dilemma remains of whether one would subscribe to the sensationalist doctrine that to see a thing is to know it, or to the view that one can join the empirical construct to the relevant data through a practiced intuitive guess. The criticism centers on the fact that at the very point of its application a theory of the world based on the correspondence notion lacks rational controls.

The seriousness of this shortcoming can be pointed up by considering the fact that it can easily lead to something that might be called the fallacy of imposed order. The fallacy of imposed order stems from the failure to have so conceptualized the difference and the relationship between that which is observed from the act of observation that something akin to "automatic" interpretation of what is seen is made so that the observer is hardly aware that in seeing he has "seen" what his empirical constructs told him he would see. A more legitimate alternative procedure is one where the empirical construct does no more than limit the possibilities of what will be seen while leaving it to a Nature who has no regard for the meanings of his statements, in the manner of a fall of events to yield him joy or disappointment. But having no control criteria by which he is able to state the conditions under which one set of possibilities rather than another are relevant ones (the construct, remember, being a faint reproduction so that a synthetic proposition as a set of related constructs reflects nature's uniformities—to be compared with the notion that the synthetic proposition is itself the statement of a uniformity), he may rely on the construct to define his data with the result that such observations have the status of illustration rather than evidence, and any logically recommended empirical statement, i.e., any empirical statement whose constructions do not offend in their meanings, the meanings stated in another empirical statement, may by the lack of offence be accorded the status of fact. A statement that is regarded as warranted on the grounds of the compatibility of its meanings with other empirical statements will then be warranted as fact.

The leading premise of the "coherence" theory of reality is that the perceived object of the "outer world" is the concrete object, and that the two terms mean precisely the same thing. Rather than there being a world of real objects cut this way and that, the cake is constituted in the very act of cutting. No cutting, no cake, there being no reality that is approximated since the world is just as it appears; there is nothing behind it. The nature of the observed event as well as the relevance of the event to others (found in statements of fact) is possible through the operation of a set of related standards, these standards being the things that provide the categories of reality and irreality, of relevance and irrelevance, of actuality and fantasy. Approximating reality means approximating the standards, and the view is that the facts approximate the theory and not that the theory approximates the facts.

In this view the way in which something is of interest to a witness is all of the way in which that thing is real. It is real according to William James' doctrine that every world is real only while it is attended to; it is only the reality that lapses with attention. Obviously one can still run into a deer without first attending to the deer. In this view concreteness does not depend upon the variety of sensory presentations. Rather the view holds that sensory presentations are the conditions but not the contents of perceptions. Only insofar as there is a standard that remains invariant under the variations of sensory variations is concreteness possible. The concreteness is found in the object so constituted as a unity of meanings and not in the sensory characters through which the object is apprehended.

An actual object is a meaningfully unified set of experiences, sensorily or ideally founded. The fullness of the concrete object is not marked off from the schematic emphasis of a conceptual representation of the object. Rather the object never appears except through its schema. *The schema of specifications in fact is precisely the object itself.* Hence the statement under the correspondence theory that a conceptual scheme can never exhaust the number of factual statements that can be made about the object reads under the coherence theory that only in God's eye are all possible specifications of an object simultaneously relevant.

Compared again to the view that the function of any conceptual scheme is to render some sort of approximation to what is really out there, the coherence view holds that however the experiencer experiences what is out there is out there.

The doubt that he experiences about what he heard specifies what he heard as doubted. As an object it stands before him complete with its doubted character.

The question for this theory, then, is not one, as it is in the correspondence theory, of what is the objective world and what is objective knowledge, but is rather, what are the varieties of objective worlds and what are the varieties of objective knowledge. Here the talk is of a pluralism of worlds: multiple realities. There are many objective worlds. The only worlds in fact are objective worlds. The world of the dreamer and the knowledge he has of the dream in transit [is] objective knowledge. Most certainly the worlds of artists, of religionists, of businessmen, of children are objective worlds.

The question of whether a world is objective or not is not in this view a question that philosophers must decide for an experiencer. A world that is not objective is experienced as such immediately and with full conviction by the person who suffers it, for the question hinges on whether or not he can continue to act. The alternative to a world that is not objective is a world that is meaningless. In this view the term subjective is reserved to mean just this: the inability to actualize an object, i.e., to intend a meaning: a world without sense: confusion.

But the ways in which these objects are constituted, the rules that govern the tests of whether an experiencer has seen correctly, the tests that he considers legitimate ones for the accuracy of his judgment of what he has seen, the conditions under which he can experience surprise and error, the consequences of the surprises that he experiences, the socially legitimate methods for resolving incongruity, the rules that govern his judgmental behavior, and so on—these show different characteristics as one compares worlds and the attitudes of attending that constitute them, and hence they show not only between themselves but between them and the world of the sociological attitude different effects for the constitution of objects and objective knowledge.

According to this view, there is no miracle to logico-empirical method that insures to the user objectivity that lesser method distorts. One can have objectivity through consensus as one finds, for example, in the social definitions of crime where the objective character of the criminal action is most confirmed by those who feel most deeply and who require that others agree on the profanity of the action in question. Rather a *consequence* of following logico-empirical method is that statements cannot be tested by the *meanings* of empirical constructs but must be tested by subjecting them to a course of experience with a Nature that the user conceives of as blind to the meanings of his statements. The particular and socially and historically unusual objective character of the sociologically empirical world is found *as a consequence of this rule.* For it organizes experiences to present one out of many possible objective worlds—

an objective world in this case that stands only as long as the experiences that it hypothesizes can be repeatedly confirmed by any person *regardless of social affiliation* who does what the statements say they should do. Such a world is certainly at variance with the arrays of them encountered in the course of a day's normal experiences. George Bernard Shaw hit the matter squarely when he said that no reasonable person would entertain a scientific notion for a minute.

The business of "sciencing" a problem in this view is not described as a procedure by which reality is successively approximated, but is described as a procedure of successively transforming or better successively reconstituting a world, any world, in accordance with the particular rules of the scientific attitude and the devices of the scientific method.

We are left, then, with two large consequences for addressing the task of describing a communicant's information: (1) Each world has an order of information peculiar to it; and (2) the order of information is a function of the mode of attending to it.

(f) The Individual as a Source of Change

Finally—though finally only in the sense that we need to be finished with these points while leaving many gaps and many further problematical decisions untouched—we need to decide on how the individual is to be regarded as a source of change in a social system. This is the familiar problem of how to handle the fact that the individual is capable of autonomously reordering the rules of his own operations, the problem of creativity. The problem is important because examining the decision made at this point would permit us to tell how much nonsense we are putting up with when we treat as a closed set a system of alternative meanings, or alternative lines of conduct, or alternative lines of development of situation. Actually, there has yet to appear a theory in the social sciences that accomplishes better than a partial ordering, despite the claims made for the doctrine of sociological determinism.

Although various solutions have been proposed (Sorokin's premises of the nature of ultimate reality; Parsons's organism that develops its sets of most probable alternatives through the socially systematized administration of rewards and punishments; Freud through the libido theory), we have no preferred solution, but ask instead that attention be paid wherever possible to the conditions, that the best of what we know or may learn tells us about, under which the world of an experiencer appears as a closed rather than an open set of possibilities.

I V

The "Object-in-General"

With these decisions as the conditions of the search for the ideas involved in the conception of information, we turn now to the actor's definition of the situation as the place to start looking. This definition of the situation is conceived of as an order of objects, or using Parsons's phrase, a situation of objects, or a situation of action. To clear the ground, we'll need first some clarification on the general notion of "the object." The discussion is not without immediate relevance to our work-day concerns in the Project. The actor's "view" of such things in his situation as "his job," "the organization," "the organization's purposes," superiors, co-workers, obligations, etc. etc.—these notions are old friends by now as far as their being designators of objects that the actor treats, treated, or will treat. What we're looking for in this section are the general terms in which such objects can be conceived and described.

After discussing the object-in-general, which we'll refer to finally as a schema of possibilities of experience, we'll turn in the following section to a closer look at the notion of the "possibility of experience." The notion of information depends on a grasp of these conceptions. I trust that you begin to see now what I meant when I talked about a trip through the jungle.

According to Husserl, all meaningful acts have the peculiarity of presenting the experiencer with an ideal object, whether the object be real or fictitious, existent or imaginary. This peculiarity is not to be considered a quality of acts as intensity, for example, is held by psychologists to be a quality of sense data. The act does not transcend the experience of the subject to seize an object belonging to a universe that is external to the sphere of experience, but rather the subject is aware of the object by the reference that the act itself bears to the object.

In being aware of an object in the present experience, one may be aware that the object is the same as that which one was aware of in some past experience, and as the same as that which, generally speaking, one may be aware of in an indefinite number of re-presentations. This "repeatability" Husserl calls identity, and it is identity that is constitutive of objectivity.

But how may identical and identifiable objects exist for and stand before the experiencer in a "consciousness" whose acts succeed one another in an incessant stream of temporal variations? Husserl met this problem with his theory of intentionality as it is found in his doctrine of the noesis noema structures.

When an object is perceived, there is on the one hand the act as a real event. The act as an event occurs at a certain point in phenomenal time; it appears, lasts, and disappears never to return. On the other hand, there is what in the concrete experience stands before the observer as the thing experienced. This "what" presents itself in a well determined fashion, whether this "what" is the house that I see during a walk or the house of memory. The object, exactly and only as the perceiving subject experiences it—as he intends it in a concrete, experienced "mental state"[—]is the noema of perception. Noesis is the act. Aron Gurwitsch writes:

> It is only with respect to the noema that a given perception is not only a perception of this determined object, but also that it is such an awareness of this object rather than another; that is to say, that the subject experiencing the act in question, the noesis, finds himself confronted with a certain object appearing from such a side and in the orientation it has, in a certain aspect, and so on.

The noema is to be distinguished from the "real object." As a "real object" a tree, for example, may appear now in one determined manner and appear in the next moment in another determined manner as one shifts his spatial position with reference to it. There may be a multiplicity of perceptions through all of which the same tree is presented. The "perceived tree" varies according to the standpoint from which it is viewed. Indeed, a real thing may not present itself as such except as a succession of perceptions. In a word, the noema is part of a non-perceptual order of objects.

The noema, as distinct from the "real object," is an "unreal" or "ideal" entity. It belongs to a sphere of meanings or significances. The unreality of entities that belong to this sphere lies in a certain independence from them of the concrete experience by which the noemata are actualized. Every noema may correspond in its identical character to an indefinite number of experiences. Noemata are found not only in perceptual life, but there is a noema corresponding to every act of memory, imagination, judgment, thinking, and so on. In all of these it is through the act that the object stands before the subject.

It is this noetic-noematic relationship that is referred to by Husserl's concept "intentionality." Consciousness is to be defined with reference to a sphere of meaning. To experience an act is the same as to actualize a meaning. Every fact of consciousness must be treated in terms of the relation: experiencing subject to thing experienced as it is experienced. No mental state can be accounted for except with regard to the objective sense of which the experiencing subject becomes aware through his act. Intentionality means the objectivating function of consciousness.

With this brief sketch of Husserl's theory of intentionality as a context, we are in a position to discuss the notion of the object-in-general.

We are attempting the most general case of the definition of the "object." Though the thread is a fragile one, it is nevertheless put in our hands whenever we allow that the way in which a person "defines" a situation is a good predictor of that person's conduct. This object will also be referred to as "the object of treatment," "the treated object," "the object that the actor is treating." Every noesis is an instance of treatment.

In previous pages we talked about the object as a thingified set of possibilities of experience. "Thingify" is another word for "reify." By "possibility" of experience is meant any *datum* of experience that serves the function of specifying the object. We underline the term "datum" to call attention to the fact that the datum may have the status of an interpreted signal. Where this is the case we say that there are conditions of an actor's make-up under which he responds not to the signal but to his interpretation of the signal. The datum however may also have the status of a specification without referring at all and without being dependent in the least upon a sensory signal, as the object "average" for example may be specified by the data of a set of numbers which are subjected to specific operations of addition and subtraction. Cinderella, similarly, is constituted as a set of specifications that are free of sensory signals. The term "possibility" is not used to include the meaning of likelihood. It bears only the meaning of "candidacy."

The term "thingify" and the term "reify" are synonymous. To relate in some unified order is to "reify." An object is viewed then as an array of possibilities of experience constituted through some "unifying" principle, some logical operator into an *order* of relationships to each other. The object is experienced as an object, through an order of specifications; this *order of specifications* being all of what is meant by the term "object."

This leaves us with the necessity of trying to make clear the nature of the ordering principle. Suppose we refer to it with the letter "e."

I am unable to describe the general "e" with any assurance. However, there are a number of things that can be said about it that are of some use. First, it is not a "form" in the Platonic sense of the prototype.

Also, although Husserl used the term intentional "essence" to refer to it, the metaphysical overtones that cluster around the word "essence" are no part of what is meant or what he meant by the term. It has nothing to do or say about the object in the sense of its "substance." Nevertheless, "essence" is a suitable term if one puts aside considerations of substance and sees instead that to reify and to "essentialize" involves a selective emphasis and making relevant to each other of certain specifications while neutralizing the relevance of others. In this sense we have the "essence" of the object when we have specified with full clarity all of what an object consists of in its meanings. No reification, no object; no reification, no action.

The problem for the investigator who would describe the properties of the objects that the actor is treating is not that of separating those persons who reify from those who do not, but is that of describing the multitude of ways in which reification is accomplished.

Second, to name is to reify, reifying and naming being, as far as I am able to make out, synonymous terms. However, the "e" is not a name; nor is it a category, though we are brought up to its meaning by encountering the names of objects.

Third, it is a principle for grouping experiences, yet in its absence there is neither specification nor grouping. For the case of empirical objects, the absence of the "e" reduces the idealized signal to a signal that signifies only itself, i.e., to the meaningless experience. In the absence of the "e" for the analytic object, like Cinderella and the triangle in general, the object is lost in the cessation of activity; the picture fades from the screen.

Fourth, in operating as a unifying and relating principle, it remains invariant with reference to the transformations of phenomenal appearances.

Fifth, the name in "preparing the world for treatment"—Mead's "collapsed act"—is, as far as we can make out, the designator *not of the object but of the grouping principle* by which an array of possibilities are arranged to present together with the principle that relates them, the object.

Sixth, as far as I am able to make out, the "e" seems to be a logical operator. As an operator its operations consist of selecting from an array and relating them to each other in some determinate fashion. In this sense the "e" may be said in its function to determine a unity of meaning. Where one is oriented to a world of sensory encounter, the failure of an "e" (which of course is not the same thing as "not having a name for it") makes it impossible to idealize a signal; hence the experiencer experiences not the data of the world but experiences signals. Where one is oriented to a world of idealizations entirely, as, for example, during an inner fantasy, the failure of the "e" stops the course of the fantasy and it fades immediately from view, leaving in its place the catatonic state of inactivity. The failure of the "e" operator implies at the point of its failure the disruption of a world, or, in more precise terms, implies the formal consequence of confusion. We'll touch on this again later in the paper.

The object in general is conceived as a schema of possibilities of experience. If I may be permitted the magic of the Kabala to make it clear, we may represent it as $e(p_n)$, where "e" is the operator, "p" means a possibility of experience, "n" means number, and the brackets ( ) say that the aggregate of p's is a set of p's relevant to each other by virtue of the ordering operations represented in the "e."

As a matter of formal rule we shall say that the removal of the "e" for the case of sensorily founded objects transforms the data character of the signal to a signal that represents only itself, which is to say, makes the sensorily presented materials meaningless. For the case of ideally founded objects, as "average" for example is an ideally founded object, the removal of the "e" leaves a "blank screen"—i.e., the cessation of activity.

In Part XV we shall consider some theorems that result from the various ways of operating on the "e."

V

The "Imbedded" Possibility of Experience

In the varieties of utilitarian theories of action it is possible to assume such things as isolated events or isolated interests. By and large sociologists have preferred alternative theories that stressed the "imbeddedness" of an event in other events, talking for example of a "complex" by referring to five senses of "imbeddedness," which we shall consider the criteria of organization of a set of possibilities of experience, a world.

Early in the memorandum, I spoke of the communicant as the *animal symbolicum*, meaning to stress with that term that the world of the communicant is an experienced world and that its objects are real for him *not* on the grounds of their ontological structure but in their constitution as unities of meaning. To say that an object is real is to mean that it is of interest to the experiencer, of interest relative to some *order* of past, present, and anticipated experiences.

Hence we forego the use of an ontology, even a scientific ontology, with which to measure deviations of the communicant's experiences from those of "true reality" or "real objectivity" except as a theory of existence, *any* theory of existence, including a scientific one, could be used as an arbitrary standard for effecting comparison. All manners of things are real (i.e., of interest to him) and are objects for him in particular ways, though this is not the same thing as saying that his world is witnessed by him alone and in his own time. Rather, we would stress the point that the continuity of his experiences rests squarely on a view that he has of a world that is interpersonally constituted and maintained.

"Worlds" is perhaps a better way of putting it than "world." Within the action frame the term "world" means only an organized set of possibilities of experience. The various kinds of organization that are possible for an experiencer even within the course of a single day involves a pluralism of worlds with a vengeance. This need not frighten us by the prospect of the minutiae of accounting for such pluralisms, for the scientific observer is himself capable of some very ruthless typification as he goes about the business of constructing a sociologically empirical world. The notion of role, for example, is such a device for removing slabs of time from the flow of actual experience and thingifying the slabs so as to present them for orderly description.

The objective character for the actor of the thing that is experienced is found in the unity of meanings that a set of possibilities hold for an experiencer. Insofar as every experience is an experience of something, every world is an objective world. We shall use the term subjective to mean meaningless. A world experienced subjectively is a world experienced without meaning, and hence without objects, without objectivity, and without interest. Conversely, the objectivities and realities of the experiencer's universes are to be sought in the meanings that the possible objects of his experience "have" for him as these objects are experienced relative to an interpersonally valid and validated order.

What now are the criteria of organization of this order of objects as a province of meaning?

a. The Criterion of Continuity of Experience

We shall say that the continuity of experience refers to the invariant character of the relationships that are possible between the various parts of an intentional experience. That is, a sequence of experiences may be spoken of as being continuous by virtue of there being an intended object, the noema, that remains the same while the quality of the act varies. Thus, in Kriegsspiel, the marker that I designate as an instance of something that I call a queen can be brought under my gaze, it is picked up, moved, I can make statements about it, I can like or dislike the piece, I can lose it to an opponent, or gain it back with a pawn promotion, etc. Another example would be a conversation where one person after another contributes to "the topic."

A sequence of experiences may be continuous by virtue of the quality of the act that remains the same while the intended object varies. For example, there is the continuity of the euphoric state or of the "negativistic" state where one votes "aye" for all things or "nay" for all things.

A series of experiences may be continuous by virtue of the fact that the act and the specification of the object experienced through the act vary while the whole order of specifications varies. For example, a person in the course of a political conversation repeats pensively, "I'll vote for Truman." We learn from questioning that the first time he meant, "I'll vote for the present incumbent of office;" the second time, "I'll vote for Papa;" the third time, "I'll vote for any candidate of the Democratic party."

There can be continuity where any combination of these factors remains constant as long as one varies. There is no continuity (1) where one expression alone is given; (2) where in a succession all the factors remain constant as to their meaning values; (3) where in a succession all the factors vary in their meaning values.

Let me construct an example of a communicative exchange in which one of the recipients of a set of messages plays it straight while the other shifts the grounds of continuity. Assume two players: a local delicatessen proprietor who has just locked up his store (the straight man) and the experimenter. The experimenter rushes up, brushes past the proprietor, and peers through the locked door. The proprietor leads off.

"The store is closed."
"Of course it's closed. Do you sell *Time* magazine?"
"The store is closed for the night."
"Then sell me the magazine out here. I don't have to go inside."
"No more selling today."
"If you want to *give* me the magazine, that's up to you, but I'm prepared to pay."
"Mister, I'm not selling or giving anything to you."
"What about my wife?"
"Do you want me to call a cop?"
"Does he sell *Time* magazine?"

Etc. Etc.—It's doubtful that an actual straight man would last this long. At any rate, continuity is one criterion of organized experience. A second criterion is consistency.

b. The Criterion of Consistency of Experience.

Lying on the desk as I write is a package of cigarettes. I perceive the package of cigarettes. We need to remember that we have rejected the notion that what the package of cigarettes means to me is to be regarded entirely as a function of the sensory impressions. Rather, whatever the object perceived, it is to be referred to for our purposes as an intended object. Thus, while it may be presented by sensory materials, it *means,* it is objectified by me, it stands as a real thing on the basis of the way in which the sensory materials have been idealized. Thus it is no "flight into metaphysics" to insist that the package of cigarettes is an intended object. We are not denying its material existence. Rather, we seek to embrace more closely than ever its empirical existence by insisting that we be able to say with reference to what rules of procedures its order of existence is to be confirmed. Thus we shall find that a crucial difference between a display package of cigarettes and the pack on my desk is found in the specification of availability of smokes.

Now, the visual image of the package of cigarettes is one thing while the perceived package of cigarettes is quite another. The two are not congruent in their meanings. The second "protrudes" beyond the first. The visual pack is presented in three places, each plane being marked off by a configuration of print and color against its background. Perceptually, the pack has six sides. For me the tax stamp does not end at the plane of the table but continues around the pack to the approximate distance of the stamp on the other side. I see two cigarettes in the torn opening, but I "see" many more inside.

These things that I "see" in addition to what is visually presented are not adventitious with regard to my initial perception. Each rather attaches to the perceived pack by a change in viewpoint and each change in viewpoint develops the "potentialities" that were, to use a dangerous term, "pre-delineated" in the original percept. The visual image presents one aspect of a thing "charged" with potentialities, and these potentialities may be actualized by coordinate perceptions revealing further aspects of the same thing. This initial aspect, one among countless others, signifies something other than itself. It remains for me to actualize these potentialities as I can or wish by further action, such as examining the package or performing such an examination in imagination or recollection. In any case the possibility of this change in viewpoint exists as a *relevant possibility.* Knocking the package off the desk is a possibility and would be a specification of the possibility of handling the package, but we will limit our use of the term relevance by making it mean a possibility that forms a constitutive element of the appearance of the thing.

The potentialities are clustered around the visual image. They can be eliminated only at the cost of destroying the unity of meaning of the perceived thing.

We speak then of an "inner horizon" to designate the totality of serial potentialities involved in the object as noema. Both the nucleus and the horizon compose the percept—the object in mind—the job, the topic, the thing about which are talking, the thing toward which we direct our love or hate, the thing we doubt or affirm, etc. The explication of these anticipated aspects leads to the "intrinsic" structure of the object. The explication of these anticipated aspects amounts to what one writer, Helmut Kuhn, has spoken of as the "intensification" of the object—the making of it ever more concrete.

c. The Criterion of Compatibility of Experiences

The object has its "outer horizon" as well. By this, I mean that in meaning, the object means more than this momentary appearance and multiplicity of its aspects. The relation of potentiality to actuality, the "comprehensive anticipation," the gradual "unfolding" of our anticipations occur *mutatis mutandis* in the make-up of the outer horizon.

The concept of the outer horizon arises out of the insight that there seems to be no such thing in our experience as an isolated object. The perceived thing is related to other things, to its closer and wider "environment." As I view the object I see also its relatedness to other things, both directly, as the package of cigarettes is seen an arm's length from me, on the table, located between the book and the ash-tray, as well as by implication, as I expect that the book of matches [is] somewhere close by. This relatedness is not an incidental addition to the object taken by itself. Rather, seeing the object, I see also the things to which it is related.

The fact that an object implicates others, we refer to as our third criterion of organization of experience. Empirically the criterion is found in the expectations of the person of what goes with what.

d. The Criterion of Temporal Continuity

Both inner and outer horizons are interwoven with a temporal horizon. The present perception is a link in a chain of successive perceptions each of which had or will have a presence of its own. Accordingly, the apprehension of the thing points both to the immediate and remote past, on the one hand, and to the immediate and distant future, on the other. The present apprehension is informed by the remembrance of the past as well as the expectancy of coming things. The actual percept at any given point in time is always touched by some temporal mode of apprehension and is concretely inseparable from a long series of former objectifying acts, or rather with their product, i.e., the well known, easily recognized thing. The present percept also points forward to its successors.

Though there may be discontinuities, there is no real break in the temporal background encircling the "here and now" of the actual experience. The absolutely new is inconceivable. Strangeness exists only with familiarity; novelty only by the standard of the ordinary. To perceive an object means to locate it within a system of expectations. The perception is a fulfillment of the expectation and may in turn furnish the foundation for new expectations. Anticipations and continuance, the before and the hereafter, do not belong to separate acts in the succession of experience. They are ingredients of the one act under consideration, and compose the temporal horizon of the intended object. The temporal "horizon" is not to be conceived of like a railroad track extending off to right and left with experiences stuck onto it like stations. Rather each experience has its own relevant past and future attached to it as an articulated set of actualized and future possibilities all experienced as a gestalt in the momentary Now. It is of no use to search for a beginning of the anticipatory pattern of the world within experience. Again, Helmut Kuhn writes, we may trace its differentiation and transformation, but not its commencing in time.

The empirical criterion of the temporal horizon is found in the formal fact that an object motivates the possibilities that serve to specify it further.

e. The Criterion of "Clarity" of Experience.

The term "clarity" is not a particularly good one but will have to do temporarily. It refers to the fact that the intended possibilities can be fulfilled with varying degrees of distinctness. One may conceive of the conditions of the actor's make-up or the conditions of communicative net being such that the possibilities of experience are "broadly" or "narrowly tuned," meaning by this metaphor that the characteristics of the signals that are "received" (to take one source of fulfillment) may vary in their characteristics within certain limits as far as the criteria for the fulfillment of the relevant possibilities are concerned.

The relevance of this criterion for the discussion of communication can be seen clearly in considering the ranges of variability of style in a message and the ways in which the conditions of a net may prescribe the manner of delivery if incongruity is to be avoided. It bears too on the possibility of extracting information from a message. A referee in Kriegsspiel who indicates "No" by shaking his head may disrupt the continuity of the player's experiences if the referee shakes his head to indicate "No" but also shakes his head in the same way due to a nervous disorder. Beyond this the possibility itself may be so constructed as to prohibit fulfillment.

But now we are on the verge of the topic of the things that condition the characteristics of organization of experience. We shall see in a moment that information designates a peculiar facet of these possibilities of experience. The result of this is a most important rule: *Any factor that conditions the characteristics of organization of experience, conditions the characteristics of information.* This is jumping the gun, however. There are some further topics to treat before this rule can be clearly exploited for the theorems it makes possible.

A Working Classification of Possibilities

We shall assume that there is nothing in the nature of any set of possibilities of experience that places restrictions on their being differentially constituted even in completely arbitrary fashion to present a unity of meaning. Hence we have the rule that all noemata are in an important sense created.

It has already been pointed out several times above that the reality of an object is *not* found in its ontological structure but *is* found in its constitution as a unity of meaning. To say that an object is real is to mean that it is of interest to an experiencer relative to some order of past, present, and anticipated experiences. To furnish another perspective in the matter: the reality of an object as a unity of meaning is not found in its ontological structure; rather, the ontological structure is found in its reality as a unity of meaning.

An object is always a determined object. However, the various ways in which objects can be determined remains for investigation. While much has been done with the determined object in the disciplines of formal logic and mathematics, very little has been done with the problem, so far, by or for sociologists.

Although the ways in which an object may be determined must remain without further elaboration, there [are] a set of adjectives for modifying the notion of the possibility of experience. These adjectives, initially at least, may serve to aid the task of talking about the structures of the object and of the relationships of those structures to other objects as well as to the mode of attending them.

Primary and Secondary Possibilities

There is first the distinction between what I'll call "primary" and "secondary" possibilities.

It is a rare case when all of a set of unified possibilities will be or must be fulfilled through activity before the object is confirmed by the actor "for what it actually is." That is, it is a rare case for a set of possibilities where all are primary. By a primary possibility is meant any possibility that the actor does in fact test as a specifier of the object.

A secondary possibility is one that can be shown to be integral to the object constituted as a unity of meaning, but which is not tested in the course of treating the object. One caution: The categories of primary and secondary are interpretive and not ontological categories. They are merely a means of distinguishing that about an object and a communicant's regard for it that is momentarily relevant as a specification from that which is not. Among other things the catalogue of primary possibilities is dependent upon the length of the defining moment of the action. It is dependent on many other things as well as we shall see when we discuss the things that condition the various properties of information.

That a possibility is to be counted as primary or secondary is altogether a different question from a consciously entertained possibility and one not presented in awareness. We shall state the view without justifying it here that the object of which the communicant is aware is not the same thing as the object that he is treating. In fact it is exceedingly rare that the two will be the same. It is the latter object that is of interest to us.

Both primary and secondary possibilities may be present in awareness. The test of the difference is found in the fact that for some possibilities the actor experiences either a datum or an image as the thing that fulfills the possibility, and such a possibility is called primary. The class of other possibilities, which exhausts the class of relevant possibilities, will then stand as unproblematical for the communicant according to a normalizing assumption that as things were in the past they are now. We shall refer to this as the et cetera assumption and return to it later as an exceedingly important structure that bears upon communicative work, the possibility of continuous communicative experience, and the nature of information.

Crucial and Equal–Moment Possibilities

Another set of modifiers that cuts across the modifiers, primary and second-ary, [are] needed to make the difference between those possibilities that are critical specifications in the sense that they count with something greater than a weight equal to each of the other specifications, and those specifications that count each for one and only one. For example, the experience of the crucial specifier, is common to everyday evaluations of persons and is expressed in the view, "I'd known John for years and always thought he was thus and so, but after he did *that* I saw him for what he really is." The crucial possibility is found in the language of substance and essence.

The other class of possibilities which we shall call equal-moment possibili-ties, is found in the language of the "batting average" or the count over the long run, or, in the language of logical classes where the thing treated is a horse because it meets all of the criteria of the class.

Objects defined according to the crucial identifiers are never constituted in matters of degree. The conception of "mostly a something" is not drawn from the language of statistical probability but is drawn from the language of essential Being. In an important sense for an understanding of the ways in which interpersonal solidarities are maintained, the use of crucial identifiers involves voting the objectivity. This is in fact the realm of values and the realm of valued and de-valued objects.

For all the various modes of possibilities, primary and secondary, crucial and equal-moment, and the others that we shall speak of, their status as one or the other is always relative to the other possibilities that specify the same object.

Relevant and Non–Relevant Possibilities

In talking about the specifications of an object, it will help to differentiate between those specifications the removal of which destroys the unity of mean-ing, that is, the removal either occasions the notion of a new object or literally leaves the experiencer faced with an aggregate of unrelated possibilities; and those specifications that specify the object though they are not constituent to it as a unity of meaning. Although it is the case that all the possible ways in which an object may be treated or experienced are constituent of the object as a unity of meaning, nevertheless it is a peculiarity of the action frame that for a given moment or sequence of moments of activity that it does not engage the notion of "wider knowledge" (something that is engaged only in reflection, e.g., past accomplished experiences), but involves the treatment of the object according to terms that are relevant to the actor's interpretive scheme at hand in a Here and Now. Hence the exhaustive listing of possible specifications is the task of the person who seeks an ontological cataloguing of a world of objects, in principle, both an unnecessary and impossible task.

Although the observer in principle brings the notion of the catalogue into account when he seeks to specify the object that the actor will treat, he uses the notion of the catalogue only to enter upon the pragmatic procedure, in the ideal, of facing the subject under conditions that control the elements of attitude with a repeated situation in order to gain a statistical notion of the specifications that the actor will treat. The observer then refers to these as relevant specifications. The others are subsumed under the category of non-relevant specifications. An irrelevant specification would be one that would not specify the object in any case.

Fullfillable Possibilities

Some possibilities will have as constituent elements of their meanings the sense of comparison of an ideal with an experience intended as some order of approximation of the ideal. The approximation is then referred to as that which fulfills the ideal. The property of fulfillability—that is, the require-ment proposed in the very experience of the possibility of comparison with some further experience—will be meant when we talk of a fulfillable pos-sibility. Fulfillability may be achieved through a datum, an image, or an idea. A non-fulfilled possibility, then, is one which lacks "closure" in this sense. An unfulfillable possibility is one that does not include the meaning of comparability. A fulfilled possibility is one all of whose meanings have been completed.

A fulfillable possibility that has not been fulfilled will be known as an open possibility. A closed possibility is any possibility, fulfillable or not, whose meanings are complete.

Some Important Terms

We are now in a position to define four critical terms to use in the theory of information: retention, protention, anticipation, and expectation.

By a retention is meant any possibility that (1) is constituted in durée alone or in durée and phenomenal time, and (2) if constituted in durée and phenomenal time it must have the temporal specification of past with or without a temporal meaning drawn from the schema of standard time. A protention is a possibility constituted in durée and phenomenal time that carries the meaning of future without a temporal meaning drawn from the schema of standard time.

By anticipation is meant a protention within a course of activity, overt or covert, governed by a teleogical principle. The term expectation designates any possibility constituted within a scheme of standard time. An expectation is by definition open and fulfillable. An anticipation would have to be examined to determine its status according to these modifiers.

Open and Problematical Possibilities

Our final distinction is between open and problematical possibilities as Schuetz speaks of them in his article, "Choosing Among Projects of Action," *Philosophy and Phenomenological Research,* vol. 12 (December 1951), especially pp. 170–173. Reprints are on file in the project library and were read in connection with the conference on model construction, so I shall not repeat the distinction here.

VI

Some Preliminary Terms

Having spent considerable time going over the notion of the object as a schema of possibilities of experience, and having pointed to the notion of the definition of the situation as a set of possibilities of experience whose organization we shall describe according to the criteria of consistency, compatibility, continuity, temporal continuity, and clarity, the place where we shall look for the thing we will call information should be obvious enough. In its general meaning the term information will refer to some property of the way in which a set of possibilities are ordered. (Remember possibility should read "possibility of experience" and by this term is meant any experience that can serve the function of specifying an object. The term possibility means alternative, not likelihood.)

Before we begin, let's introduce a few necessary notions: signal, sign, expression, message, and communication.

Signal—Consider the biological body and its physical environment as two systems that can be independently described. We shall consider that the two systems are coupled by the receptor properties of the body's nervous system. Insofar as a pattern of nervous excitation can be matched with a state description of the physical system, we shall refer to the pattern of *receptor-coupled physical events found in the state description of the physical system* as a sensory stimulus. A sensory stimulus that is experienced by a communicant as an indicator only of itself will be known as a signal. By definition, signals are meaningless.

Sign or mark—When a stimulus is experienced by a communicant as an indicator of something other than itself, and only as an indicator, the stimulus will be referred to as a sign or mark. To say of a stimulus or stimulus pattern that it is a sign, i.e., that it serves the meaning or function of representation, always implies that it is a sign *of* something. The meaning function of representation may occur with regard to *any* experience regardless of its sensory or ideal character, that is, regardless of whether it is presented as a stimulus, as an image, an idea in recall, etc., and regardless of its complexity as an experience. Insofar as an experience is experienced as the representer of something else, whether this something else is sensorily or eidetically given, the representer will be referred to as a sign of the thing represented.

For a sensorily presented sign, two things need to be described for a complete description: (a) its physical character (i.e., what it is stimulus wise that is a sign) and (b) its representational function (i.e., that it is a sign of something). The thing that it is a sign of will be known as the meaning of the sign.

For example, suppose I write "mib" on the board. Any of the many possible ways that I could achieve a physical state description of this configuration of letters would define the stimulus character of the word. To call the thing described a signal it would be necessary to show that the structure of the experience of the witness stands in a one-to-one correspondence with the physical state description with nothing left over. But it is possible for the actor to attend not to the stimulus pattern in its state character as such, but to attend to it as a word, i.e., as having sense to it, as for example the sense of its being a word. Or one can start with its word character as the thing that is the sign, in which case it stands before us now as a sign of "something that I will soon give a sense to." Or in orienting this configuration of markings, I could attend to it as an indicator of "a configuration of markings." Further, suppose I go ahead and define "mib" as "any triangle with a short perpendicular line attached to one of its sides." The word "mib" then is a sign of the thing indicated in the definition, and its sense is no more than and just this thing that it stands for.

Expression—There are some patterns of stimuli that can be so attended to—so experienced—that the thing they represent has itself a sense, a meaning, that refers *through this meaning* to something beyond itself. That is, the thing represented has the sense of a specification that stands as the specification of a thing that the specification specifies. Such stimuli will be referred to as expressions.

Three meaning functions need to be separated out: (1) the function of representation (all expressions and all signs are alike in this respect); (2) the function of signification; and (3) the function of reference or naming. A stimulus that is experienced by a communicant in these three senses will be known as an expression.

The function of representation has already been defined. By the function of signification is meant that the thing represented has a meaning in that it says something. Finally, by the function of reference is meant that the thing represented that says something says something *about* something. Thus we distinguish between the meaning of an expression and its property of naming an object through its content or meaning. Farber, in *The Foundation of Phenomenology,* to which much of this discussion of signs and expressions is indebted, writes:

> It is only by signifying something that an expression can refer to something objective, so that the expression signifies or names the object by means of its meaning.

The necessity for the distinction between the meaning of an expression and the object of an expression stems from the fact that two expressions can have different meanings but the same object. For example, the expressions "A is greater than B" and "B is smaller than A" have different contents but name the same thing, namely, a relationship of differential magnitude between A and B. "The man in the White House" and "Margaret Truman's father" are two further examples. Two expressions can have the same meanings but refer to different objects. For example, I can say "Two plus two is four" and refer in one case to an arithmetically proper relationship while referring in a second case to the bit of folk wisdom that "Things always add up if you figure them out." Two or more expressions may differ in both respects, but they may also agree in both respects. The former case is obvious; the second case is seen in tautological expressions; i.e., expressions that mean and name the same thing. The clearest example of this is seen in the equivalence of expressions in different languages.

Although the functions of meaning and reference are independently variable, they do not occur independently of each other in the sense that one could have an expression with a meaning but with no object meant. In this sense they are best conceived of as "dependent contents" of the thing called an expression, in the same way that hue and extension are the dependent contents of general idea, color. Just as a color which has hue but not area is unthinkable, just so and as a matter of a priori law, it is impossible that an expression has a meaning but no object meant. Insofar as an experience is said to be meaningful, every such experience is an experience of something. The statement that an experience is meaningful means that the experience is an experience of a something. To be unable to actualize a meaning is the same as to be unable to objectify. A signal is precisely a stimulus for which the experience is unable to actualize a meaning. Thus as we shall see later, whatever conditions the ability to actualize a meaning is a condition that can be manipulated to induce confusion, i.e., a state in which signals rather than signs or expressions are experienced. The relevance of this rule for manipulating the characteristics of information will soon be seen.

Some further remarks may help draw things together. (1) One may have the function of representation operating without the functions of specification and reference. One can *not* have the functions of either specification or reference without the other two. (2) The actual contents of meanings and object can be simultaneously constituted into a unified expression as for example in proper names that both mean and name the object through the same term. (3) This does not say however that the meaning of the expression is found in one term of an expression while the object is found in another. (4) Objects are not given except as a unity of specifications; hence there is no such thing as an object in and of itself.

(5) A meaning may be given but the thing meant may not be clear. The phenomenologists speak of acts of meaning intention and acts of meaning fulfillments by way of underlining the structure of an experience in which a meaning is grasped as referring to something though the thing referred to is not grasped. The child's game of "What am I?" illustrates this effect: "What am I?" runs the question, i.e., I am a what? and then the sentences go: "I clean myself," "I like milk," "I say meow" while the child selects from a set of pictures under each of which he is asked: "Am I a cow? (picture of a cow), etc., etc. Here then each of the specifications intends an object as something that stands as the thing referred to through these specifications. Until he hits on it, the thing may be for him "that which cleans itself, likes milk, says meow." Fulfillment of an object may be achieved in any of these three ways: through a perception; through an image; through an idea.

(6) There is nothing in the nature of an experience itself that prescribes its sign or expression character. (I say this however only to take a temporary position in the matter since I'm not clear on the question of what is involved in referring to the "language of gestures.") But with another however, we can say that we would like to say that the sign or expressional character of an experience is dependent upon the "rules" by which signals and meanings are "matched." These rules include not only the usual sense of grammar, but matters of temporal order, context of meanings, redundancy built into the statistical structure of language, expectations that are entertained without question, etc., in effect, the rules that prescribe what kind of interest one is to take in a set of signals. (7) Expressions will be known as sensorily founded expressions or ideally founded expressions. They differ in that a sensorily founded expression

requires for complete description its physical character as it was referred to in Memo #1, its vehicular character, or style. An ideally founded expression is given directly as an image or an idea. Ideally founded expressions and ideally founded signs are, so to speak, "all meanings." The memory system, to take another position, consists only of meanings.

(8) A distinction needs to be pointed out between equivocal and multivalued signs and expressions. An equivocal sign or expression is one that has more than one meaning, but whose particular meaning for one reason or another (we shall see later what such reasons are) cannot be selected out of a set of possible ones. A multivalued sign or expression is one that has many meanings, all of them being pertinently named, for example, universal names like "The Gross Anatomy of the Cat." (9) Another distinction that will prove useful is that between what Husserl calls "objective expressions" and "occasional expressions." An objective expression is one that is understood without regard on the communicant's part to the person uttering it or to the circumstances of its utterance. An occasional expression is one that is understood by the communicant who orients himself to the make-up of the person uttering it and the circumstances of the utterance. According to Husserl no expression containing a personal pronoun has an objective sense, only a sense appropriate to an occasion, i.e., an occasional sense. This is so, he claims, because the word "I" names a different person from case to case. Its general meaning function is to denote the person happening to speak. Farber (238) writes:

> The word "I" has an indicating function which as it were says to hearer: the person opposite you means himself.... The further distinction between exact and vague expressions is one which relates to the ambiguity of expressions. Most expressions of ordinary life are vague, such as tree and bush, animal and plant, and the like, whereas all expressions that are constituents of pure theories and laws are exact. Vague expressions do not have a meaning-content that is identical in every case of their use. Their meanings relate to typical but only partially clear examples which usually change frequently.

Although the various distinctions that have been made may appear at first glance to be concerned with too fine a categorization, I think it will become clear in our later discussion that the distinctions are not only necessary and useful to handling the problems that arise when we attempt to insert the phenomena of meaning into what is otherwise little more than a theory of signaling, but that these initial classifications will prove fundamental to elaborating a vocabulary to handle the types of communicative work that are characteristic of various communicative nets.

To cite several examples: (1) We would expect that there will be a proliferated use of communication by means of highly standardized signs, and various devices by which uniformity of interpretation was insured in situations which for one reason on another required secrecy, or control of large and heterogeneous numbers of persons, or where a high value was placed upon conserving the time required for communicating, or where complicated instructions had to be communicated in a situation marked by extraneous noises or long distances over which say a voice could not carry sufficiently. (2) It strikes me that the rationalizing of organizational structure and operations involves the "depersonalizing" of communicative work, i.e., rendering expressions anonymously objective, a phenomenon that I would expect to go hand in hand with the phenomenon of substitutability and rate of turnover of personnel in bureaucratic organizations. (3) The intriguing notion of "organizational sense" that Wilbert Moore suggested may involve in the "degree of occurrence" the ability of the person to engage himself with those complex communicative constructions that are found in irony, humor, shadings of motive, intent, and circumstance that are the hallmarks of communication between in-group members and that are so obviously difficult to grasp by "the stranger." It seems to me that much is to be learned about the structural and operational features of a social system by examining the instrumental and "expressional" features of the language of the exchanges that occur. I suggest for example that situations marked organizationally by the fact that they consist of coalitions formed for the pursuit of mutual and technical interests will show in their language a marked instrumental emphasis. This comes out very clearly in the case of the language of professional criminals whose language names the relevant features of their work situation in terms that name the object through that specification that stands in most immediate relevance to the technical manipulations that must be performed or taken into account for maximizing in their view the chances of a successful outcome.[8]

From the point of view of a legitimate citizen, a group of professional criminals may be designated by the mass nouns "a gang of hoodlums," and the life circumstances of the legit are such as to make this expression functional with reference to the attitudes that are appropriate to the maintenance of his bonafide status with other legits. But for a professional criminal such a term would be considered vague and totally inappropriate except as provocative of laughter. Such a massive noun does not differentiate at all the important facets of his work situation; the group consists of an "inside man," a "roper," "a mark," a

---

8. [Editor's Note: Gresham Sykes was doing his classic study of prison argot at the same New Jersey prison Garfield studied.]

"shill," all of these terms being specific designations of the functions that the various persons so designated must perform for the successful swindle.

I'm not saying that the legitimate person has a less instrumental language, but am insisting only that the properties of language and communicative work will be functionally related to the properties of the social relationships under study. And the distinctions that have been drawn above I feel will permit closer study of those relationships between communicative work and social relationships than would be the case were we to settle for the difference between signs and signals as one in which signs are signals that have referents and attempt to handle communicative work with this massive and to my mind misleading and inaccurate distinction.

Message—In strict and preferred usage this term will mean a spatially and/or temporally patterned set of *signals.* The patterning involved is that imposed by the experimenter. The patterning is defined in the physical state description drawn from the experimenter's vocabulary. In loose usage the term will be used synonymously with the term *a communication."*

Communication—As a noun, in the sense of *a communication,* the term refers to a spatially and/or temporally patterned set of signs or expressions. Patterning here is the patterning of the communicant. Whereas the patterning of signals in a message is patterning by the design of the observer, and hence can be assumed by him insofar as he controls it or takes it into account as part of his investigative design, the patterning of signs and expressions is for the observer empirically problematical, something that he seeks to learn about, though it is nonetheless subject to his manipulative control. Under certain circumstances of inquiry and for certain problems he can assume the fact of this patterning and address himself to other properties of communications, as for example, contents, timing, logical properties, and such other facets as were considered in the discussion before.

As a noun, in the sense of *communication-generally,* the term refers to the inter-communicant processes of operating upon messages through the operations whereby messages are "invested" with their meaning character.

As a verb in the sense of *to communicate,* the term refers to the patterning of signs and expressions in process.

Communicative work—The processes of transmission, reception, and interpretation of messages.

Meaning of a message—The "products" of the meaning-functions defined above of indication, signification, and naming.

Communicative tactics—Insofar as the patterning of signs or expressions is governed by a communicant's assessments of the identified other's definition of the situation, we shall talk of the tactical character of the communicant's communications.

Communicative strategy—Insofar as the communicant's communications are governed by the communicant's projected plan and the intention to realize the plan, we shall refer to the plan as conferring a communicative strategy upon his communications.

Communicative plan—Insofar as a communicant decides in advance which of several alternatively possible communications he will choose as the necessity for choice arises, and makes up his mind in advance for all possible contingencies, we shall speak of such a set of decisions as his communicative plan.

Communicative design—Insofar as communicative work is regulated only by normative prescription and without reference to a project and intention to realize it, the system of prescriptions will be known as communicative design.

VII

A Working Definition of Information

THE DISCUSSION MAY BE HELPED ALONG IF WE PROVIDE AN ILLUSTRATIVE context from which to draw examples whenever the discussion gets too hairy. I suggest the game of Kriegsspiel, because it is a situation in which something called "information" is a prominent element of conversation.

Kriegsspiel is also known as double-blind chess. It is played with boards each having a full complement of pieces for both players. The player is not allowed to see his opponent's pieces, but must infer the opponent's position from whatever sources of information are otherwise available within the rules of the game. The referee alone can see both sides. He indicates whose move it is. He announces possible captures by a pawn, pawn promotions, the fact that a piece has been captured though without identifying the piece, checks by row, file, or diagonal, and check-mate.

Let's first consider some recipes of play that a Kriegsspiel player might give to a novice, for these recipes throw some light both on the formal character of the thing called information as well on the conditions that bear on the informing character of the message.

If you ask him for advice, the addicted Kriegsspieler may tell you as follows: "Unless you know how to talk during the game, keep your mouth shut." He's not talking about being polite. He's saying that there are various ways of getting information about the effect of a move, the location of pieces, contemplated strategies, and so on. Some people, for example, blow or grunt when they lose an important piece. Some players become animated when they figure something good or something bad is in prospect. In a word, they start communicating directly instead of through the referee. And the good Kriegsspiel player knows that wherever there are messages, there is the possibility of information.

Another piece of advice runs: "Never forget that the only pieces you ever see are your own." This does not mean that you are forbidden to look at your opponent's layout. Such virtue is assumed. It means that it is a dangerous conceit to treat a hypothetical arrangement of your opponent's pieces as anything other than one plausible arrangement among many plausible arrangements. So this advice says, never take anything for granted except what you can see directly.

More advice. "Keep an accurate piece count." The referee announces all captures, though he identifies only the capture of pawns. A failure to remember how many pieces the other person has lost makes it impossible later in the game to maintain the continuity of a line of assessment, so that one is unable to evaluate possible moves and to even realize much less correct for error. The game becomes literally a jumble.

And another piece of advice related to this: "Once the game starts, if for any reason you have to leave, suspend the whole game until you return. Don't let anyone play for you during your absence." This advice has nothing to do with the selfishness of Kriegsspiel players. It has everything to do with the fact that information in the game is systematically cumulative and in such a way that two definitions of the state of the game can only be grossly matched. Continuity is lost if a substitute is allowed to carry on the game.

Let's say I am playing the white pieces. The game has proceeded through several moves. I have just moved my queen to my opponent's king-rook-one and the referee says, "Black's move."

I have arranged a set of possibilities such that the message in return will provide me a means of knowing which of the possibilities has been actualized. Let's go further. I am attending to an object that we'll say is the state of the game as it consists of an arrangement of black and red squares, a line consisting of a rook, a knight, a bishop, with "other pieces so placed as to make reprisal on the next move impossible," with my queen so situated as to bear through an open diagonal on the rook in the corner, and so on. Or to put it concisely, the thing in view, the object, consists of something called a position that is specifiable in terms of a set of relationships between the pieces in the territory of play.

Now if you play Kriegsspiel Garfinkel style, you will be surprised and a little indignant to hear the referee say: "Black's move" because I would have expected him to say: "Piece gone at the king-rook-one, and black's move." That is, in moving my queen, I expected the order of possibilities to be altered in such a way that where my opponent's piece was, my queen now stood. In fact, I expected it more specifically: I expected my queen to capture my opponent's rook.

But to my surprise and immediate regret I hear the referee say: "Black's move." Now, a rule of the game is that the referee must announce all captures. I know the rule and I also assume that the referee knows it and will act accordingly. Thus, no announcement? Hell! No capture. Well, I moved my queen to the corner, that I know for sure. No capture? His rook wasn't there. In fact, nothing was there. That conniver. I'll bet his rook is where his knight should have been. Wow, if that's so I've fallen into a trap. We'll see. Sure enough, the referee announces: "Piece gone at the Black king-rook-one, and white's move." I've lost my queen. But by a rook? By his knight? Was the row open to the king? No. If it had been open, I would have learned this because the referee would have had to announce the king in check—assuming that his king—was on that back row to begin with. Come to think of it, he usually gets his king out fast to help him know what I'm up to. Well, if his king is back there, it would have cost me a queen to learn whether or not the row was open, which it wasn't. I can see that *now*. His king knight pawn is somewhere in the knight file other than in the original position, otherwise I would have gotten a "No" from the referee when I tried to go down there, and besides there haven't been any pawn captures on that side. But where is it? It's at least one move away from my pawns on that side because my pawns are arranged to pick up the presence of an approaching pawn. Etc., etc.

The notion of information lurks in various places and in various senses throughout this recital. It does not refer, for example, to the object "the game as it exists in the corner," for this "game-in-the-corner" is known to me only as a set of specifications of pieces in their places. It does get located, however, in the predications of the object.

Let's see first the various senses in which it is said that I obtained information. (1) First there is the sense of information obtained directly from my reading of the messages, "Black's move" and "Piece gone at Black's king-rook-one and white's move." (2) There is information in the sense of the rule that goes, as I recall it, that the referee announces all captures and checks. (3) There is information in the sense of what I got to know by inference. (4) There is information in the sense of what I got to know in retrospect. (5) There is information in the sense of what I know as my ignorance, i.e., what I don't know. (6) There is information in the sense of what I know as merely possible or likely or doubtful. Through all this, one thing seems to remain as an invariant meaning: The thing that I know about stands before me in the affirmative sense, i.e., I experience it with one sense attached to it as a determining sense, namely, the sense of the judged thing.

We have then our first specification of the thing, "information," I experience it not as liked, loved, hated, wished for, doubted, but *judged*. Or to borrow from the terminology of logic, I experience it in the mode of its affirmative meaning. To use Husserl's language, I "live in" its sense of affirmation. I do not affirm *about*; I affirm *that*. As I look at the Kriegsspiel board, I see directly the sense, the meaning, "I have completed my move without capturing a piece." When I consider the possibility that his king is not on the back row, I experience in its affirmative sense the question of where his king may be if it is not on the back row.

And now what else is required? (1) *For the case of signs:* Insofar as the experiencer actualizes something as the thing indicated by the sign, the thing indicated as it is experienced in the affirmative mode will be called the experiencer's information or "what he knows." (2) *For the case of expressions:* Insofar as the experiencer actualizes the object of an expression, that is, insofar as he effects the coincidence of the meaning and the thing meant—which can be done as was pointed out previously through a perception, a fantasized image, or an idea—the unity of meaning and thing meant as the coincidence presents a specified object will, insofar as the experiencer "lives in" the affirmative mode of the coincidence be known as his information or "what he knows."

So much for the notion of information in general. A very touchy problem remains to be handled: the problem of information storage. Temporarily I would like to propose the following view. Instead of conceiving the coincidence of meaning and thing meant as a little package that gets tied together and filed away in the recesses of memory, "put on the drum," to be drawn out again when the need arises, I would prefer (though again only to take a stand on the problem) to regard information as something not recalled but re-created out of the resources of the available order of possibilities of experience, available sensory materials, actions, etc. Thus preferred usage would be to talk of a communicant as knowledge*able* rather than talking of his knowledge. What he knows he knows only in the moment of knowing and not otherwise. I'm still peering at this notion with a stranger's eyes and so I'm in bad need of some very searching conversation. What I'm after is somehow to resolve the bothersome dilemma between information as a momentary product of experience and information as an atemporal sum of things experienced.

Inasmuch as the empirical procedure for testing recall consists of matching the "recollected" item with the original expressional input, it might be that we can abandon the notion of knowledge held in potentiality of recall as unnecessary and perhaps as even scientifically sterile, while addressing our-selves to the task of considering what conditions of the communicant's make-up and what conditions of social structure give us the probabilities of a certain kind of "re-creation" when the task of recall is set to the communicant. At any rate, I much prefer the notion of memory as a describable set of operations by which a previous meaningful experience is reproduced or re-presented to the notion of a memory as a container. However, I'm not insistent, only puzzled.

With this much to go on, let's turn now to some kinds of information.

VIII

Kinds of Information

The offering in this section consists of a preliminary vocabulary of information. The list of characteristics is a loose one. Some of these characterizations have been borrowed; others have been invented. In any case, they were selected because they promise immediate research application.

I would like in this section to do little more than run through some types, briefly pointing under each to possible applications, while reserving the task of drawing out the more systematic implications for research for a later section when we shall have in hand not only various characteristics of information but the factors that are conditional of these characteristics.

1. Perfect and Imperfect Information

This distinction is borrowed from Von Neumann and Morgenstern's *Theory of Games and Economic Behavior*. The distinction is intended here to relate a communicant's definition of the situation to the kind of access that the communicant has to what is going on in the remainder of the net.

Consider the game of two people playing tic-tac-toe. The number of outcomes (in the form of accomplished moves as the actualized meanings of the messages represented by a player making a mark in one of the cells) may be immediately available to both players as well as to a referee. But the game can be so constructed that the referee has access to more messages than does either player. Thus he would have access to more information than either of the players. (Remember we are talking here of outcomes. In a later typing of information, this kind of information will be defined as material information.)

Von Neumann and Morgenstern distinguish between what they call the "preliminarity" of a set of moves and the "anteriority" of a set of moves. By anteriority is meant the full chronology of moves as the referee would know them. Preliminarity refers to the outcomes that are part of the player's state of information.

By perfect information is meant that preliminarity and anteriority of moves is the same. That is, a player with perfect information is one who knows the outcomes of all previous choices. His information does not differ from that of the referee. A player's information is said to be imperfect where there is a disparity between all the outcomes and the outcomes that the player knows of.

The communicative net as it is constituted in the ordinary game of tic-tac-toe or chess illustrates a net whose communicants have perfect information. Kriegsspiel illustrates a net where the players have imperfect information.

Two points need stressing. First, the perfect or imperfect character of information is always relative to the communicative net-work under examination. Second, most of the communicative nets that we have considered so far in our seminar discussions are characterized by communicants with imperfect information.

The distinction is not a dichotomous one, but is rather describable as a single "number" which specifies the discrepancy between the referee's information and the communicant's. The concept is appealing in its possible operational clarity. Some nasty though intriguing problems in sampling a net are suggested as first order business. The notion promises help in handling a notion that has achieved almost platitudinous status in current sociological theorizing, namely, that interpersonally coordinated and integrated activities presuppose uniformity in the definitions of the situation of the involved parties. The property of uniformity may in fact be misleading, for a situation of imperfect information is by definition one that lacks uniformity in this regard.

So the questions arise of uniformity in what respects; and indeed, need there be uniformity at all? By addressing ourselves to the property of uniformity of definition we may be overlooking entirely other properties of the definitions of the situation and particularly properties that arise when definitions are considered by sets whereby coordination is effected, and where uniformity rather than making for integration may be dysfunctional to it. I'm thinking of cases where perfect information may be achieved only at exorbitant costs of money, time, and effort. We might find that the stability of a communicative net, let's say the manageability of a situation, is achieved through various devices that overcome the requirement of perfect information and uniformity of definition. Particularly is this suggested in systems marked by occupational specialization.

A moment's reflection on the phenomenon of perspectival view suggests again that even in a game like straight chess a minimal discrepancy must be a very difficult thing to maintain. The usual insistence on uniformity of definition as a crucial integrator might merely reflect the tremendous value Americans place on conformity. At any rate, the distinction promises to help in removing the grand vagueness that now surrounds the notion of the definition of the situation. In addressing the question of consensus, the point of investigative interest is not the fact of the uniformity but the fact that the communicant makes the assumption of uniformity that is productive of incongruity in amounts that can be handled. On the basis of this reasoning, the role state and the various tactics of incorporation and methods of resolving incongruity are brought under attention. A proposal was made at a previous seminar that if one followed this view, one might expect the very opposite of coordination to be the result of opening the lines of communication to permit the freer passage of messages up and down.

I suggest that we include in the final report a proposal of research on the problem of what it is that is actually going on within and between communicants in a situation that would according to going platitudes be characterized as a situation of open channels of communication. A study of the recent conferences in model construction might be revealing for pilot findings in this matter.

2. Relative Equality of Distributed Information

Whereas the notion of perfect and imperfect information permits us to handle the relationship of the communicant's information to what is going on in the rest of the net, the notion of relative equality of distributed information is designed to handle the relationship between what two or more communicants in a net know and do not know *between* them. Communicants may be equally informed, for example, while still having imperfect information.

In Section III the question was discussed of what we shall take to be meant by the notion of ignorance. A communicant's ignorance was to be conceived of as relative to another communicant's information. What A is ignorant of was to be defined as what A does not know that B knows.

Hence, the total ignorance in a system is defined as the information that all the communicants have but do not have in common. When the area of information held in common is added to this, the result is all that is known among and between communicants, these two categories being exhaustive. This view of ignorance has those characteristics, which I feel are desirable: it preserves the relational character of information in a net; it emphasizes the notion of information in use rather than information in storage and sum; it binds the notion of information to the characteristics of a social relationship; and it makes it necessary to account for actions and their consequences in terms of what communicants know while avoiding explanations based on what they do not know but could know or are prevented from knowing, etc.

The various notions involved may be clarified with the use of a simple diagram, (Ansley Coale tells me this is known as a Venn diagram and may be used as a logical device instead of a mere picture. I am indebted to Ansley for making clear some of the techniques involved in reading the diagram.)

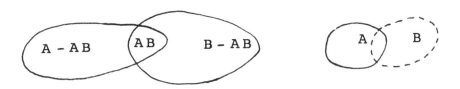

The diagram may help visualize our definitions: (1) If everything that a communicant knows, he knows in common with the other communicants, we shall say that a state of equally distributed information exists. Diagrammatically, this is the same as saying that the area AB is congruent with the areas A and B (assuming a two person net). (2) If everything that a communicant knows is not known by any of the other socially related communicants, we shall say that a state of perfect inequality of information exists. Diagrammatically, this is the same as saying that the area AB is equal to zero. (3) To the extent that AB is greater than zero but less than equivalent to A plus B, we shall talk of a state of unequal distribution of information. A state of unequal distribution of information means that there is a communicant for whom there is another communicant who knows something that the first one does not know.

The definitions need the prefix "For a time t."

Assuming that the topological properties of those diagrams match the properties of information according to our general definition, then two theorems can be proposed: (1) If additional persons are added to a net, the things they know in common can either remain the same or decrease, though it can never increase. (2) If additional persons are added to a net, the total ignorance in the system, i.e., the things that are not known between persons can either remain the same or can increase but it can never decrease.

The following are some partially rationalized theorems. (They were suggested to me when Ansley Coale brought to my attention a theorem that Veblen had proposed about the relationship between the division of labor and the level of technology.)

The nature of the solutions of tasks we shall say is a function of the coordinated exchange of information. Assume a system of communicative exchange. (1) For a state of equal distribution of information, the nature of the solution will be fixed by the information of any single member. (2) For a state of perfect inequality of information, the nature of the solution will be fixed by the information of any single member. (3) For a state of the unequal distribution of information the nature of the solution will be fixed by nature of the system of information exchange, i.e., the organization of information. (4) Veblen's theorem: In a state of unequal distribution of information, dividing the area of information held in common will reduce the nature of the solution of tasks to a more primitive level.

These speculations would underwrite Morgenstern's insistence in his paper, *Prolegomena to a Theory of Organization,* that the social organization of the factors of production rather than the factors alone is an important determinant of the output of an enterprise. It might be, too, though this a vast hunch, that the probability of innovation is in significant part determined by the degree of inequality of distributed information, and that as the state tends toward equal distribution the probability of innovation declines, while at the extremes of equality and perfect inequality the probability of innovation is minimal, perhaps, zero. However, this statement needs lots of further work to give it a status of more than more suggestion.

While we are making a little bit of speculation, we might as well make a little bit more. I envisage a line of development of the notion of distributed information that will link it more closely to communicative patterns as well as incorporating a time variable. To anticipate a result of such a development, suppose we were to represent a communication as the change of information from the region of the remainder to the region of intersection. If we assume that the communicants do not have access to information coming from outside of the system while at the same time the communicants as a matter of rule must engage in communicative exchanges, then in a specifiable time, depending on the nature of the rule, a course of communicative work will transform a state of inequality to a state of equality. We obtain the theorem then that under such conditions the fact of the organized transmission of information, as communication proceeds, will decrease the probability of innovation that it determines, while technical solutions to tasks will become progressively fixed. If the channels to information from outside the net remain open—one way of doing this being the introduction of new personnel into the net—then some minimum area of intersection would appear necessary to maintain a given level of technology. We theorize further that between the organization of information flow and the area of intersection there would be some devices by which innovation would be kept from running wild. One set of such devices, for example, would consist of the operations whereby the criteria of social selection are administered to effect entry and egress of network personnel. Simon's remarks on the constraints upon rational solutions might be relevant.

3. Complete and Incomplete Information

This distinction is inserted to relate the state of a communicant's informational portrait of an order to the devices for assessing and correcting for error and regulating discrepancy. These terms were defined in Memo #1 and in the Glossary.

Consider the case of a communicant who is faced with the necessity of choosing between alternative courses of action or between alternative meanings of a message, etc. The order of objects he orients as his problematical state of affairs can be conceived of as defined through some set of more or less intricately related variables. (We pay no attention, temporarily, to the things that condition either the weighting or the relationships of these variables.)

Insofar as there are insufficient specifications (for whatever reason) of the variables so that the communicant is unable to project a determinate outcome or solution in a Now, we shall say that his information is incomplete. Where the variables are sufficiently specified, and again on whatever grounds—for as we shall see later, one can have complete information within the attitudes of daily life by transforming the arrangement of a set of variables as well as by other means—we shall refer to his information as complete information.

The things that we shall be particularly interested in discussing with the aid of the conception of complete and incomplete information, as far as the things that condition information are concerned, are the devices whereby continuous action is maintained in the face of what appears for a fully rational communicant to be an insufficiently specified situation. Both Max Woodbury and Martin Shubik, who are doing work in this area, have expressed wonder over the fact that people "go ahead and do it," even though on strict rational grounds these people are without the information that adherence to the norms of scientific rationality would require [for] an informed decision.

The thing that strikes me in the matter is the frequency with which a communicant does *not* experience anything like a state of incomplete information; in fact, the usual response in answer to a question of how a decision was made in the face of informational shortcomings is a vociferous claim that everything that *needed* to be known was known.

The studies that Dick Snyder proposed into the nature of the "intellectual processes" involved in decision-making in the practical situations of a bureaucratic organization should throw some light on this phenomenon. A particularly good setting for investigating this problem is provided by police activities where the very characteristic of decisions made in the face of insufficient information is built directly and fairly obviously into the structural characteristics of policing systems and appears as a prominent element in police ideology. I would suggest the investigation of the characteristics of hypothesis formation and test of police as a good "short" problem for possible inclusion in the document to be submitted to the Ford Foundation.

4. The Probable Character of Information from Randomness to Certainty

This concept is concerned with relating the communicant's assessment (in terms of his own calculus of probability—the so-called "psychological probability") of the likely character of the meanings to be drawn from a message, to the various properties that the dimensions of "style" and patterning can show. An important property would be that of relative ambiguity. Consider, for example, the reversible staircase as a message. (If the steps are the up side, do x; if the steps are on the underside, do y.)

Or better, perhaps, let's consider the arrangement between Paul Revere and his friend: "One if by land, two if by sea." His friend hung two lamps and Paul Revere spread the word that the British were coming in boats. But let's say that, just about the time his friend hung the lamps, Paul Revere developed a liver complaint and saw a whole field of spots before his eyes. What part of the signal field, he would have had to settle for himself, was contributed by his liver and what part was contributed by his friend.

Or take another case. You address a question to a friend who has a nervous tic and is given to shaking his head, now up and down, now side-ways, but in a fashion that varies independently of what you say to him. If you ask him a question requiring a yes or no answer and he has lost his voice so that he needs to nod in answer, you may have a certain amount of trouble sorting out the informing character of the messages from their "noise" character. ("Noise" is more responsibly defined later.)

Now in a case where no separation can be made in a signal field between the noise character of a message and the informing character of the message, we talk of the random character of the meanings that can be drawn, or a state of zero-order information. (The things that can condition a message to make it yield zero-order information are discussed in the next section.) If the informing character can be made out, the thing communicated will be experienced one of two ways. Either the inference will be experienced as a weighted inference of an order greater than zero but less than one, or it can be experienced with complete certainty. Thus Paul Revere might have been able to recognize that among the set of spots, all of a distant yellow hue, two were without green perimeters. "Aha! By sea." On the other hand, he might have seen green perimeters around all of them, but two of them seemed to be bordered only *when* he looked directly at them, though he couldn't be sure and he couldn't wait around for the liver attack to pass. So off he gallops shouting: "To arms! The British are coming by land or by sea; I'm not sure which or even if they're coming, but I'll bet they're on the way and put money it's by sea!"

The particular value from zero-order certainty to complete certainty that a set of meanings found in a message can have is among other things a function of the patterned occurrence of the signal. Unlike the case of patterning in the sense of the operations of patterning that the observer performs (in the definition of a message) the patterning referred to here is a patterning "found" in the field by the experiencer. Where the communicant is unable to make a separation in the signal field between the random character of the occurrence of the signal and the patterned character of the occurrence of the signal we shall talk of the random character of the information that can be drawn from the message.

Unlike the observer's patterning of signals to present a communicant with a message, where one need know only the operations that the observer has performed upon the physical state in order to effect a complete description of the message, a complete description of patterning in the second sense requires that the observer take into account the nature of the message, the manner and fact of its coupling to the communicant's nervous system, the attending attitude of the communicant, and the communicant's "tactics of incorporation," i.e., the processes by which the communicant transforms, "encodes," the message to yield for him its data character, its meanings.

The probable character of information can be controlled by alterations of variables at any one or any combination of these points. Not only operations upon the signal field, but operations upon the coupling system, upon the interpretive devices, and upon the communicant's attitude or Role will determine the probable value of the communicant's information. And of course any factor that is conditional of these factors is conditional of the probable character of the communicant's information. Later we shall draw some theorems from this rule.

5. Primary, Secondary, and Inferential Information

In Memo #2, a distinction was made between primary and secondary information. Any information that a communicant finds in a message by which he knows how his communicative efforts are being generated and received will be known as secondary information. All other information is primary information. That is, any information that a communicant finds in a message that is other than information concerning what Bateson and Ruesch refer to as meta-communication—communication about communication—will be called primary information.

We add the category of "inferential information" as a possible modifier of primary and secondary information. The term distinguishes between information that stands as the product of a message and information obtained by the communicant's processes of inference. While the information obtained from a message may be viewed as related to the message through a set of "coding" or "transforming" rules whereby the signal and its referents are matched, it is also possible to obtain information from what one learns directly from the meanings of the message by a chain of judgments whereby sets of meanings other than those meant through the message are implicated with the meanings of the message. The example taken from the game of Kriegsspiel can be used for illustration. The referee's message, "Black's move," that I as a communicant experienced as the expression, "Black's move," yielded the direct primary information of its own meaning as an expression, "White has moved, it is now Black's turn." But I learned along with this that my opponent's king either was not on the back row or if it was there, then a piece stood between his king and my queen. Thus, the information that my own move had effected only my move and not a capture locked into a train of inferences through a complicated judgmental structure that linked up my assumptions about the rules of the game, my knowledge of the play up till then, the current arrangement of my pieces, and so on.

The nature of inferential information is not as precise as it needs to be. I hope its vagueness can be cleared up with not too much additional effort. The category is necessary for it permits a solution to what is otherwise the nasty prospect of having to handle the possibility that what a person does *not* say or do is a message.[9]

The importance of the concept of inferential information for handling communicative work in large scale organizations can be indicated by the following theorems, which are treated more elaborately later: (1) Direct information and inferential information stand in a relationship such that if one is of zero order, the other is of zero order. (2) In any net the extent of inferential information relative to the direct information of a message is a function of the communal character of the relationship between communicants. The function may be stated as the following relationship: As a relationship is made more communal—i.e., as it takes on the properties of a communal as compared with an associational relationship—information drawn from a message will increase toward a maximum which is represented in the theoretical state of total affective integration.

At this point, the direct information of the message and the inferential information of the message are the same in the sense that any meaning simultaneously and directly means and implicates the entire system of information. As the relationships are rationalized, i.e., as they increase in their associational characteristics, the inferential information relative to the direct information decreases, reaching its minimum and equality to the direct information in the state of complete rationalization.

Both states are theoretically states of zero-order information: the first because any signal means everything in the universe in the moment of its occurrence (a state that is approximated in the rather rare psychopathological state of paranoia) and is experienced in a state in which every meaning counts equally with every other one. The second is a state of zero-order information

---

9. [Editor's Note: CA has demonstrated that what is not said is very significant conversationally. For instance silences where other things "should" be— also pre-sequences in which success means something is done best by not being done.]

because the temporal horizon is reduced to the momentary occurrence, and hence the message does not inform but represents only itself, hence it is experienced as signals.

An important consequence drawn from this line of theorizing is this: The way in which a person draws inferences from a message may be used as an empirical measure of the normative integration of a group.

6. Eidetic and Material Information

Unlike the first four characteristics of information that are constituted as matters of degree, the difference between eidetic and material information is a difference in kind, just as primary, secondary, and direct, and inferential information are different in kind.

The distinction between eidetic and material information is a critical one in this theory. Somewhat sloppy and in need of heavy criticism, the distinction is nevertheless useable.

The distinction is between information that bears upon the question for the communicant of what the world means (eidetic-information) as compared with information that bears on the question of what the world consists of in fact (material information).

The distinction was set up to relate the characteristics of the communicant's attitude to his ways of maintaining, validating, testing, and altering a meaningful world. The difference between the two is made by the answer to the following question: If the communicant abides solely by the rules of the game, how much of a course of experience, from his point of view, is determined in its possible significances for him? We'll spell this out.

By eidetic information is meant information that elaborates the definitional status of a situation. In this sense, it is information that answers the question for the communicant of what the world means, that is, what the world consists of without reference to considerations of standard space and time. In this sense, it is always experienced by the communicant either in the mode of full certainty or it is not experienced at all. (Certainty, however, does not mean the same thing as clarity.) Its significance is absolute in the sense that all matters that stand by definition are absolute, Just So, and, in an important sense, decreed, determinate, certain, invariant with reference to the fluctuations of circumstance. All ideally founded information is eidetic information, but not all sensory founded information is material information, as we shall soon see. However, all material information is sensorily founded. Only material information, however, can have a probable character. This does not mean, however, that material information cannot be experienced in the mode of certainty. We saw this above in the example of Paul Revere.

Let's shake down what we have so far. (1) Eidetic information always stands in the mode of certainty. For the case of eidetic information a signal is experienced either as bearing a certain meaning or it is experienced as meaningless. Only material information and not eidetic information has a probable character ranging from zero-order or meaningless through a continuum of probableness to certainty. (2) Both eidetic and material information can be acquired by messages, i.e., sensorily founded materials. But only eidetic information can be acquired either from messages from the outside or without reference to messages from the outside, e.g., only eidetic information is the product of mental problem solving, recalling a message that was received and drawing further significances from it, etc. Material information is the product only of sensory signals. (3) Although eidetic information can be obtained through the use of a projected plan and the intention to realize the plan, it can be obtained without the use of a plan, as for example, one gets information in the sense of experiencing and being able to recall the contents of a dream. Material information can be obtained only through project oriented activity where there is an intention to realize a plan.

Finally, the difference between the two types of information can be said to consist of the difference in the factors that condition the possibility of experiencing a discrepancy between an expectation and the memory of an event, i.e., the possibility of experiencing error. We have material information and the possibility of acquiring material information only under the following conditions: that the experiencer entertain an expectation of timing (i.e., the assumption that sensorily founded events will occur in a particular sequence), though this expectation of timing applies to a world experienced by the communicant as an organized set of possibilities that show two properties: (1) they are determinately related to each other, and (2) they are open, though not in the sense of the distinction between open and problematical, but in the sense of dependence upon a future fall of events for their fulfillment, hence open in the sense of fulfillable. Another way to designate this characteristic is to talk of an "unthematized horizon," or lacking closure. There are many ways of affecting a thematized horizon.

I'll mention a few and put aside the task of exploring their variety for a later task. One device consists of "tuning" the standard that is used in assessing the significance of an event so narrowly that actual events serve only as illustration of the intended thing. Another device consists of so broadly "tuning" the standard that precision of reproduction is lost. Another device consists of extending the specification of a future event "so far," i.e., giving it the time sense of will occur, but without specifying when, or locating it in a future time that is not approached by the passage of standard time. Another consists of giving a definite standard time specification to the possibility of one's own death. Another way of thematizing or putting a boundary on a horizon is to orient a Nature with which one is in personal league. All such thematizings render the information acquired under such an order, eidetic information. Consultations with clinical psychopathologists should yield a long list.

The general difference between the two types of information is found in those facets of attitude, tactics of incorporation, and the definition of the situation that furnish for the communicant a requiredness to events. I shall take a temporary position in the matter and state that insofar as events have any requiredness, the requiredness is always a moral requiredness. Insofar then as any event, in the eyes of the experiencer has about it any sense that its occurrence is governed by any rule other than the rule of chance, it has a sense of moral requiredness. This is another way of saying that for a communicant there is an important sense in which every event occurs as a matter of principle and without regard for consequences. Only the alienated can properly sing "It ain't necessarily so." And if there is sufficient alienation from a body of principles that furnish an ultimate rationale, they must sing, "I ain't necessarily so" which is to say they must stop singing, in fact, they stop everything. From all of this we draw the general rule that both types of information not only can be but always are obtained from a message. If there is a message, and one type of information is obtainable, so is the other. Every message insofar as it is experienced as a sign or an expression will as a minimum convey eidetic information. Where no eidetic information is possible, no material information is possible. Material information is never found to exhaust the information of a message.

I think it can be seen now that the categories of eidetic and material information are designed to help us in coping with the factors of the make-up of communicants, the properties of the orders they orient, perceptual practices, interpretive devices, normative logics, social relations, etc. that influence the determinate character of our communicant's experiences. I pointed out in a previous section that determinism is found in meanings that events have for our communicants and not in the ontological structure of the events themselves. Hence, there is a determinism that is peculiar to every different attitude that is constitutive of an order. Every order has a mode of determinism peculiar to it. The problem for research is that of specifying the ways and properties of these ways in which a set of possibilities are made determinative of each other, i.e., the ways in which they necessarily (from the communicant's point of view) implicate each other.

One final point needs making. The categories of eidetic and material information are theoretical categories and not epistemological ones. Hence they are not designed to cope with the question of all the valid inferences that can be drawn from a message, a task we would have to face up to if our communicant was conceived according to the model of the rational man. The difference between eidetic and material information is based on the assumption of a psychological model of the communicant. We are not interested in the inferences that our actor can draw from a message, but only the inferences that he does draw.

The rational man in the sense of a disembodied manual of proper rules of procedure is used only as one arbitrary standard among many that we could select from to compare what and how our communicant knows, with what he would know were he to show the characteristics of a person acting only with regard to rational precepts.

IX

The Factors That Condition Information: Introduction

I'VE GONE OVER SOME OF THE DIFFERENT THINGS THAT WE CAN SAY ABOUT information. The task now is to address the factors (in the various values they can take) that are conceived to determine the values that can be assigned to the various types of information. For example, if we assume a discrepancy of x-value between what a communicant knows and what a referee knows about a course of outcomes, how will this discrepancy be altered toward greater or lesser discrepancy as we manipulate the communicant's image of himself to reinforce the image or to make it unstable? How will the timing of messages in a net effect the ambiguity of information that a communicant draws from a message? What is the relationship between a status hierarchy of communicants and the relative equality of distributed information? If for a communicant you perform a set of operations whereby you truncate the temporal horizon of the order he orients, what does this change imply for the kind of secondary information he will find in messages, and how is this in turn related to the likely efficiency of one means of effecting coordinated action as compared with another?

While questions of this sort can be drawn up by allowing the combination of experience and imagination to play over a set of categories, I'm looking for a device that will provide us with hypotheses that are governed in number and construction not only by the intuitive play of good sense in the matter, but by the logical manipulation of lawfully related analytic categories. In other words, by the workings of a theory. As is the case for any theory, we must expect to get various mixtures of statements from it: some plausible, others implausible;

some strange, others familiar; above all, many that experience shows or will show to be unqualifiedly cock-eyed.

The remaining parts of this paper are concerned with sketching in the principal constructions that we shall use to represent the factors that condition the properties of information, of stating the general laws that relate these factors to each other, and to start the resulting theory percolating to see preliminarily at least what kinds of theorems it provides.

The tasks of the paper to follow this one will consist of reducing the sketchiness of the theory, making it more responsible for what it says, and devoting ourselves specifically to the task of pulling out of it as many theorems as we can. The programmatic character of our research will then be well launched and we shall be able to turn our attention to the design of investigative procedures for the test of those theorems whose test appears to be of theoretical and perhaps of practical importance.

Four sets of factors will be considered. They are referred to in the parts devoted to each as (1) factors of the order of possibilities itself; (2) "Role" or "Attitudinal" factors; (3) factors of communicative work; and (4) net factors.

X

Factors That Condition Information: (A) Factors of the Order of Possibilities

Under this topic two sets of factors will be considered: (1) the factor of the "allocation" of possibilities between two "domains" that are conceived to be exhaustive of all possibilities in the order. These are referred to as the "domain of constancy" and the "domain of variability." (2) The criteria of the organization or "imbeddedness" of possibilities, previously defined in part V.

1. The Domains of Constancy and Variability

These two notions may be clarified by turning for help to the game of tic-tac-toe.

Suppose we address ourselves to a formal or normative description of tic-tac-toe. (It would be compared with tic-tac-toe as an operating communicative net, i.e., an empirical instance of the game.) A normative description might run as follows. The game is played by two players on a three by three table of cells. The players move in the sequence: 1, 2, 1, 2, etc. A move consists of placing a mark in one of the cells. A player is not allowed to put a mark in a cell already occupied. A player's object in the game is to get three marks in a row, a state that will be known as a win. Play proceeds until all cells are filled or until one player has three marks in a row or until it is obvious within the rules of play that nothing that either does will produce a winner.

An examination of the game as it stands by definition will reveal two sets of rules that can be differentiated from each other by the characteristics that one group shows that are not found in the other. For convenience's sake, we'll call these two groups "basic rules" and "rules of preferred play."

The set called "basic rules" have these characteristics. First, out of the set of possible territories of play, sequences of moves, numbers of players, etc. they frame a set of required alternatives. These alternatives are experienced by the player as alternatives that must be chosen regardless of the player's desires, circumstances, purposes, interests, consequences for either player," and so on. Second, each player is expected to assume that the same set of alternatives [are] binding on his opponent as are binding on him. In fact, the formally defined player may be completely described as the person who acts with regard to these required alternatives.

Now from the point of view of the players, these rules have the status of expectations that are invariant to the course of play. They are in effect standards of play and as such serve as the basis for recognizing the "strange" move, the move that is "outside of the game," or better, the occurrence of non-standard alternatives that are incongruous in the sense of error: their occurrence violates the game as an order.

Another class of rules is illustrated in the statement that the object of the game is to get three markers in a row. This statement may have different statuses. It may be a formal fact of the game considered in abstracto: i.e., under a given sequence of moves, the outcome is determined by the basic rules of play. The statement may have the status of an empirical fact, in which case it says something about the actual purposes of the players and involves for its specification that materials entirely outside of the basic rules of play be considered. Finally, it may have the status of a rule, though not a basic rule, but rather a projected outcome of a sequence of plays, i.e., as an element of the player's strategy of play. In the latter sense, and this is the sense that interests us, the statement frames a range of alternatives whose very constitution, let alone choice and ground of choice between them, [are] within the legitimate freedom of the player to consider and exercise.

Like the basic rules these rules of preferred play also have the status of expectations when regarded from the standpoint of the assumptive order of the player. But rather than their being invariant to a course of play or circumstance or interests, etc., they are characterized by their variable character, both in the sense of the elections that can be made between one strategy of play and another, as well as in the very important sense that they have contingent status up till the time that an actual outcome occurs. They then become constant by the fact that they achieve the sense of the past accomplished event, a sense that is possible only by virtue of the fact that someone actually (not supposedly) makes a move.

When we ordinarily speak of tic-tac-toe or any game, for that part, the game is defined in terms of those expectations that are the sufficient conditions of play. We assume that there are many other conditions that will be operative both in the constant and variable senses. For example, the identity of the opponent, the time it will take to play out a game, the self images of the players, the spatial proximity of the players to the board, the aid that will be obtained from kibitzers, and so on, may be considered as necessary but unspecified conditions. We can widen the area of conditions of play to include such factors as these without altering the definition of the game as a game of tic-tac-toe, and indeed the significance of game theory for sociological investigation is found in recasting the conditions of play to include such specifications as the things that the player we are interested in "also has in mind." We extend them on the ground that, as these expectations are given by the observer constant or variable status an alteration makes it necessary that the observer alter the statements that he would otherwise make as to the "nature of the game."

For example, a player who is distrustful of an opponent would be expected to balk in honoring the opponent's claim that he had beaten him at the game; i.e., he would have difficulty in assessing the meanings of the communicative work that his opponent engaged in. Perhaps the example of tic-tac-toe is a difficult one to make clear the relevance of distrust to continuous interpretation of messages. The game of Kriegsspiel, however, leaves no doubt in the matter. For Kriegsspiel addicts one must present practically a bill attesting to one's good character and alertness in order to be allowed to referee a game. A referee can reduce all previous play to hash and make the prospect of continuing a thing of anxiety and distaste by merely indicating at some point in the game that he thinks there is some kind of mix-up, that he needs only a minute to straighten it out, and then fails to come through dismissing the mix-up as something he overlooked but what the hell.

From all of this we get a rule of huge importance: *The nature of the information obtained from a message is conditioned by the arrangement of possibilities according to their constant or variable character.*

Having shown the important sense in which rules of play have the status of possibilities of experience when we consider the rules as they are found in the player's situation of play, i.e., his order of possibilities, we can now drop the notions of basic and preferential rules and talk instead of all the possibilities of an order as being exhaustively ordered between two "domains": the "domain of constancy" and the "domain of variability." We get another important point: insofar as we talk of a consensually defined situation, or an order that is common to two or more communicants, or the uniformity in their definitions of the situation, we mean by this that each orients an order of possibilities which shows these properties: (a) the objects, whether they be other persons, physical objects, events, rules, actions, beliefs, motives, etc., are, among a set of alternatives, required alternatives; and (b) the two communicants each *assumes* (and regardless of the "correctness" or not as an observer makes such an assessment) that what holds for him holds equally for the other. Or, to put it briefly, we talk of consensus when two or more communicants assume a set of possibilities as constant, and each assumes that the same is the case for the other person. The continuity of a relationship (as for example its duration) as well as the characteristics of the information that can be drawn from a message will be conditioned by these two assumptions. Some theorems that this rule allows are discussed in Part XV.

The domains of constancy and variability have the following characteristics: (1) Any possibility of experience at any given time is included in one or the other but not both. (2) A domain may be an empty set. If so this implies that all the possibilities are included in the other domain. (3) A possibility can be moved from one set to the other. We talk *then* of a change of state of the possibility. A "domain" thus is not an area but is a property of a possibility of experience.

Let's return now to the game of tic-tac-toe for help in learning something more about the tie-up between the domains of constancy and variability and the notion of information.

Suppose we agree to play tic-tac-toe, but we set the game up in the following fashion: we make all of the rules of the game basic rules. That is, in addition to all the usual basic rules, we agree beforehand where you will put your mark when I put my mark somewhere. Numbering the cells across, we might agree, for example, to follow an order of play something like this: I mark cell 3, then you mark cell 5, then I mark 7, you 8, 2, 1, 9, 6, 4. This order, of possibilities is treated by us as constant. With this agreement we proceed to play.

Now we have a project; it is that of accomplishing the sequence of play. But there is something peculiar here. To the extent that I assume that you will abide by these rules, the actual outcomes (if you play according to the agreement) confirm for me what I already know on the basis of what the rules require. The point was made before that the basic rules are necessary conditions for information and that they condition the information that can be drawn from a message. But a game constituted and played entirely according to the basic rules is a game in which no variability of outcome is possible. It is a completely ordered set of possibilities. By the very invariant character of the expectations, the game is ordered in the eyes of the players. That is, you and I as players do not "allow," i.e., we reject the possibility that the fall of events may occur in a fashion at variance with these standard requirements.

We make minimal the possibility of surprise or incongruity. In that the possibilities of experience, as we noted in part IV, are specifications of an object, what these basic rules consist of is an ordered set of expectations that constitute the situation (in this case, the state and course of the game) as a matter of definition and do so in such a manner that the occurrences confirm the nature of the situation as it stands by definition at any point and at any time—that is to say, without reference to time.

We have, then, a general principle: *any occurrence witnessed within such a completely determinate order, to the extent that the basic rules provide for it, serves the effect for the communicant of verifying the nature of the situation.* Hence to the extent that any message requires for its informing character a set of invariant expectations, to that extent and regardless of whatever other information may be obtained from it, it informs as well about the nature of the game; it has "something to say" about the order in its definitional aspects. Information of this sort, as we saw before, is called eidetic information.

As soon as we intrude the rules of preferred play, we bring in the notion of the contingent event. We introduce the possibility of surprise, incongruity—i.e., the possibility of a disparity between what I expect to occur and what occurs.

We have then the notion of incongruity as any experienced disparity between an expectation and an outcome. Insofar as the incongruity has the effect of impugning the integrity of an order —that is, its occurrence impugns the criteria of organization—and this occurs only under the conditions of the natural attitude (whose structural features were described in Memo #2), we shall refer to the experienced discrepancy as the experience of error. Strictly speaking, the disparity is between the expectation of an outcome and the outcome in its sense of the past accomplished, i.e., the *memory* of the outcome. And further: it is not the outcome in particular, but the outcome (let's say, "event") as a *representative instance* of the event as the thing of which it is a representative stands in a non-perceptual order—in other words, the standard, and again in other words and finally, *the empirical ideal type of the event.*

And now we have a peculiarity: Insofar as we allow for the possibility of actualizing one possibility among a set of them, we necessarily allow for the possibility of incongruity or error. And with this we have a corollary statement:

only insofar as there is the possibility of error, do we know which of a set of possibilities has been actualized, or, to put it otherwise, only to the extent that error is possible is it possible to know what occurred if the matter that stood by definition did not occur. We have then another principle: *if there is no possibility of error, there is no possibility of material information.* And a corollary theorem: the greater the chances of error, the greater the amount of material information from any specific outcome.

If we tie the notions of open and problematical possibilities to the notion of error we get a few more theorems. Both problematical and open possibilities can be treated in terms of the concept of a number of possible outcomes. For problematical possibilities the notion of number is clear, and barring the case of anxiety which is marked by the very fact that there is a large number considered though without any standard for assigning psychological likelihood, the number of problematical possibilities is relatively small, and structurally speaking stand before the communicant in a manner of specific naming and within the mode of attending in which the outcome is specifically doubtful. One of the possibilities will occur: which one? Or one set of a set of sets will occur: which set? The case of open possibilities is otherwise. Here the notion of a number of possibilities is included in the form of a "mass noun" so to speak. The possibilities are viewed under the aspect of what Schuetz refers to as the "et cetera" assumption, i.e., as things were yesterday they will pretty much be in the future. The number thus is a huge one, including as it does the set of possibilities that can occur under the aegis of "things are normal."

Now the first theorem: (1) the greater the possibility of error, defined as the fraction 1 over the number of possible outcomes, the less the probability of confusion under any specific outcome. The less the possibility of error, the greater the probability of confusion under any specific outcome.

By tying these notions to the notion of routine, we get another theorem. (2) If one of the things that we mean by routine and routinize is that the conditions of a net are such as to permit the operation of et cetera assumptions, then: it is possible to say that one of the effects of routinizing the conditions of a net is to minimize the probability of confusion.

We expect, therefore, that every net that is set up to accomplish more than trivial tasks will have a proliferated set of communicative devices whereby the routine aspects of the net are maintained as well as a proliferation of communicative devices whereby incongruity is controlled. Further, we would expect that every manner of routinization will have an order of confusion particular to it.

Let's introduce now the concept of "information loss" and mean by it that between the point of transmission and the point of assessment the information undergoes a transformation through the fact that the message must undergo the process of meaning investment before the receiver realizes the information possible from the message. Following Wiener we shall say that information can never increase in its passage between two transformers. One way of minimizing such loss is by standardizing messages and the rules of transformation, hence meanings are standardized. This means routinizing the conditions of the net. From all this we can infer the following. That in routinizing the net we minimize the extent of the loss of information, i.e., the degree of transformation of information as it is passed by messages around the net. By maximizing the routine conditions of a net we tend to establish some standard loss of communicative efficiency. But there are inherent limits to the efficiency that such routinization may accomplish, the limits being established in one case at least by that person or those persons in the net through whom the messages must pass and who transform the information the most. Hence to routinize the situation means to design the message work in such a fashion as to handle those tasks that can be accomplished on the basis of the information available in the net after the least efficient transformers have operated upon it.

Let's return now to the game of tic-tac-toe. Intruding rules of preferred play into the game reduces the situation as it stands by definition. This is another way of saying that the situation is made probable.

We can conceive now of two poles: the pole of all basic rules, which means a situation in which the significances of outcomes are determined by definition. The other pole is one in which the situation is defined by only rules of preferred play. If the Hobbesian theory of rationality is employed, this pole is the pole of the "interessenkampf," the state of a completely rational pursuit of self interest. In terms of a system, it is the pole of the war of each against all. However, the theory of rationality that we have elected to use proposes that, except in the case of the *ideal* of scientific rationality, the rationality of everyday life is possible only under the assumption of an invariant order; rationality in everyday life is possible only as there [is] a set of principles that [is] not subject to rational appraisal. Thus, a durable conflict in the sense of the Hobbesian state is according to the theory we shall use impossible without an invariant order, which is to say, there is no durable conflict if the domain of constancy is an empty set. We would propose therefore that the state of the "interessenkampf" is not the pole of all preferential rules. Rather, the state of all preferential rules is a state of the complete extinction of activity—a state of confusion. It is a state in which messages are experienced just as messages, i.e., as sets of meaningless signals. This will be called a state of anomie or randomness.

We have then another theorem to work with: The statement that the domain of constancy is an empty set implies that no information, eidetic or material, can be drawn from a message. The specific ordering of possibilities to the domains by content determines what information can be drawn from a message. When we speak of the factors that condition information we are talking of the conditions of the communicant's make-up, the conditions of the net, and the conditions of communicative work which, given as a state, determine the distribution of a set of possibilities between the domains of constancy and variability. For each such state, there will be a distribution specific to it. Hence, altering a set of conditions implies the re-arrangement of possibilities between the domains. Where the conditions are such as to move a set of possibilities to the domain of variability while leaving the domain of constancy an empty set, the message will have the status of mere signal character and hence such a state is a state of zero-order information.

We get from this the meaning of an important concept: "noise." For our purposes this term will refer to the randomness or meaninglessness of a set of signals—the unidealizeable character of a set of signals. Noise refers to the extent to which a communicant can invoke a set of constant possibilities as standards for effecting the idealization of signals. Insofar as we can manipulate the factors that condition the order of possibilities so as to remove them from constant to variable status, we have in each such manipulation a condition for increasing the noise character of a message. Later in this paper and in the paper that follows we shall use this principle as a source of theorems about the efficiency of communicative work, and pay particular attention to the efficiency that one can have in a net under various structural conditions of the net.

It is possible now to see some relationships between error, noise, and information. (1) In a state of complete variability of possibilities (i.e., where the domain of constancy is an empty set) the probability of error is zero and the probability of noise is 1. Such a state is one in which neither eidetic nor material information is possible. (2) In a state where the domain of variability is an empty set, the probability of error is zero and the probability of noise is zero. Such a state is one in which no material information is possible.

At the extremes either of randomization of possible outcomes or the complete determination of situation of outcomes there is no error. These extremes are our sociological friends in new guises: the states of anomie and complete normative integration. Insofar as we can state the conditions of the actor's make-up and the course of experience under which his beliefs are validated, we shall have a further range of theorems to work with, most particularly those that deal with the problem of socialization. The discussion of these is reserved until after we have described the defining structures of Role.

Previously I said that the basic and preferential rules are exhaustive of the order of objects. I wish to qualify this view here, and to point out that this conception is possible only if we portray our communicant as a rational man. Were we to conceive of him as a rational man, we could talk then of the case where the domain of variability is an empty set which would leave us with a state of total normative integration. For various reasons we will put this assumption of the rational man aside, with the result that we get an important new range of theorems. First, why put the assumption aside?

(1) Rationality of everyday life shows the operations of the "et cetera" assumptions, which do not completely specify a situation. (2) There is the fact of the similarity of the experience of the experiencer as he experiences them and the matter of differences in life histories. (3) There is the matter of the institutionalization in degree and the disparity in any moment of experience between public and private me-relevant memories. (4) There is the indeterminacy of the date of one's death, which provides an open temporal horizon. (5) There is the variability of the body as a frame of reference, and with it variability in the basic categories of space and time. (6) The nature of routine and the operations of routinization are not clear and would have to be in order to appreciate what is involved in portraying the rationality of our communicant. (7) There is the fact that a state of total normative integration has never been empirically achieved and hence one may ask whether it is profitable to treat it as a theoretically possible state.

The consequence of these considerations is that on empirical grounds, and possibly on theoretical grounds, it may pay, or at least we shall assume that it will pay, to assume that some "amount" of noise is always present. That is to say, our communicant will be conceived to be always in some measure confused. He is always in a world that is in some respects without meaning for him. The trick, then, is to spell out the conditions of his make-up and the conditions of the net under which noise in a given amount makes a difference. And the problem that lies just beyond this is that of learning about the devices that can be used to reduce or magnify this amount.

Thus we postulate that a part of the communicant's communicative work and "internal" action will be devoted to minimizing the amount of confusion or meaninglessness. Or, in terms of a social system, much communicative work will be oriented to the maintenance of interpersonally valid definitions of the situation.

2. *The Criteria of Organization*

We shall have to jump the gun a little to introduce these constructions. We introduce an assumption that is explained later that only insofar as the elements of "Role" (or "Attitude") remain constant in value are we allowed to conceive that signal input is continuously transformed by the communicant into the data of his world, data that is capable of fulfilling or being at variance with the expectations that are proposed by the intentional field. (The intentional field is that part of order of possibilities oriented by the communicant in a Role at any moment of time.) Its properties are temporal irreversibility; transformability; span; and organization. It is to be differentiated from the expressional field or phenomenal field (the terms will be used synonymously) which is defined as an idealized signal situation. The intentional field, unlike the expressional field, may include all orders of non-sensorily founded objects—plans, rules, Gods, the law, persons bodily in absentia, ancestors, etc. These attitudinal components are also referred to as the communicant's "premises" or "assumptions." The communicant with his "premises" intact, so to speak, will experience the world in such a way that his experiences of it meet the criteria of continuity, consistency, compatibility, temporal continuity, and clarity, i.e., his experiences of the world remain organized.

Organization is to be regarded as a continuous variable up to the point of the failure of one of the criteria at which point there is a discontinuation in the form of the failure of all, and with it the cessation of all activity.

What are the behavioral criteria by which the analytic criteria are to be considered as having been fulfilled?

Continuity

The following are the conditions under which we must say that a communicant's experiences are not continuous.

(1) There is no continuity if there is simultaneous change from one moment of activity to the next of the three structures of an experience: the noesis, the specifications of the object presented through the noesis, and the "e" operator that together with the specifications comprises the object. Behaviorally, this characteristic would be found in the "flight of ideas."

(2) There is no continuity where there is no change of any of the three structures from one moment of activity to the next. Behaviorally, this is found in the characteristic of "compulsive repetition."

(3) There is no continuity where one expression alone is given and is allowed to stand without further activity, which is to say, under the cessation of activity where the object is presented in an unending moment, so to speak. Behaviorally, this is not the same as repetition, for the object stands before consciousness like a frame in a movie that has become hung. It is found behaviorally in the symptoms of blocking.

Consistency

This criterion refers to the elaborated specifications of the object. There is no consistency when the specifications are experienced as a blind juxtaposition of events. That is, the specifications are experienced as logically and/or factually incompatible.

Behaviorally, the failing of this criterion is found in the complaints of uneasiness about the irreality of the witnessed object, hesitancy and discontinuities of treatment of the object, a tolerance of error that is occasioned by the failure of the conception to stand and the inoperativeness of the canons of everyday judgment; complaints of strangeness with and distance from the familiar, routinized, and recognizable experiences.

Compatibility

This criterion refers to the "external" relationships of the object to other objects. It refers to the phenomenon of an experiencer requiring, if an object is to be recognized, that it have its *place* in an order of objects. We have the condition of relative non-compatibility when the object cannot be fitted into its background. It stands instead in incongruous relationships to its "surroundings," evoking the complaint of strangeness. Behaviorally, the condition is met in the subject's inability to draw any implications of his view of the object for the meanings of the objects that accompany it. One might refer to this as the splintering of the intentional field.

Temporal Continuity

This criterion is found in the formal fact that the intended object motivates the possibilities that serve to specify it further. Anticipations and continuance, the before and the hereafter, are ingredients of the object as it is given in a moment of durée, a Now. The temporal horizon, as we called it before, refers to the fact that the time specifications that get attached to a set of possibilities locate the object with reference to the body of recollections and protentions that comprise the stream of experience.

In the failing of temporal continuity, experience takes on the "flavor" that Jean-Paul Satre described for the hero of his novel, *Nausea*. Events acquire this behaviorally in the clinic in the symptomatic complaint of the patient suffering depersonalization or ego-splitting when he experiences himself simultaneously as the subject and object of his actions.

Clarity

This criterion refers to the formal fact that the intended possibilities can be fulfilled with varying degrees of distinctness. This criterion is met to the extent that the order of images, ideas, or sensorily founded perceptions fulfill the intended specifications.

Behaviorally, the failing of this criterion is found through the principle that the failure to fulfill the intended possibilities undermines the effectiveness of the "e" operator, leaving the experiencer addressed to unmortared detail. There is the concern for detail before the object fades from comprehension, and with this concern is the recapitulation, so to speak, of the remembered accuracy of previous definitions.

The five criteria are proposed as analytically distinct in order to underline the five different classes of operations for defining the failure of any one of them, i.e., the state of confusion. In the first operation, we were examining the character of sequences of experiences as sequences. In the second, we are examining the rules of construction and transformation of experience. In the third, we are concerned with what the processes of transformation consist of in content—or what, for want of a better term and temporarily, we shall call "judging behavior." In the fourth, we are concerned with the processes of memory. In the fifth, we are concerned with feed-back processes.

We postulate the following analytical relationships between them:

They stand systematically implicative of each other. Hence, if one is operative, all are operative. If one fails, all fail. This means that the criteria of failure converge to mean the same thing at the point of failure, namely, the dissolution of the world. For the case of sensorily presented world, their convergence upon the point of failure implies the reduction of messages to their signal character, hence, zero-order information. For states that approximate this, that is, states of failing rather than failure, we are dealing with matters of degree of organization. All such states will be known as states of anxiety, and will be designated as states of anxiety relative to a limit to be known as zero-order anxiety state defined as the complete fulfillment of these criteria, a state that by theoretical necessity can only be approached asymptotically.

An important problem for the theory and one that I have found to be immensely difficult must be mentioned even though I have little by way of a solution to offer at this point. I refer to the problem of finding an order of constructions that will serve as the general dimensions that could be used to achieve a determinate description of the order of objects. Or, as Cottrell referred to this hairy problem when he last visited us, the problem of stating the defining dimensions of the definition of a situation. As the definition of the situation stands now, it is to be regarded as a system of "complex" variables, some of them taking constant values, others depending on problematical outcomes for their constancy. The meaning of the notion of the actor's state of information must necessarily remain a rough and ready notion until this area of problems is worked over. Not only is there the problem of ordering the varieties under a set of general classes, but there is the nastier problem of stating the operations that relate them. For example, it has been pointed out that an event stands in an order of events as of a given time, t. The anticipated event stands not only in a temporal relationship to others—as the temporal horizon implies—but it stands in an intricately structured order of implication to other possibilities, and the state description of the order must remain ambiguous in its meaning until we are able to handle both. That the state is difficult of conceptualization does not mean however that we are without any measures for handling the order as a describable state. It just means that when we abandon concrete descriptions we must be prepared to talk nonsense.

XI

Factors That Condition Information: (B) Role Factors

Tнат оur actor is capable of experiencing is to be assumed as unproblematical. What he experiences, when, how one experience succeeds another, the organized character of his experiences, etc. are the problems that need accounting for. Along with some others, this assumption was laid out in Memo #1.

Our task here is to provide a set of constructs that will be used to specify the conditions of his "make-up" under which the order of possibilities of experience is determined in its possible properties of organization. We will consider in this part those structures of the communicant's mode of attending to an order that are determinative for an observer of the particular meanings that an experience can have for an empirical person. These constructs are such that when the observer assigns a particular range of values to them he is permitted, indeed required, to say what an object will mean according to a class of X meanings and no other class; and that the treatment afforded the object will be of the class of Y treatments and no other class.

There are six constructs that we shall use. Taken together they will be referred to as the defining dimensions of a communicant's Attitude, or Mode of Attending, or Role. All of these terms will be used synonymously and interchangeably. These dimensions are taken directly from Alfred Schuetz's article, "On Multiple Realities," *Philosophy and Phenomenological Research* (June 1945), pp. 533–575, where he refers to them with the term "cognitive style." I cannot say that he would approve of the way I have defined and used them.

The constructs will be referred to as (1) the form of epoche; (2) the form of sociality; (3) mode of attention to life; (4) form of spontaneity; (5) mode of time consciousness; and (6) mode of givenss of the self. These constructs were arrived at by Schuetz through a phenomenological analysis of the structures of the experiences of daily life, of scientific theorizing, of fantasying, and of dreams. These general structures are found in all of these attitudes. More accurately, these attitudes are defined by the specifications that are assigned to these structures. A structural comparison in this regard of the attitude of daily life and the attitude of scientific theorizing is found in Schuetz's article "On Multiple Realities," and in an article I wrote, "Notes on the Sociological Attitude," in which I borrowed heavily from the "Realities" article and tried extending the comparison.

Although we are using these six constructs, further experience may reveal that there are more. The utility of the ones that we have, as well as the possibility that there are others, is to be judged by their utility in reducing the proportion of "unexplained error" that we encounter in our experiments.

The constructs are so conceived that a logically completed description of Role has been achieved when the observer has provided the specifications of each. The constructs do not themselves describe the world. They have nothing to say about the world. They are rather the terms in which the observer as a matter of theoretical necessity if he plays the game of theorizing, using the scheme we are setting forth, must conceive the conditions of experience when he addresses himself to the problem of the conditions of the communicant's make-up.

In the remainder of this part I shall define these constructs briefly, give the minimum characteristics of the natural attitude since this is the one that shall most concern us, and go into some detail in spelling out the relationships between the Role constructs and between Role and the construction, order of objects.

Role Constructs Defined

I have restricted myself to bare definitions. To do more would require a revised duplication of the better part of some 120 pages in my [Ph.D.] thesis, and I do not feel up to the task. I shall therefore assume that those who desire further clarification will consult the thesis, and permit me to postpone the task of a revised presentation until time is not so pressing.

By the *form of epoche* is meant that the communicant assumes a set of procedural rules whereby a class or classes of possibilities are removed from the operations of judgment and are treated within the conditions of this abstention. The epoche of the natural attitude involves the suspension of doubt that the objects of the world are as they appear according to communally valid canons of judgment, and communally valid principles of relevance.

By the *form of sociality* is meant a set of assumed I-thou relationships, where the thou or thou-s are "attitudinal thou-s." That is, the other person is an object, and like any object, is an order set of specifications of conduct. This set can be analyzed to show two orders of statements: one set that tells us what the other person does behaviorally; another set that consists of statements that identify the other person motivationally (remember, in the eyes of the communicant). A motivational term is any term that furnishes the interpreter with the grounds of conduct. Such terms answer for the assessor the question of who or what the other person is. When the two are given together, the other person is constituted thereby for an experiencer as an object. The form of sociality includes as well the relevant me's, the communicant experiencing himself as an object in the world simultaneously with the experiencing of others.

By the term I is meant those sequences of experiences experienced by the communicant *in their course*, i.e., in Husserl's sense, "lived in," or in Mead and James's sense, experienced as the stream of consciousness in process so that no matter how quickly I turn I can never catch it except as it appears in the past tense. Those familiar with Mead's distinction between the I and the me will have no difficulty with the distinction since it is substantially Mead's distinction between the I and the me that is intended. I means those sequences of activities that the person as he acts recognizes as his own and that can without incongruity be attributed to a Me which he recognizes as an authentic representation of himself (regardless of the "occasional" or "total" character of the self-defining actions.) By the term I-thou relationship is meant that there stands in the stream of experience an invariant interpretive scheme designative of a thou or a me. By the term invariant is meant that the interpretive scheme is not affected in its meanings by the momentary fluctuations of intention and object found in the flow. The specification of the natural attitude that interests us is the assumption by the communicant of a common intersubjective world of other persons and me's. That is, the communicant assumes reciprocity of definitions of the situation between himself and his socially defined system of alters.

The stream of experience must have another relationship to the "thou" and/or "me" for there are times, for example, when the "thou" changes directly with the flow, as for example during the initial stages of conversation between two strangers who seek to "place" each other. This other relationship is one that provides the change or steadiness and is provided for in the next construct.

Mode of Giveness of the Self

This construct is defined as a set of memories that are selected and made relevant to each other by an attitudinal me so as to specify a me in the world. These memories may be treated according to public or private standards of treatment. A public standard is one through which the object enjoys its objectivity by virtue of being testable according to consensually constituted and validated testing procedures. A private standard is a standard through which the object enjoys its objectivity by virtue of being testable according to a set of individually validated testing procedures. The actor treating the object-me according to public standards is said to be given as Person. The actor treating the object-me according to private standards is said to be given as Individuum. However, for any moment of experience the communicant is not given as one *or* the other; he is always given as *both*. In fact the processes of socialization are processes by which the communicant acquires a disparity between them. If one does not develop, neither does the other. Two specifications need to be made: the relative constancy of the disparity, and for any given relationship, the relative primacy of one or the other. The concept is of particular usefulness in handling the structural conditions under which one gets the occurrence of the so-called "social affects"—shame, guilt, indignation, love, etc.

The condition that interests us for the natural attitude is the stress on the Person (i.e., the institutionally identified Me), with particular reference to the assumption of tribal measures of validation (i.e., I am right because other agrees with me).

Mode of Attention to Life

This construct is defined as the mode of interest or no interest in meeting, elaborating, and/or testing the consequent possibilities of experience that are immanently proposed in and through the intentional field. The specific value of the natural attitude involves a pragmatic mode of attending to the alterations of the situation brought about by the communicator's as well as the communicant's bodily movements. The assumption depicts the world as something that can be affected by or that affects the communicant. Schuetz proposes it this way: the world is experienced as something that one must master through one's bodily intervention.

Mode of Time Consciousness

This construct refers to the nature of time as constitutive structure of the object, and its relations to other objects. Three meanings of time are distinguished in this regard as the "times of experience": (1) durée, (2) phenomenal or inner time, and (3) standard or interpersonally standard time.

By standard time is meant those socially validated schemes of temporal reference of events which lend empirical status to the objects that its structures modify and which make it possible for an experiencer to gear his experiences to the occurrence of events in his factual world, thus making it possible for the experiencer to coordinate his activities with those of his fellow men. Standard time is the time of "working acts" (to use Schuetz's phrase), i.e., action in the outer world based upon a project and characterized by the intention to bring about a particular set of relationships between objects by bodily movements.

Phenomenal time or inner time refers to the temporal structures that modify the objects of all covert activity. Its values attach to the objects of fantasying, dreaming, planning, theorizing, problem solving, and so on.

By the term or notion of *durée* is meant the succession of Nows, with there being arranged around the Present the various Thens of what was experienced and what is to come, *all given in a Now.*

By way of aiding the discussion we might briefly note the properties of these three time experiences that will be relevant to our later work.

The properties of standard time that interest us are the following: (a) its various values can be related to each other by any arbitrary linear continuum of equal intervals. (b) Its meanings are such as to meet the criteria of the axioms of arithmetic. An important consequence of this property is that the experiencer can experience, i.e., can *live in* an interval of time. It is only in the scheme of standard time that this is possible. (c) Its values are so ordered sequentially in experience that Time 1 can only precede Time 2. Hence, for example, ends can only be realized *after* means. (d) It is irreversible.

The properties of phenomenal time are quite different. (a) Not only is it reversible, but it can be accelerated, decelerated, or halted. (b) Its sequences are such that the end can be realized before means are even considered. Effect can precede cause, things that have to occur successively in standard time can occur simultaneously in phenomenal time. The future can become the past while the past can assume the status of yet to happen, or a state of affairs can be given in phenomenal time without its precedent. (c) Its values cannot be ordered to a linear continuum, nor can its values be arithmetically treated (which is *not* to say that they cannot therefore be mathematically treated). The experiencer in phenomenal time can *know* an interval, but he does not and cannot *live in* the interval. Its order is analogous to an ordinal scale.

The defining properties of durée are (a) the irreversibility of any succession of Nows; (b) the fact that it is constitutive of *every* object (phenomenal and standard times are not); (c) the fact that it is an enduring moment; and (d) each Now is an instance only of itself, hence the categories of sameness and difference do not apply to objects constituted solely in durée since all objects so constituted are of a just so character.

The general properties of phenomenal and standard time above will be found in all the varieties of phenomenal and standard time. The lists of properties for each would have to be extended to take their varieties into account. For example, the experiences of fantasy, dreams, and problem solving show further characteristic differences in the times that modify the objects of these experiences. For example, the time of events portrayed in the theatre, an order of phenomenal time, allows for any arbitrary rearrangement of events taken from the world of standard time, whereas the order of phenomenal time in the task of extracting the meaning from a conversation that one has witnessed and recalls requires that the events be ordered in their "actual" order of occurrence.

Similarly the orders of standard time can be differentiated to take account of the differences between the time of the historian, the time of an experiment, the time schedules of daily life, etc. Like the case of phenomenal time, the general properties of standard time hold for all its varieties.

The time assumption that interests us in the natural attitude is the assumption of a timing schedule based upon interpersonally validated schemes of standard time.

Form of Spontaneity

This construct is defined as a principle, expressional or teleological, that governs a course of experience. We might understand as a rough distinction between the two that activity governed by an expressional principle is activity undertaken for its own sake, "self-consummatory" or to use Schuetz' phrase rather loosely, activity governed only by a "because of" order of motives. Activity governed by a teleological principle is project oriented activity where there is an intention to realize the project. By the intention to realize a project is meant that the communicant entertains an expectation of sequence in events. The structures of the two orders of experience are quite distinct. The natural attitude is marked by the assumption of a projected future state with the intention to realize the state that involves bodily movements that are geared to the nature and timing of outer events.

With this much, then, we have completed a good enough portrayal of the constructs and of the specific values of them that we shall be interested in. We take up now the relationships between them.

The Constructs of Role in Their Relationships to Each Other

By the relationships between the constructs I am referring to the rules by which the observer is allowed to make statements about the correlated changes in the specifications of the constructs. These changes are of several different sorts. First, there is change in the sense that the property of organization in experience is not given at birth, but develops in the course of a life history. Two big initial questions here are: "(1) How are the bodily experiences relevant to the formation of the conceptions of time, space, the self, other persons, and so on? (2) How in a course of development is a given Role experientially prior to another?

Second, there is change in the sense that the specifications of a Role can be "torn out," so to speak, thus destroying the properties of organization in experience and reducing the experiencer to some state of enduring confusion. It is this kind of change that we shall be primarily interested in.

Third, we speak of change in the sense of the ways in which altered specifications of one construct involve alterations in the specifications of others. On this score I have only empirical information to go on, and am not yet able to state which of such changes are related as matters of formal necessity.

Finally, we speak of change in the sense of the succession of Roles that occur empirically in the course, for example, of a day's experiences.

Despite the lack of our knowledge on which to ground a formal vocabulary of relationships, I have nevertheless elected to assume several relationships so that, through a commitment, we may at least get some predictive work under way.

With reference to the four kinds of changes, we postulate the following:

1. The natural attitude is developmentally prior to all the others.

2. The development of the natural attitude is perquisite to the development of all the others.

3. All attitudes are constituted as modifications of the structures of the natural attitude. In this sense we shall refer to its logical priority over the other attitudes.

4. There are various levels of organization of experience. The properties of organization for experiences within the Roles are not the same as the properties of organization for experiences organized on a biological basis, though the two levels are intimately related. Hence, the destruction of the natural attitude does not involve the cessation of all activity, though it always implies the formal consequence of confusion.

5. The natural attitude being logically prior means that we assume a "hierarchy" of attitudes in the sense that the consequences of the destruction of a world will not ramify beyond those attitudes prior to it in the hierarchy, with the natural attitude as the "fundamental." Thus the road to anomie will be found in the destruction of the structures of the natural attitude and not in the destruction of the attitudes dependent upon it.

6. An attitude shows the aspect of a set of invariant systematically related meanings. The system will be altered (a) by changing the specifications of one or a set of constructs within the limits of the possible specifications for each. We do not know yet what these dimensions or limits are beyond rough empirical knowledge. Such a change defines what is meant by a change in attitude or Role. (b) By rendering the invariant specification or specifications variable. (c) By "destroying" a specification or set of specifications.

These conditions can *not* occur in combination. The possibility of each excludes the simultaneous possibilities of either of the other two. "Destruction" is a temporary metaphor. It means that the invariant meaning ceases to operate as a standard while no standard takes its place.

7. The assumption that the specifications are systematically related means that each specification is so related to the others that the observer for specifying one of the constructs is limited in the possible specifications that he can assign to the others: that these possibilities decrease as each is specified; and that the specifications of five determines the specifications of the sixth.

8. The assumption of systematic relationships means also that each "sustains" the others. Hence, the destruction of one implies the destruction of all. When speaking about the observer, the absence of a relevant specification renders the observer's account of the Role elliptical. When speaking about the experiencer, the absence of a relevant specification implies a disorganized world, or confusion.

9. We postulate that the adoption of some but not all attitudes is within the free discretion of the experiencer. The maintenance of some but not all attitudes is also within the free discretion of the experiencer: By "free discretion" is meant that the experiencer, as a matter of choice, or by following a set of instructions, can control the invariant meanings that constitute an attitude.

It appears to me that the attitudes of waking fantasy, of play, of scientific theorizing are accessible to free discretion. The natural attitude and the attitude of dreaming are not. This classification is not complete.

10. For any succession of attitudes we postulate (a) that the styles of the succession rarely occur by the design of the experiencer; (b) that the succession of one attitude by another is something continuous with reference to the experiences encountered in one that is temporally immediate to it; (c) that the order in the succession will show empirical regularities; and (d) that these empirical regularities can be treated according to the precepts of logical necessity.

11. Nevertheless, we postulate that the differences between attitudes are not matters of degree. Their specifications do not shade into each other. One does not go gradually from one to another, but goes rather by a "leap." By "leap" is meant the modification of attentional interest in the object is modified so that the accent of reality is placed elsewhere. The attitudes of fantasying, for example, or scientific theorizing are not modified recapitulations of the natural attitude but rather each had an integrity of its own, there being no transformation formula by which the objects constituted within one attitude and compatible with each other within this attitude can be made equivalent to the objects constituted within another attitude. Schuetz writes:

> [S]een from P, supposed to be real, Q and all the experiences belonging to it would appear as merely fictitious, inconsistent, and incompatible, and vice versa.

That each attitude has its own integrity does not mean that the objects constituted within one attitude cannot be compared with the objects constituted within another. Schuetz stresses that it is the meaning of our experiences and not the ontological structure of the objects that constitutes reality. The various attitudes are not ontological entities, but are modes of organization of individual consciousness. They are not separated states of mental life in the sense that passing from one to another requires the extinction of memory and consciousness. They are merely names for different modes of organization of one and the same consciousness,

> [A]nd it is the one and same life, the mundane life, unbroken from birth to death which is attended to in different modifications.

12. We postulate the attitude and the order of objects that it constitutes as a unified field. This means (a) that every attitude has an order of objects

particular to it; (b) that an alteration of an attitude implies an alteration of the order of objects; (c) the inoperativeness of any structure of an attitude implies the formal consequence of confusion; (d) the variability of any construct value implies a lesser degree of organization of the order of objects, i.e., anxiety; (e) All these statements are reversible.

13. At this time we are unable to say over the board that if a Role construct takes a specific value, what values the other Role constructs may and may not specifically take. However, it is possible to state that certain of the constructs go together in blocks as far as their possible values are concerned. For example, without an orientation to standard time, there can be no suspension of doubt that the world is as it appears according to the canons of everyday judgment. Similarly, the attitude structure of pragmatic involvement does not seem to occur simultaneously with the primacy of the Individuum. Also the kinds of motivational schemata that will be used to constitute the system of alters that the communicant orients are closely related to the mode of giveness of the self in that primacy of the Individuum is incompatible with an orientation to the motives of others in which these motives are constituted as instances of a type. Also, the variability of the mode of giveness of the self (as in the case of an "unstable self image") is incompatible with a stable system of alter-imputed motives. (The phrase goes, "By the treatment I can give and get from you I recognize who I am. If I don't know who I am, I don't know who you are, and if I don't know who you are, I don't know who I am.")

14. We shall assume the possibility of vacillation between alternative values of these constructs for each one. Such vacillation will be known as Role conflict. Such vacillations always imply a lessening of the degree of organization of a world. The case can best be illustrated with Scheler's theory of shame. The behavioral paradigm of shame can be summarized by the experiential formula of the removal from public gaze. "I want to run away and hide." According to Scheler this affect is the product of the following. An actor is given as a self either in a public or private sense. One can start from either. If, when one is assumed by an actor relative to an alter or set of alters, the actor detects in the actions or attitudes of alters a treatment directed to the one that is not given, there may be what Scheler calls "an attentional redirection back upon the self." The vacillation between the two is productive of the affect of shame. A set of interesting accompanying effects, for our purposes, are the immediate and marked closing down of the span of the intentional field, i.e., time perspective undergoes immediate and marked truncation (significances of past and future for events are lost to the sense of the immediate event), with it the loss of standard time orientation, loss of purpose, loss of pragmatic involvement,

loss of an orientation to the motives of others, and the immediate experiencing of the world in doubt. These effects would imply the consequence of the withdrawal of activity, and indeed this is a prominent characteristic of the conduct and covert activity of the person experiencing shame.

XII

Factors That Condition Information: (C) Factors of Communicative Work

INSTEAD OF FIRST GIVING THE FACTORS AND THEN STATING THEIR RELATION-ships, we'll reverse the procedure and discuss just the relationships, most particularly the relationship between the notion of communicative work and the notions of Role and the order of objects.

A comparison with Parsons and Shils's conception of action as a relationship between actor and order of objects may help clarify the formulation we shall use. In the Parsons-Shils view (as elaborated in *Toward a General Theory of Action*), an actor is said to orient a situation of objects. Provision is made for the actor as an object in the situation. The actor's actions are for these authors the ways in which the actor relates himself to these objects, including himself in the order as one of its objects. His actions as a system present to the observer a set of regular actor-object relationships. As his actions are for one reason or another altered in their typicality, the order of relationships is altered. What we have in effect is an exceedingly complicated "space," though to take a simple example: consider a person in a room, standing ten feet from a desk. If we describe his action as a movement toward the desk, we can with fully equivalent sense say that his relationship to the desk changes continuously on a distance scale from 10 to 2 feet. Similarly, the action-relationship equivalence holds, though with reference to more complicated dimensions of description, for a person whose orientations to a set of objects are those of loving or hating.

The view we shall take is somewhat different than this. For one thing we have already provided in the notions of actor and order the notion of a set of objects that stand in relationship to each other by virtue of the invariant conditions that are constitutive of the objects as unities of meaning. Parsons and Shils employ a different theory of objects and hence for them this is not the way their problem is formulated. The object is there; the specifications of the actor determine not the structure of the object world, but the significances that the actor *attaches* to the object world. Hence the make-up of the actor determines how the actor stands in relationship to an order of objects.

In our view, the actor and the structure of the object world are simultaneously constituted. They do not stand in relationship to each other; there is no sense of an x interposed between the actor and the world. No actor, no world; the two together are a unified field in this particular and important sense. (Cantril's view of actor and order as a unified field shows still another difference since he seems to assume a real object world independent of his actor about which the actor can have prejudiced views.)

Given the view then that the conditions of the communicant's Role determine an order of related objects, what then do *we* do with action (or for our purposes, communicative work)? Just this: action or better communicative work will in our scheme be viewed as operations by which various orders of transformation are effected upon the relationships between objects. In our scheme communicative work has the logical status of a designator of a class of operators upon the Role-Order schema.

Until good sense catches up with us we shall provide for the following classes of operators: (1) the operations of sending and receiving messages, which we shall call message work; (2) feed-back operations, by which is meant (a) the operation of comparing an outcome with an invariant standard; and (b) the devices for the correction of error; and (3) the operations of meaning-investment, which is to say the operations of assigning meanings to a message through a set of rules by which signals and meanings are matched.

All refer to behavior and actions of communicants in the sense of these terms set out in Memo #1. I hope it is possible to see now the sense of the statement made in Memo #1 regarding the problem of order at the level of the premises of conduct. All the operations above are actions. We have conceived them as the operations by which the relationships between objects are altered. But it should also be clear on the basis of the discussion of the criteria of organization and the insight of the imbedded or interimplicative character of the set of possibilities that are the communicant's world or order as well as on the basis of the discussion of the domains of constancy and variability that alterations of the relationships between some possibilities and between some objects is continuously possible only if the domain of constancy is not an empty set—i.e., something can alter if something else remains unchanged.

Hence the meaning of the statement that the operations alter the order of possibilities that regulates the course of the alteration. The discussion of the relationship between Role and Order presented the view of the Role assumptions as conditioners of the limits of meaning that the objects of the order could take. The Role conditions were said to be constitutive of this order. Hence the role constructs are systemically related to the operations. If the Role constructs are intact then there is action going on. If they fail, so do the operations. Conversely, if the operations fail—any of them—so will the Role constructs fail. Since the Role constructs are postulated as invariant to a course of operations, we must allow that the operations, insofar as they effect a continuous or error free transformation of relationships between objects, confirm the character of the assumptions. Hence the meaning of the statement that there are conditions of the actor's make-up under which the actions that alter the order that regulates their course while maintaining the conditions under which they occur, i.e., are possible.

But having this much leaves us with an important problem undecided, and whose solution would provide us with a postulate of immense importance as far as the possibility of extracting theorems from the theory is concerned. The problem is this: If we allow the point to stand that each Role-Order schema will have a class of operations particular to it, and assuming that it is possible to list many empirical devices that would come under the notions of the operators (the familiar empirical vocabularies of action will do for this task at least for a while) is there any rule by which the specific operations (that could be listed under each of the above classes of operators) can be ordered to a ranking of probable occurrence?

I think there is, and I would propose the following postulated solution: *For the case of the natural attitude and only for the case of the natural attitude, those operations have the greatest probability of occurrence which involve the minimal amount of reorganization of the socially validated realities depicted in the order.*

There is much empirical evidence to recommend this postulate. First, it seems to be exceedingly difficult to get a person to act in such a manner as to deliberately court error. Most convincing however are the findings on persons in extreme situations—and I refer here to Kogan's report on German concentration camps, Goodson's account of American prisoners of war of the Japanese, Allport, Bruner, and Jandof's article on Jews in pre-war Nazi Germany, Hersey on the Warsaw Ghetto, Janis on aerial bombing, Cantril on the effects of the Orson Welles program. This material shows over and over again how even when the information was available *if the persons involved would interpret it as outsiders to the situation* to arrive at the conclusion that they faced extermination, the actions and interpretive devices that were usual were those that were predicated on a view of the future that was a projection from and continuous with the present socially validated routines.

This postulate would seem to imply that perspectival changes occur only in small amounts. Certainly such would be implied for the case of the dedicated acceptor—let us say the "enthusiast"—who is subjected in isolation to pressures to re-organize the relevance-structures of his world. For what other cases this would be implied remains to be pulled out theoremwise from the scheme. But one can find too the case under this postulate for abrupt changes in large amounts, found for example in a situation where perspectival alterations could proceed without impairing the actor's assumptions with regard to the reciprocity of perspectives. Of relevance here, for example is Lewin's work on alterations of food preferences, and the repeated finding in industrial training programs that innovations often proceed with greatest success where those who would be affected are made "participant to the decision."

The postulate serves to underline the importance of the structure of the communicative net-work, and most particularly the importance of the timing of communicative work in the net as it is relevant to the assumptions of the reciprocity of perspectives of the natural attitude for the problem of social change. I would suggest as a problem to be included in the report to the Ford Foundation the investigation of the characteristics of a communicative net and particularly the characteristics of perspectival assumptions and interpretive tactics under which one gets the phenomenon of increasingly accelerated changes, to be compared with situations in which change is difficult to initiate and maintain.

XIII

Factors That Condition Information: (D) Net-work Factors

Wʜᴇɴ I ᴄᴏɴᴄᴇɪᴠᴇᴅ ᴛʜᴇ ᴘʟᴀɴ ᴏꜰ ᴛʜɪꜱ ᴘᴀᴘᴇʀ, ᴛʜᴇ ᴛᴏᴘɪᴄ ᴏꜰ ɴᴇᴛ-ᴡᴏʀᴋ factors was provided in order to cover the structural characteristics of a system of communicants. I thought of the topic as a rug under which the leavings from each of the prior topics would be brushed as each was "cleaned up." But when I looked under the rug I found not only the leavings but everything else that had been treated up till then. To clean up the mess required that I elect some theory of organization. When that disastrous insight occurred I knew with the full conviction of a gut response how Norman Maier's rats felt when they were being goosed off their perches but were unable to choose where to jump. I crawled off the platform, went home, beat up my family and crawled into bed.

I managed to regain a grip on my nerves when it occurred to me that, instead of seeking an election of theory, one might ask instead for a list of ideas that seemed to be immanent in the conception of "organization" in the sense (1) that any theory of organization would be in effect a vocabulary that gave specific content to these ideas; (2) that these ideas would help one to assess any theory to find out what the theory covered and what it did not cover as well as what the underlying assumptions of the theory consisted of, as well as (3) permit a description of the functions that the specific concepts of the theory served in the theory. What these ideas represented then were not variables but a set of terms for defining a set of variables. Various decisions with regard to the specific concepts to be used could be made. The list of ideas was regarded as a kind of "check-list" with which a systematic appraisal of a theory of organization could be made, as well as a comparison between theories. As a minimum recommendation for the effort, it seemed to me that such a list would even in first approximation permit the systematic pushing ahead of the problem of codifying the principles of organization. In medium recommendation it seemed that by playing them against each other in various relationships, a huge number of topics could be devised. By giving them specific theoretical content, their maximum usefulness would consist of their status as descriptive parameters of something called "an organization."

Maybe my trauma on the perch knocked me loose from my good sense, but I elected to follow up this question. The idea behind the list is this: that any theory of organization, whether it be a "partial" or a "complete" theory will either provide an explicit set of constructions for handling these ideas, or it will be possible for the theorist so interested to find implicit decisions about them. Since the ideas are conceived as logically necessary, there is no alternative to handling them. Not to handle them is to introduce an irreducible obscurity into the theory in the sense that alternative decisions on the ideas not covered are open and hence it is impossible to evaluate the meanings of the concepts that have been introduced.

The following list is presented for criticism. (Since I am interested in communication I have chosen the language of communication. One can without difficulty translate them into more general language.)

1. The idea of the communicant. I refer here to the characterization of the typical instigator, so to speak. The idea is known familiarly as the idea of the actor. Whether he be typified according to a vocabulary of personality, of roles, whether he be accounted for as an "undifferentiated region," a point in a set of enumerable points, a "black box" designative of a person or an office or department or bureau or corporation or whatever, is a matter that the theorist may choose according to the purposes for which he constructs his theory. The theorist will have a set of communicant-relevant terms regardless of whether he thinks he needs them or not.

2. The idea of numbers of communicants. The idea is fairly apparent in its meaning. It is found in such concepts as size, pool, aggregate, dyad, group, etc.

3. The idea of communicative work. I refer here to stimulus transmission and reception, handled through such concepts as action, conduct, behavior. In the theory outlined so far it is found in the notions of signal, expression, sign, symbol, message, tactics, strategy, and so on.

4. The idea of communicative territory. The general meaning here is that of the scenic locus of action. The familiar three dimensional physical space is about as simple minded as one can get in treating sociologically relevant notions of territory without abandoning sociological problems altogether. Concepts like distance, area, municipal limits, the owner's premises, county, realty, physical geographical locus, and so on are elaborative constructions.

5. *The idea of communicative timing.* I'm referring here to the temporal values of standard time location, sequence, and duration as these values taken together in the multitude of ways in which they can be framed permit one to constitute a set of observed events as a pattern or type. For example, by treating actions as Parsons deals with them, durational values are treated as point-like intervals, fat points so to speak. This makes it possible to speak of one pattern logically implying the co-existence of others. Change is then handled through the notion of the prerequisites of an equilibrated state. Deutsch handles timing by statistically standardizing the message work with reference to alterations in duration and looks to the properties of self-regulation of output as these are functions of the coordinated passage, assessment, storage, control, evaluation of information.

6. *The idea of social relationships.* The idea consists of a frame of concepts for ordering data-wise the differences that it is supposed to make in a communicant's actions when an other person is placed in his situation. Deference hierarchies, prestige allocations, power hierarchies, the division of labor, kinship systems, and so on are illustrative of such organizing schemata.

7. *The idea of a normative order (institutions).* The general notion referred to here is the notion of rules or its equivalent idea which is constitutive of the kind of treatment that an actor is conceived to give and the kind of interest he is conceived to take in the objects that comprise his situation. The terms marriage and market are empirical constructions that elaborate this idea. Sumner's folkways and mores are candidates; so is Odum's addition of technicways. Technical norms, appreciative norms, institutional norms, Sorokin's law-norms are further examples. Standards, ideals, myth, ideal images, status quo, Utopia, projected outcomes, tradition, racial unconsciousness, the structure of the super-ego, ego-identifications, interjected purposes are concepts drawn from here and there to illustrate some of the more ingenious ways in which this idea has been handled. The terms are alike in their function of depicting those aspects of a situation of action that remain invariant and are transcendental to the particularities of a sensorily changing situation. They permit the observer to define the alternatives of view and conduct that the actor is conceived to be faced with, and at their best permit the observer to make rough but useful estimations of likelihood that one or a set of them will be "chosen."

8. *The idea of communicative paths.* (In the glossary these were conceptualized as primary and secondary feed-back loops.) This is the last one that I have

dug up and is the one that I am least confident of. I have in mind the general notion that the actor experiences his own actions as he acts and that because of the phenomenon of memory he seems to be capable of delaying a response until after long serial orders of stimuli have reached him.

Some notion like "path" seems to be required to handle the time differential between the points of stimulus origin and reception or assessment. Again there are many different ways in which this idea has been handled. Peculiarly enough, the most prevalent way that sociologists have handled it is through the use of a graphic metaphor. Two circles are drawn to represent two actors and a double headed arrow is drawn connecting them. The arrow represents "interaction," i.e., reciprocal, serial, simultaneous, over-lapping, etc. stimulus, assessment, and response. It has been handled too in such rough and ready concepts as "contacts," "access," and "lines of" this or that—communication, influence, power, authority, for example. That it has been handled through metaphors I take as a sign of the commonplace character of the notion and the fact that it has been generally regarded as theoretically and practically unproblematical. With the recent popularity of the ideas of communications engineering it has come under examination as a problem in its own right.

So much for the list of ideas.

Although the theoretical vocabulary that I would like to use to give specific reference to these notions is only partially worked out, it is possible neverthe-less to jump ahead to furnish a definition of "organization" or "an organiza-tion."

In mulling over these concepts in the attempt to apply them to concrete materials I was struck by the way in which they implicated each other. As one was specified in its empirical reference, it seemed that such specification had implications for the specifications of the others. For example, it seemed to me that to describe a communicative territory, let us say by considering the quadrangle outside of the south entries to Dickinson Hall, the notion of spa-tial arrangements grew in its sociologically concrete character as I addressed the questions of the fluctuating numbers of persons that occur through the normatively governed time schedules that the students follow over the course of a routine day's activity. The paths that were followed, the groupings that occurred as the students passed from place to place in turn required statements about a normatively constituted territory consisting of the "Senior sun dial," "the grass," the paths, the "Economics building," "the church" and so on.

Never one to fail to leap to a conclusion, I decided—though with the provi-sion that my critics would show me the errors of my ways—that any related set of theoretical specifications of these ideas, considered as constructions, would be referred to as an organization. In this sense the term organization does not represent a concrete entity (except as a mere way of talking) but has the status instead of a set of interpretive rules which taken together define a field of observation. It makes no statements of fact. At its best it will present the conditions that tell which of the set of all possible outcomes of observation we shall encounter. It remains then for the actual operations of observation to settle the question of whether the restricted frame of possibilities that the terms of the organization propose can be realized. To say for example that we are interested in large scale organization in which persons gain a livelihood is merely a rough and ready delineation of the order of specifications of these constructions that we shall take as constants. When the theory has more guts to it than it has at present we may find a more accurate way of delineating the kinds of organizations that are specifically of interest.

In previous memoranda I indicated that I was interested in communicative work in large scale self-regulating systems. Let me now sketch in what this phrase refers to. The relevant conceptions lay down what I consider to be the general procedural rules that I hope to follow in applying the theory to the development of research questions and the interpretation of findings.

First, there is the notion of system. I do not intend the term to refer to a property of events. Hence all talk of concrete systems is, as far as I'm concerned, loose talk. Insofar as the observer places events in an order of some sort to each other which is to say that he formulates a set of statements and the statements stand in some logically implicative sense with each other, then the ways in which they are implicative will be used as the sense in which statements are systematically related. Or to put it otherwise, the system-like character of events will be found in any type of significance for each other that the observer assigns to a set of events. This includes independent variability. To speak then of a large scale system means that I am interested in the ways in which the events of conduct, for example, are peculiarly related to each other when for example we are dealing with a field which includes the specification of a large number of persons (if we take large numbers as an initial though crude way of designating large scale).

What about the notion now of self-regulation? I'm referring here to a set of theoretical conceptions, based on the ideas that were listed before, which are conceived to be related in such a manner that if there is a specification of communicative timing, for example, that implies by the general laws that relate these constructions certain specifications of communicative territory, and these specifications imply something about the numbers of communicants, and thus the chain proceeds until after going through the list one finds himself talking about the fact that the specifications of normative order imply what one has said before in the specifications of communicative timing, then I shall say that there is a set of specifications of these constructions under which the values are implicative of each other and this property will be known as the property of self-regulation. Self-regulation in this sense is an adjective that gets attached to system. We shall assume that there is a configuration of specifications under which this criterion is not met. Otherwise the notion of self-regulation does not pose any empirical questions and is in this sense sterile. Since the characteristic of communicative timing is conceived to be a temporalized function of communicative territory, the criterion of self-regulation may be stated as follows: that the specifications of any construct at any given time is a function of the specifications of that construct at a prior time. In specifying the conditions under which this holds for a set of data we will have described the sense in which the system is a self-regulating one. An example can be taken from a thermostatically controlled heating system. In order to say that the system is self-regulating we would have to show how the probability of the heat output of the oil burner at any given time is a function of the height of the oil in the tank, the rate of flow to the burner, the rate of flow of heated air through the ducts, the correlated alterations of the height of the mercury in the thermostat and the etc. etc. until we return finally to the temperature of the flame of the oil burner. For a communicative system, the possibility that it is a self-regulating one would lead us to ask how the temporal patterns of communicative exchanges—measured for example in frequency of message exchanges between communicants—are related to formal regulations that govern frequency, how the distances over which these messages must travel are related to the timing of messages as well as to the extent of subscription to the regulations, how there will be found at a relevant time certain numbers of persons that are by regulation required to have an "up-to-the-minute" definition of the overall state of the net-work, etc. etc. until we would finally get back to the characteristics of the timing patterns. One can of course begin anywhere. Above all one can confine himself to the description of the operations of any portion of the net.

This leads to the notions of the structural and functional prerequisites of a self-regulating communicative net. I shall be using these terms in a different manner than either Parsons or Levy, both of whom have made the most consistent use of them as far as Sociological theory is concerned. To make them clear I shall have to talk first of the structural problems of a net and the functional problems of a net.

By the structural problems of a net I'm referring to the problems that the observer is faced with in meeting two tasks: (1) The task of allocation which

I shall conceive to be that of assigning the values to the set of variables represented in the set of ideas listed above which we shall refer to as the conditions of organization so as to yield the logically possible notion of self-regulation. That is to say, the problem of allocation is that of assigning the values to these conditions under which the criterion of self-regulation is met. (2) The second structural problem is that of integration. By this is meant again the observer's task of stating the laws that relate allocated specifications. I wish to emphasize: a system does not allocate job functions, make role differentiations, distribute prestige, rewards, punishments, align communicative responsibilities, select actors from a pool to place them here and there. There are persons who are regarded by others in particular ways, who make demands, issue orders, decide between one way of doing things and another, tell others what will be expected of them, show deferential behavior to others, make little and big plans, and so on and so on. The notion of the system is found in the fact that the observer can describe these events as they stand in typical orderings to each other, the ordering being drawn from his schema of logically related conceptions drawn from the ideas listed above that he calls his theory.

There is a second order of problems: the functional problems. Like the structural problems these too are the observer's problems, not the problems of "the system." I shall refer to them as the problems of motivation, of coordination, of control. They have to do with communicative work and are inserted as operators by the use of which the notion of A as a function of B can be handled in the specific senses in which the specifications of A stand as operational consequences of the specifications of B.

Motivational functions. In Memo #1 I said that a message would be conceived to alter the receiver's definition of the situation by the "amount" of its occurrence. Another way to conceive this, and perhaps an easier way, is to say that the definition of the situation is conceived to be altered in the constructions that the communicant places upon it by the information that he extracts from the messages. To give us a way of handling the alterations "incited" by communicative work, I should like to talk of the information as motivating these changes. (One could talk of the information "causing" the changes, but it seems to me that "cause" is inaccurate.) If this formulation appears too general, one may, though with some risk of distortion of what is involved, conceive the motivational consequences of communicative work as the effect that received communications have upon the grounds of the recipient's actions.

By the term *coordinative functions* of communicative work I am referring to the effects of communicative work in maintaining an interpersonally valid definition of the situation.

By the term *control functions* of communicative work I am referring to the effects of communicative work for the regulation and resolution of incongruity.

To repeat here a point made at greater length in Memo #2, there is no one-to-one correspondence between the communicative functions and the particular communication. There is no such thing as a type of communication that serves one function while another type serves another function. Every communication, to the extent that it is not experienced in its mere message character, serves three functions simultaneously. If one effect is found, then the other effects will also be found. However, one may in a given research problem be interested in only one or some combinations of these functions.

These functions are problematical for the observer in the sense that he is faced with the task of specifying the structural conditions under which a set of communicative functions are operative and second of specifying how they operate within a set of structural conditions as a contribution to the criterion of self-regulation.

By a structural prerequisite of a communicative net is meant any first-order value of a structural component that is logically necessary to the conception of the system as a self-regulating one. By a functional prerequisite is meant any first order structurally induced effect that is logically necessary to the conception of the system as a self-regulating one.

Differing again with Parsons and Levy's usage, we shall lay down the rule that the notions of structural and functional prerequisites will be used as descriptive parameters of a self-regulating communicative system constituted as a problematical field of investigation. In short and dirty fashion, the structural and functional prerequisites as far as we shall be concerned are used to define what it is about an actual investigative site that is relevant to the problem we are interested in investigating.

I realize that the discussion so far has not been directly concerned with network factors as conditioners of information. One might be kind and say that at best I have sketched in a way in which we might collect our thoughts when this problem is addressed. A big step lies ahead of laying out an initial set of constructions that will serve us theory-wise for dealing with this problem.

If there was no vocabulary of constructs available and if in fact we had to face up to the job of inventing them from scratch, there would be good reason to take seriously the despair I spoke of at the beginning of this section. Actually the picture is rather bright. The section on Role provides us a way of talking about communicant characteristics. Of course we need not rely on this to give some workable content to this conception. Much familiar theory is available to handle the ideas of numbers, institutions, and social relationships. A beginning has been made on a vocabulary of communicative work; it's thin but usable. Only the ideas of communicative timing, communicative territory, and communicative paths are sources of worry, and even these are far from empty, though the last named idea is distinctly undernourished.

To complete the sketch of conceptions, I want to conclude this section by introducing some concepts at least by way of putting the idea of communicative paths on shaky feet.

By way of handling the idea of communicative paths, I would like to introduce a distinction between what will be known as primary and secondary feed-back loops. By the term primary feed-back loop is meant the path of a signal for a communicant between the point of transmission and the point of assessment that is uninterrupted by the transforming operations of another communicant. For example, the signal path for a communicant between a vocalization and the assessment of that vocalization as it is picked up by his ears is a primary loop. So too is the path of the signals represented when in a face to face contact one communicant addresses a question or converses with another, reading off the posture and facial expressions of the receiver the signals by which the communicator assesses the effects of his communicative work.

A secondary feed-back loop is one that has for a communicant at least one transformation point between the point transmission and the point of assessment. Until we run into difficulties with it, we'll conceive of a loop as a normatively likely signal path.

The following properties of secondary feed-back loops in general are listed to get some work under way. (1) The time between transmission and assessment is always longer in a secondary loop than it is in a primary loop. (2) This time delay is limited only by the "span" of recall of the message transmitter, the delay being ideally variable up to this point. Neither of these two features is the case for primary loops. (3) Every transformation point involves, relative to the intended meanings of the sender's message work, a loss of information.

A loop with one transforming point will be referred to as a first order loop; a loop with two transforming points is a second order loop, and so on. For example, from A to B and back to A is a first order loop. From A to B to C and back to A is a second order loop. From A to B to C to B to A is a third order loop. Additional elaboration of this vocabulary will be necessary later to permit us to make the difference between circular and linear routings, for example. The differences made so far have been made in the hope that they will be helpful in dealing with the motivational, coordinative, and control functions of communicative work. They permit us too to link the properties of these paths to the other parameters of territory, social relationships, institutions, and so on that were reviewed before. Not only are these other parameters conditional of these paths, but the reverse is also the case. The paths also are immediately relevant to the properties of information in many ways. For example, we shall expect that many of them will be institutionally prescribed. The attendant losses of information—the "perceptual distortion," for example—can therefore be conceived of as functions of these paths. The relevance of this for the problem of "uniformity in the definitions of the situation," for the relevance to the operations of a network of imperfect information, for the communicative tactics that will be employed in competitive contests for advancement and power, for the effects upon and control of something that I have come to think of as "organizational anxiety," can I think be seen initially at least without too much stretching. The concepts are useful, too, if one regards the institutionalized prescription of paths as conditions that a communicant regards as constancies in his communicative situation and hence the paths themselves become relevant for the communicant's assessment of the meanings of messages, and hence are relevant to the probable character of information.

These constructions should be of considerable help with reference to the topic of "lines of communication" particularly as they help to bring together data on group productivity, questions of efficiency of communicative arrangements, information loss, perceptual "distortions," morale, and the constraints upon and the consequences of organizational innovations.

XV

Problems and Theorems

This section consists of an unsystematic listing of points taken either directly from something mentioned in the preceding sections or suggested and/or spun out from something mentioned there. It reads therefore like jottings in a notebook, being a grab-bag mixture of this and that: questions, topics for research, theorems, postulates from which theorems can be derived, and so on.

I must apologize for not being neat. I listed many of these points originally with the intention of using the list to write this section. However, time devoted at this point to matters of arrangement seemed to me to be ill-spent, particularly because I felt impatient to be done with the preliminaries and to get on with the theorems, the research designs and the researching. I decided therefore to simply put the ideas down as a point of departure for the papers ahead. This does not mean that the list is a "maybe this would be interesting" kind of thing. I offer the list as a partial one of the topics as I see them that a long term program of research in the sociology of communication would be concerned with. It should therefore be read with the purposes of the fall report in mind.

1. Any factor that conditions the characteristics of organization of experience conditions the characteristics of information. Theorems from this.
2. The reality of an object is not found in its ontological structure but is found in its constitution as a unity of meaning. To say that an object is real is to mean that it is of interest to an experiencer relative to some

order of past, present, and anticipated experiences. ("Attitudes toward history" and their bearing on relevance structures. Theorems here.)

3. Conditions found in a net that transform $e(p_n)$ into s_n. The various ways of experimentally operating on the e.

4. Ways of operating on signals to transform their sign and expressional character. Relevance for characteristics of information.

5. Whatever conditions the ability to actualize a meaning is a condition that can be manipulated to induce confusion, i.e., a state in which signals rather than signs or expressions are experienced. Relevance here of the occasional character of the expression "I."

6. Conditions under which one would get the rationalizing and depersonalization of communicative work.

7. Conditions of instrumental and expressional character of language.

8. Message work, feed-back operations, and the operations of meaning investment re: functions of motivation, coordination, and control. Theorems.

9. Perfect and imperfect information and the problem of coordination. The costs of systems that require perfect information. Relevance to the notion of the uniformity of definitions of the situation. Relevance to open channels of communication. Relevance to power phenomena.

10. In addressing the question of consensus the point of investigative interest is not the fact of uniformity but the fact that the communicant can continue to hold to an assumption of uniformity that is productive of incongruity in amounts that can be handled within the terms of the assumed relationships and other conditions.

11. The conditions under which opening the lines of communication to permit the freer passage of messages up and down would disrupt coordination.

12. Problem suggested of what is actually going on within and between communicants in a situation that would, under going platitudes, be characterized as a situation of open channels of communication. Study of recent models conference suggested for pilot findings. Sociology of scientific discourse.

13. The nature of the solution of tasks a function of the nature of the organized exchange of information. Relevance of the distribution and organization of the exchange system of information to the problem of change and innovation.

14. Complete and incomplete information. Insofar as there are insufficient specifications (for whatever reason) of the variables so that the communicant is unable to project a determinate outcome in a Now (course of action), we shall say that his information is incomplete. Ways of achieving complete information other than by supplying information to specify the variables.

15. Ways of achieving certainty in face of situation that is under the assumption of rational canons of incomplete information. How come the prevalence of the communicant's claim that he had complete information and knew everything that needed to be known. The relevance here of trust and the "we" relationships.

16. Characteristics of hypothesis formation and the canons of realistic judgment and test procedures in the natural attitude.

17. The probable character of information from randomness to certainty. Ways of measuring this.

18. Psychological probability as a "calculus." Schuetz' notion of likelihood compared with mathematical probability.

19. The things that condition a message to make it yield zero-order information.

20. The relevance of judgments of weighted inference to the net-work conditions and operations. Consider particularly the nature of social relationships.

21. The properties of socially defined fact.

22. Social theories of knowledge and their relevance to net-work conditions.

23. The hunch that the products of judgments will show more uniformity than the processes by which these results are obtained.

24. The nature of the message (temporal and spatial patterning) manner and fact of its coupling to the nervous system, attending attitude, tactics of incorporation points for manipulating the probable character of the communicant's information.

25. Further, re: these, any factor that is conditional of these factors is conditional of the probable character of the communicant's information. Theorems from this.

26. The relevance of net-work conditions to the nature and amount of inferential information that a communicant will obtain.

27. "Incest awe" as a constraint upon inferential information.

28. Constraints upon acquisition of inferential information.

29. Relevance of secondary information to inferential information. Factors that condition secondary information condition nature and amount of inferential information. Theorems here.
30. Analysis of variance to test the hypothesis that net-work factors account for more variance in nature and amount of inferential information than does I.Q.
31. Direct information and inferential information stand in a relationship such that if one is of zero-order the other is of zero-order.
32. In any net the extent of inferential information relative to the direct information of a message is a function of the communal character of the relationship between communicants. The function may be stated as the following relationship: As a relationship takes on the properties of a communal as compared with an associational relationship the inferential character of the information drawn from the message increases toward a maximum which is represented in the theoretical state of total affective integration.
33. Spell out what is meant by the nature and amount of inferential information: See the word in paragraph above, "extent."
34. Ways of transforming eidetic information into material information and back.
35. What factors condition the possibility of experiencing incongruity that undermines an order? i.e., error. Consider the case of surprise for attitudes other than the natural attitude.
36. Way in which communicative timing is relevant to possibilities of error and hence possibility of getting material information.
37. Re: the relevance of communicative timing. The expectations of timing and the nature of the social relationship, and its relevance to the eidetic or material character of the information from the messages that pass between the communicants. Stress the relevance of the expectation of sequence and the way this expectation varies relative to the definition of the other. Expectations of timing and the differences between calculated and expressional treatment of the other. Expectations of timing and the social perception of purposes, qualities, activities, familiarity, strangeness, etc. of the other. Variations by status differences of the communicants.
38. Phenomenal time values and concept formation.
39. Ways of effecting a thematized horizon. Relevant to the eidetic or material character of the information of the messages. The devices of

interpersonal support and validation of thematized horizons. Analyze concentration camp materials re: open and thematized horizons and the phenomenon of routinization.

40. Social philosophies and social interpretive tactics for investing events with requiredness. Start with Merton's analysis of social structure and anomie and the ways of adjusting to the discrepancies between institutionalized goals and the culturally prescribed means for achieving them.

41. For a communicant there is an important sense in which every event occurs as a matter of principle and without regard for consequences. Alienation, enthusiasm, and rationalization of social structure.

42. If there is a message and material information is obtainable from the message, so is the other. Eidetic information in every message. Design procedure to find out what the eidetic status is of information in inter-office memoranda for example. What happens to material information when the eidetic info of the message cannot be taken for granted. Eidetic information and the phenomenon of routinization. The effect of making messages anonymous as to authorship and addressee on a memory background of communal and personalized communications taken for granted. Look into this effect at Trenton State Hospital.

43. A problem for research is that of specifying the ways and the properties of these ways in which a set of possibilities are relevant to each other (determinative) i.e., the ways in which from the communicant's point of view they necessarily implicate each other. Look into the various techniques that have been developed to handle this problem at the empirical level. Freudian laws of association. Method of induced incongruity. What are the solutions that are available by fiat. (Parsons' pattern variable scheme.) Schuetz' analysis of the structure of the world of daily life. Recent work of Guttman.

44. Sociological epoche for transforming materials collected in interview into the definition of the situation. (Pre-medical interviews for illustration of the technique.) Consult analysts for their experiences. What are the assumptions behind Mel's distinction between the intrinsic, extrinsic job satisfactions and relations on the job? What are devices for dealing with this in questionnaires that provide structured alternative answers. Re-examine the open ended interview. Re-examine scoring procedures for questionnaires. See Elliot

[Michler] for material discussed re: this and his proposed article re: scaling.

45. How will the timing of messages in a net effect the ambiguity of information that a communicant draws from a message? Investigate the various ways in which a "context" will be found and used in a message to extract the sense of the message where the message is in various respects incomplete, e.g. omitted letters, omitted phrases, misspelled words, nonsense words, scrambled phrases, etc. Compare "continuous passages" with the ad hoc listings of facts a la Information Please. Look into the objects that the recipient in each case is attending to. Look up work of Hyman et al. re: interviewer bias in this regard. Look into problem of repetition, boredom, and the categorization of the situation.

46. *The following problem suggested as a design for exploring the factors that condition information.* Problem: There are a number of informants. Each has information about a situation whose parameters of description can be independently decided upon by the experimenter. The situation may be one of witnesses to an accident, a military problem in getting intelligence information, an executive forming estimation of plant operations, trial testimony, police interrogation, insurance inquiry, D. P. questioning re: Russian industrial practices and social structure, etc. No limit to the situations that are possible since the problems involved are highly generalizable. Now say that no two stories will be exactly alike (or if so then this becomes a condition that is of interest as the case is found for example in collusion between prisoners being interrogated by police officials). The interrogator is faced with the task of constructing a picture of what is most likely the case. Now: what are the factors in the communicative relationship (will spell out the kinds of things these may be in a moment) that determine the picture that is selected, especially the factors that operate to determine the closeness of the approximation, i.e., the likelihood of being right. For example, how many informants, with what characteristics, what timing of question administration, nature of the relationship, structure of the order that is oriented, etc. etc. (See Net-work factors), also include with what varieties of answers, do you need for the best approximation? Look into the 40 million Frenchmen can't be wrong effect, i.e., that a single person may not know it by himself, but in the company of others (aggregate, consensus based on interaction), there is a group sense that is

wiser than the sense of any single person. Look at this for its actual use and conditions under which it works as well as this as a rule that the participants follow in making their estimations.

47. To design an experimental situation that will give the answer to the following question: what is the relationship between the expected variations in testimony and some kind of descriptive parameters of the situation about which the testimony is given. Make separation between credibility and factuality. How related? Are the grounds for predicting each the same or different?

48. What kind of characteristics of the witness and the situation can you find out about that will tell you the kind of expected variability that you can get in the answers. Look then for any invariant relationships that could be used to discount the answers given over a range of informants. What are the net-work determinants of credibility? Inkoles, Sheldon, Hyman, Asch, Kendall, preliminary list of names to write re: bibliography. Mosteller's work on superstition. Wonder if Columbia Bureau, various research agencies doing work on informants about Russia, Rand, State Department, Counter Intelligence Agency would have relevant information. Tactics of inquiry as relevant variable. Include the tactics as the interrogator who experiences his own as relevant variable. Different variable then first named. Write Florence Kluckhohn and Ben Paul for relevant bibliography on problems of field investigation, particularly re: the situation of inquiry as a social relationship.

49. Rule: the nature of information obtained from a message is conditioned by the arrangement of possibilities according to their constant or variable character.

50. We talk of consensus when two or more communicants assume a set of possibilities as constant and each assumes that what holds for him holds for the other. The continuity of a relationship, e.g., its duration, as well as the characteristics of the information that can be drawn from the messages will be conditioned by the character of these two assumptions. (See Schuetz re: the idealizations of the common sense attitude, especially the assumptions under the idealization of the reciprocity of perspectives.)

51. Operations on timing, territory, relationships, numbers, paths. Role characteristics that move a possibility from one domain to the other. A way into the problem of relevance structures.

52. Communicative work as operations for moving possibilities from one domain to the other.

53. Operations on net-work factors and the operations of communicative work in inducing incongruity. Intra- and inter-personal devices for the resolution of incongruity. These devices can be stated in terms of the reorganization of net-work factors, and communicative tactics as operations for the regulation and resolution of incongruity.

54. To the extent that any message requires for its informing character a set of invariant expectations (i.e., a domain of constancy that is not an empty set)—and in fact every message requires this—to that extent and regardless of whatever other information may be obtained from the message, it informs as well about the nature of the game; it has something to say about the order as it stands by definition.

55. Only to the extent that error is possible is it possible to know what occurred if the matter that stood by definition did not occur. Test this. If there is no possibility of error, there is no possibility of material information. Test this. Theorems re: conditions of no error.

56. Shall say that learning is the process whereby the acquisition of material information transfers possibilities from the domain of variability to the domain of constancy. Theorems here re: error, conditions of error and characteristics of learning curves.

57. One of the effects of routinizing the conditions of a net is to minimize the probability of confusion. Theorems here re: routine, rate of learning, and probability of confusion.

58. Every net set up to accomplish more than trivial tasks will have a proliferated set of communicative devices whereby the routine aspects of the net are maintained as well as a proliferation of communicative devices whereby incongruity is controlled.

59. Every manner of routinization will have an order of confusion particular to it.

60. Consider points 58 and 59 for theorems that relate those devices as communicative tactics, learning rates, efficiency of communicative work, learning, and innovation.

61. Theorems stating the relationships between information loss and primary and secondary feed-back loops.

62. Theorems re: the various devices for routinizing the experiences in a net and the variable efficacy of these devices for minimizing the transformation of information as it is passed by messages around the net. Is

there a "minimal" relationship between the two? My hunch is that the two are related in the following way:

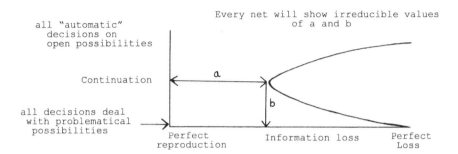

63. Routinization, the psychological likelihood of outcomes, and information loss.
64. Problem: Given a two person net. What are the operations that will reduce the state to the complete extinction of activity? i.e., confusion, anomie.
65. Problem: The game of "Schlagspiel," characterized by the properties (1) that if the players play by the rules, they must form coalitions in order to survive in the game even though they will not be able to trust the persons with whom they form coalitions, (2) the power of a player is a function of the distribution of power among the other players, and (3) the configuration of power positions under the conditions of no coalitions and play oriented to furthering one's self interest alters with each play. Problem is to explore the devices that make continuous play possible.
66. If the domain of constancy is an empty set, no information, eidetic or material, can be drawn from a message.
67. Insofar as we can manipulate the factors that condition the order of possibilities so as to remove them from constant to variable status: we have in each such manipulation a condition for increasing the noise character of a message.
68. At the extremes of either randomnization of possible outcomes or the complete determination of the situation of outcomes, there is no error. Theorems here relating Role structures and the phenomena of adult socialization.

69. The communicant is always in some measure confused. That is, he is always in a world that is in some respects without meaning for him. Theorems here relating the conditions of his make-up and the conditions of the net under which noise in a given amount makes a difference, as well as the problem of finding the devices that can be used to reduce or magnify this amount.

70. Every net will have devices particular to it that are oriented to the maintenance of interpersonally valid definitions of the situation. Inventory them.

71. The clinical symptoms of anxiety are positively correlated with the variability of any one or any set of criteria of organization.

72. The failure of any one or any set of criteria of organization implies the failure of all. Test.

73. At the point of the failure of any one or any set of criteria of organization, there is a cessation of activity. Explore procedures for inducing failure.

74. The variability of any one or any set of criteria of organization is positively correlated with the noise character of a message. Test.

75. No information can be obtained from messages received under the condition of the failure of any one or any set of criteria of organization. Test.

76. Re: role theory and role theories: what findings on bodily experiences and concept formation; what findings from developmental psychology on experiential priority of values of Role constructs; what findings from clinical psychopathology re: relations of values of role constructs.

77. Comparison of the grounds and consequences of incongruity in various attitudes. Comparison of the Role structures in the experiences of humor and indignation. Structural constraints operative in the natural attitude against neutrality of view with regard to the fall of events. Structural conditions of a net under which the possibilities of experience acquire equal-moment in place of crucial status, particularly with regard to socially defined categories of human action and socially validated classifications of motives.

78. Test of the proposition that the road to anomie will be found in the destruction of the structures of the natural attitude and not in the destruction of the attitudes dependent upon it. The relevance of this rule to the theoretical problem of hierarchies of value and relevance.

79. The structural and operational characteristics of identity classification schemes (e.g., socially defined status hierarchies, job classifications, reference groupings, etc.).

80. The relevance of these characteristics in point 79 to sociologically defined status orderings. The devices for handling socially defined behavioral data that is incongruous to these socially defined identity classifications. The constraints that the role construct values place upon socially valid and invalid social judgments in assessing the deviations from these expectations that are organized by those identity classifications. "Social realism" (in this regard) as it is found at various points in a sociologically defined status ordering. See Honigsheim's work on the structural relevance of social philosophies—nominalism as a philosophy of the socially disinherited; idealism based on the pragmatic concerns of everyday life as a philosophy found in the middle class. Problem to devise a list of the characteristics of each of these philosophies to determine incidence by class. Kurt Wolff for bibliography and comment. Review Weber and Mannheim on the Utopian mentality. Sources in the social structure of crime reform movements for further info; differential incidence of moral indignation for political, sexual, bodily assault, and crimes against property. Also examine popular support of Eisenhower for president in re: moral grounds of attitudes toward permanence and change. Examine devices and difficulties that publicity agents for large scale businesses have in selling the moral leadership of big business. Compare bureaucrats, politicians, businessmen, military men (socially defined) as vessels of good and evil. The relevance in this regard of the "clean sweep" and the "need for a change" as motivations in ritual definition of the situation.

81. What is there in the literature on clinical psychopathology with regard to the invariance of role structures, the biographical determinants of such invariance, and the theory of the "trauma."

82. Look up clinical and experimental literature re: the operations for inducing "destruction" of these structures.

83. Experimental test of Scheler's theory of shame for light on the problem of the actor's discretion in the adoption of the conditions under which a proposition holds.

84. Theorems that are possible under the assumption that the structures of the natural attitude are not subject to adoption by a communicant according to his free discretion.

85. Elaborate the list of related values of constructs as theorems. Compare with what one would have to say using Parsons's pattern variable scheme. Possible source of a series of critical experiments.

86. Analysis and experimental test of the structural conditions of the social affects: indignation, disgust, guilt, enthusiasm, boredom, apathy, etc.

87. Message work, feed-back, and meaning-investment as operations whereby the state of the Role-Order specifications is changed through time. Theorems that this conception makes possible.

88. For the case of the natural attitude and only for this case, those operations have the greatest probability of occurrence that involve the minimal amount of reorganization of the socially validated realities depicted in the order. Theorems here.

89. Examination of the literature on persons in extreme situations for inventories re: the nature of routinization, the factors that disrupt routine, and the devices for effecting routinization.

90. Theorems drawing on point 88 re: persons sociologically characterized for whom perspectival changes occur gradually and in small amounts; those for whom changes occur abruptly and in large amounts.

91. What are the structural differences between situations in which "participation in the decision" does and does not produce the effect of acceptance of innovation?

92. Suggest power as a problem for study as focus for the tasks of developing a vocabulary to handle net-work factors, for finding the uses and dead ends in the scheme presented above, as well as for the usual purposes involved in a study of this phenomenon. *Power will be defined as the probability that communicant A can by his communicative work so alter communicant B's definition of his situation as to restrict B's alternatives of conduct to those that B desires.* Since the social relationships are conceived to be dialectical in nature, the power [manuscript ends here in midsentence at the end of a manuscript page].

Appendix 1
Memo #1, Organizational
Behavior Project (Undated)

A Statement of the Problem of Communicative Strategies in Self-Maintaining Systems of Activity

This paper is the first in a series that will be concerned with inventing some theory to handle the nature and effects of communicative strategies in self-maintaining systems of activity. It is limited to the presentation of those ideas that will serve as a point of departure for the tasks of theorizing that lie ahead.

I. Remarks on the Problem of Social Order

The problem of the relevance of communicative strategies in self-maintaining systems is one facet of sociology's central object of study: the problem of social order. Empirically, the problem of social order consists for the observer of describing the first order determinants of the characteristics of statistical regularities of normatively governed activities.

Analytically, the problem has been variously portrayed. Karl Deutsch's paper at the forthcoming seminar on "Problems of Model Construction" will discuss the variety of such portrayals that have been used in the past and that are currently available.

Two analytical views of the problem can be summarily presented here. Each stems from the work of Max Weber though with somewhat different readings. Each provides a formulation at two "levels"; the first we shall refer to as the "level" of *de facto* action; the second as the "level" of the "premises of conduct."

The level of *de facto* action is reached by making two assumptions and thereby excluding two sets of considerations from problematical view. These follow:

(1) A set of invariant definitive characteristics of the actors are assumed.
(2) The assumption is made that the method of understanding works between the actors in the system.

At this level the observer's attention is paid to the regularities of activity. He attempts to explain "permanence and change" by a theory that deals only with those conditions of the system other than the ones that we have indicated in these two problem areas.

The level of the "premises of conduct" is constituted by bringing these considerations into central problematical view.

The analytical problem of order appears differently at each "level"; and for the two theories that we are concerned with, the analytical portraits differ again within these "levels." The theorists responsible for these formulations are Talcott Parsons and Alfred Schuetz.[1]

At the *de facto* level the analytical problem of order as Parsons conceives it is the problem of the structural conditions of a system of activity under which normatively oriented patterns of activity continue to show systematic character. The functional prerequisites of the system are first order problems of action (frequently though misleadingly referred to as the "goals" of the system). The structural features of the system are conceived of as conditions for activities that serve as solutions to these problems in the sense that their character as solutions permits the observer to make assessments of the probability that the system's characteristics will remain unchanged or will alter. The eventuality is provided of an assessment of the ultimate survival of the system.

At the *de facto* level the analytical problem of order as it can be drawn up out of the writings of Schuetz is the problem of conceiving the structural conditions

---

1. [Editor's Note: Garfinkel was a close friend of Schutz and uses the German spelling of his name throughout these manuscripts. In the interests of preserving the character of these early manuscripts and preserving their historical flavor as much as possible, spelling and other matters of style have been left in their original form.]

of a system of normatively oriented activity under which the activities maintain the structural conditions under which activity occurs that maintains the structural conditions under which it occurs etc. The functional prerequisites of the system so depicted are first order effects that are conceived to be logically prerequisite to the notion of the systemic character of the activities that maintain the structural conditions under which they occur.

At the level of the "premises of conduct," the analytical problem of order as Parsons sees it is the problem of the conditions of the actor's make-up under which his actions as part of a system of normatively governed activity are maintained in their systematic character. At this same level the problem of order for Schuetz is the problem of the conditions of the actor's make-up under which his actions as part of a system of normatively governed activity maintains the conditions of the actor's make-up.

The problem of studying the relevance of communicative strategies to large scale systems of activity consists in the first instance, at least, of selecting between these two representations as well as between the kinds of assumptions that we want to make in defining the central set of problematical considerations. I prefer the Schuetzian formulations because they promise a way of handling the problem of introducing the time variable into the treatment of a system of activity.

II. The Rationale of Action Categories

Because the term "communicative strategy" is a construction that is found in a vocabulary of action although it does not mean the same thing as the term action, it may help matters if we establish a context for our later points by first reviewing briefly the methodological rationale as well as the definitions of a few of the more familiar action categories.[2]

In the view that I have come to use, the task of presenting a vocabulary of action consists of laying down the rules by which the observer is to go about the business of transforming those signals that he witnesses through his vocabulary of "cues" and that can be referred for their origin to a bodily defined other person to the data of behavior. According to this view, the observer does not perceive signals and he does not describe signals. He describes the interpreted

---

2. [Editor's Note: There is a margin note at this point referencing the issues of negative entropy, G. A. Miller, Shannon and Weaver, and rules—all issues he will address in Memo #3.]

signal; his empirical perceptions are interpreted signals. Under this view the objective character of an event of behavior is found not in the signal but in the sense that a witness, any witness, scientist or otherwise makes of the signal. Signals are not the contents of perception; they are no more than the conditions of the observer's perceptions. Their contents are found in their meanings. The observer's empirical world is thus a normatively constituted one.

This implies that the observer interested in empirical research is constantly engaged in the task of constructing, testing, validating, altering, and maintaining an empirically possible world, possible in the sense that the objects that are portrayed in terms of the events that specify them are constructed on the basis of the considerations that govern the observer's perceptual behavior. For the observer these considerations are found in the basic and procedural rules of science, in the rules of the sociological attitude, in the observer's stock of empirical knowledge, and in the interpretive principles that comprise his theories. The sociologically empirical world as an organized set of possibilities of experience is, like the actor's empirical world, an order of possible experiences that an "attitude" or "perspective" in orienting these possibilities, orders.[3]

Its properties of arrangement and content are determined by the specifications of the constructs that specify the attitude that orients these possibilities. The vocabulary of events that specify a scientifically possible world consists of empirical constructions. Their sole function is to present to that observer whose actions are governed by the rules of the scientific attitude a restricted frame of experienceable possibilities. When these possibilities are modified by the appropriate qualifying conditions of standard time and place, they can be ordered to statements that describe an expected and reproducible course of actual events that the observer will experience if he reproduces the conditions that these statements propose. His empirical laws are no more than descriptions of expected and reproducible sequences of experiences. His analytical laws tell him no more than how he may legitimately order any set of empirical constructs.

Under this view a set of empirical constructs do not describe the world; they *are* the world. There is no reality beyond them since the ultimately and irreducibly real world is found in the perceived object and not in the signal. This holds for both actor and observer, regardless of whether the empirical construct is a scientifically adequate one or not. The dated Judgment Day of the Seventh Day

---

3. [Editor's Note: There is a margin note here that mentions in particular the equation $O = e(p_n)$, the information equation that he also mentions in the last paragraph and which will be elaborated in Memo #3. The new term in this margin note is O. O = order.]

Adventist is as much an empirical construction and a specification of the world for the Seventh Day Adventist as the physiologist's graph with its coordinates of blood sugar level and rate of pancreatic secretion is for the physiologist and empirical portrait of his sympathectomized cats. Hence a construction like "a movement of the arm" or "a gesture of greeting" or "a symptom" is ontologically irreducible. The construction is not an approximation to something beyond it; there is no question here of a pie that may be cut in many ways, but rather the pie is found in the act of cutting. Unfortunately for Man's peace of mind, his constructed world is forever at the mercies of a Nature that is transcendental to Man's best constructions. We assume a Nature that is deaf, dumb, and blind with reference to the meanings of these constructions.

Under certain conditions, as for example under certain properties of these constructions, and properties of the rules for testing and manipulating them and for the "worlds" of certain roles or perspectives, the probability is high that an experiencer can experience surprise, one variety of surprise being error. And that's the Big Rub. Borrowing usage from Ames, Cantril, etc., Man "assumes" a world, and hopes for the best.[4]

The terms "behavior" and "action" must be regarded as terms that are peculiar to the investigative vocabulary of the scientific observer. This reservation is necessary because the agents being studied have their own vocabularies of behavior and action. They have their own notions as to what it is that they witness behavior-wise, where they see it, what is responsible for its appearance, in a word, their own worlds with their properties of construction, their own procedures of definition, judgment, test, alteration, maintenance, etc. For our purpose it is a point of crucial importance that these principles employed by the agent show upon examination that they differ in most remarkable respects from the attitudes and modes of idealization that the scientific observer employs with reference to the "same material." Like the actions that the observer engages in, in constructing a sociologically empirical world, the agent's construction procedures have the status of data and require explanation in the same way that action requires explanation. The problems that are involved in maintaining the distinction between these two vocabularies we shall refer to as the problem of "parallel vocabularies." In later papers we shall take up this problem in detail.[5]

---

4. [Editor's Note: There is a margin note here referencing eight examples.]

5. [Editor's Note: A margin note says: "illustrate from crim lectures." Garfinkel was teaching a criminology course at Princeton and wrote the outline for a "crim" textbook while he was there.]

Whatever else we may come to mean by the terms "action" and "behavior" one thing stands: these terms designate the empirical data that we shall be dealing in. We hold as a matter of methodological principle that all those statements and only those statements that describe behaviors or actions or that are reducible to statements that describe behaviors or actions are to be counted statements of sociologically empirical fact. We hold such questions as "What is man?" or "What is society?" in their substantive sense to be unanswerable.

What is meant by these terms "behavior" and "action"?

III. A Short and Nasty Vocabulary of Action

Conceive the dimensions of standard time and physical location. A person or persons, and this includes the observer, defined bodily by any further set of criteria that we shall leave temporarily unspecified, comprises within the space-time coordinates what we shall refer to as a "behavioral field." A *behavior* is any alteration of this behavioral field. This includes the "mere" temporal difference between two states of the field.

In making clear what is meant by action, we need to say first what is *not* meant by action. The term "action" is not used in the sense of the actus-status distinction. Nor do we mean action in the sense of behavior, nor do we mean it in the sense of that redundancy "meaningful behavior" (since all behavior is meaningful in the moment of the observer's recognition). We most certainly do not mean anything like "psychical activity" in the sense of the "psychic functions" about which the 19th century act psychologists spoke.

Rather, we are referring to an order of empirically irreducible categories that result from the transformations of behavioral categories according to the rules that the observer's theories provide. Alterations that the observer finds in the behavioral field such as gestures, talk, locomotions, posture, facial contortions, and so on, are transformed into the categories of what Parsons has referred to as sequences of "impulse-object structures" or what I have referred to as sequences of "noesis-noema structures" and what in not so plain English should be called the structures of experience and thing experienced, intention, thing intended, etc.

It is this transformation process that we shall refer to as the observer's task of "understanding" in a "motivationally relevant" sense what the other person is saying and doing.

What is this transforming operation?

The observer's task in constituting his data within the categories of action does not lie in asking what occurs to man as a psychophysical unit, but, following Schuetz,

> does lie in seeking out what attitude he adopts toward these occurrences and his steering of his so-called responses.
>
> Meaning . . . is not a quality inherent to certain experiences emerging within our stream of consciousness but is the result of an interpretation of a past experience looked at from the present Now with a reflective attitude. As long as I live *in* my acts, directed toward the objects of these acts, the acts do not have any meaning. They become meaningful if I grasp them as well circumscribed experiences of the past, and therefore in retrospection. Only experiences that can be recollected beyond their actuality and which can be questioned about their constitution are, therefore, subjectively meaningful.

If we ask for the meaning of a person's conduct in the sense of the scientific meaning of the person's conduct, then we must look to the observer to furnish it. Max Weber's definition of action as behavior with a meaning attached to it would do for us with this proviso: it is the observer who does the attaching and not the person whose behavior is being observed. It is the observer who experiences the act in reflection; *his* categories are the things that make these behaviors "well circumscribed experiences of the past"; and he grasps them as they are recollected "beyond their actuality"; and *he* questions their constitution. The observer's categories (in the form of his empirical and analytical types) together with the procedures that he uses in applying them are designed to effect nothing else than exactly this result of "attaching a meaning."

The operation for transforming a behavioral category into a category of action consists of the following. Given a behavior. To realize a category of action it is necessary that the conditions of the actor's Role be specified (we are using Role in a special sense and will discuss it during the meeting—meanwhile the term "perspective" will do[6]) and that order of possible experiences to which the behavior is oriented be specified such that the effect of the behavior for the actor is to test, alter, or maintain this order of experiences. (Read

---

6. [Editor's Note: There is a long discussion of the conception of Role and Garfinkel's issues with it in the 1948 manuscript to which readers should refer on this point. One of his main objections to Role is that it references the whole person, rather than the identified actor in a given situation. But, there are other objections. Garfinkel appears to be using Role in this memo as a matter of convenience—in the same way that other conventional ideas are made use of—with the special proviso that he means "perspective."]

as synonymous with "order of experiences" the term "definition of a situation"; read also, "social theory"; read also, but carefully, "order of organized expectations"—carefully since many possibilities of experience that are part of this order to do not have the character of expectations). In making these specifications the transforming operation has been performed.

The conditions of Role limit the range of alternative meanings that the observer can assign to the behaviors. In this sense these Role conditions place limits upon the ways that a set of possibilities may be ordered. (In this sense they *constitute* an order of possibilities.) At the same time they limit also the devices that the actor may use to interpret the feedback effects that arise through the fact that the actor experiences his own behaviors as he behaves. Further, an experience that is governed in its course by an order of possibilities of experiences will in the nature of its being experienced in occurrence alter the order that regulates it.

We say then that any experience that serves the effect of maintaining the conditions under which it occurs while simultaneously altering the order that regulates its course will be known as an action.

Insofar as experiences can be shown to serve these two effects their "motivationally relevant" meanings have been assigned to them and they are referred to as actions.

Neither the term "behavior" nor "action" has made any reference to purpose. We explicitly exclude the assumption that all behavior or action is purposive. Also, we count the view erroneous that actor, norms, means, and ends are apodictic to conception of action.

Action may be overt or covert. Overt action will be known as *conduct*. Overt action that is regulated by an expectation of timing will be known as *purposive conduct* or *performance*. We shall use the term *working act* synonymously with performance to accent an important property of all performances, namely, their *gearing* into the world through bodily movements. Temporarily, we shall residually define *expressional conduct* as all overt action that is not regulated by an expectation of timing. (Actually expressional conduct may be explicitly defined as overt action that is regulated only by an order of because-of motives, but the task of clarifying the meaning of "because-of" would lead us so far afield as to risk snapping entirely the principle thread of this presentation that is already badly stretched.)

We distinguish several types of covert action. This list does not exhaust the range of types. Covert action for which there is a projected plan but no expectation of timing (i.e. no intention to realize the plan, the expectation of timing being the observable property that makes the concept of intention to realization empirically manageable) will be referred to as *fantasy*. Covert action in which there is neither a projected plan nor an expectation of timing will be known as *day dreaming*. Covert action, in which regardless of a projected plan and an expectation of timing, the sequences are not controlled by pragmatic modes of attending to an order of possibilities, will be known as *dreaming*. Covert action that is regulated by a projected plan and the intention to realize the plan will be known as *thinking*.

Any action that is oriented in its course to an identified other as a controlling element in the experimental scheme (or "definition of the situation" or "order of possible experiences") will be known as a *social action*. A social action can be overt or covert. By the term *social relationship* is meant the probability as the observer assigns it than action will be oriented to and identified other as a controlling element in the experiential scheme. It is thus possible to speak of *one-sided and reciprocal social relationships*.

Where we find that the actor invests the *ordering* of possible experiences with moral requiredness, that is, where he can be said to regard what he has experienced in the past, is experiencing, or will experience in the future as sanctioned by some ultimate rationale for its occurrence, we shall say that the order has been legitimated, and will refer to the order that he orients as a *legitimate order*. Following Weber at least long enough to get some work under way in the matter, we shall say that such requiredness may be achieved through the authority of tradition, of revelation, or legality, and of rational belief in a metaphysical first principle. A legitimate order then is an organized set of possibilities of experience, oriented by the actor and furnished by him with rationale of some ultimate authority.

The probability that an action will be oriented by an actor to the belief in the existence of a legitimate order will be known as the *validity of an order*.

IV. The Concept of Communication

To make this concept capable of bearing up under thoroughgoing criticism would require that we prepare its introduction by an excursion into the various meanings of "Time" as a structure that is constitutive of experience. There are three such constitutive "structures": duration, phenomenal time, and standard or clock time. The necessity of handling them will only be implied in this brief display of wares; the rest we'll leave to the discussion of this paper.

The various ways in which the term "communication" is currently used seem to have an important characteristic in common: generally, a distinction is intended between communication and action. Definitions of communication in common use designate something like the transmission of verbal, written, or gestural messages, with this notion acquiring various degrees of refinement by placing the phenomenon of message transmission into a context of structural arrangements. Simon has summarized this formulation in describing the problems attendant on phenomenon of communication as those of who says what to whom, when, where, and why.

I do not mean to debunk the distinction nor to debunk the value of the questions that are possible in the who, what, when school. Because the whole area is a new one, simplicity is not only necessary but virtuous. I do mean however to disregard this usage.[7]

A distinction that seems at first glance to keep apart things that need to be kept apart, appears at closer glance to maintain a distinction at the cost of clabbering up the phenomena that each is intended to accent in its handling.

In the view that we shall be attempting to elaborate the terms communication and interaction do not mean the same thing.[8] Nor will it be our view that they chart different aspects of some phenomena. Rather they are conceived as *constitutive* of two different orders of phenomena such that in conceiving of a communicative system one has of formal necessity excluded the possibility of treating it as a system of activity, and in treating it as a system of activity, one has of necessity excluded treating it as a communicative system. There are specific operations by which a system is transformed to show one concrete face or the other, there being no concrete phenomenon that stands beyond the system of categories that constitute these phenomena as sociological events to begin with.

It should be obvious, though it may pay nevertheless to point out, that because we may choose to study a system of activity that we are not barred from simultaneously treating the study site with reference to questions relevant to the study of a communicative system. Most certainly nothing is implied by way of invidiously comparing the two treatments.

---

7. [Editor's Note: This form of disclaimer is typical of Garfinkel's approach to conflict. In discussing positions with which he disagrees he usually says that he does not mean to debunk or criticize them—but, as in this case, he will disregard them. But, as he will say in the next sentence, he thinks they are "clabbering up" the phenomena they are intended to accent. In fact, he is very critical.]

8. [Editor's Note: This next section is a bit confusing. Garfinkel appears to be presenting his own position. But, what he is doing is presenting a version of the *de facto* approach—and that is not his approach.]

A set of behaviors received their accent as a communicative system through the nature of the assumptions we make about the actor. Those assumptions follow.

1. We conceive the actor as a signal generator and as a signal receiver. (We shall refer to signals through the use of the psychologist's vocabulary of "cues.") Beyond this the actor is conceived as so constructed that the signals that are generated feedback into the generating system as they are generated. Diagramatically this may be represented as follows:

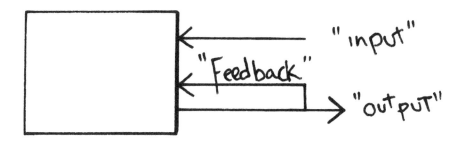

The characteristics of the generated and received signals are conceived to be determined by the biological characteristics of the nervous system.

2. We conceive that the actor is forever experiencing. We do not recognize that the question of how experience is possible in the first place for our actor is an unanswerable question. There are only the questions of what he experiences, of what properties of organization his experiences show, of how they succeed each other, when they occur, the conditions under which he will have a particular experience, etc. but that he experiences and experiences continually is our second assumption.

3. Experience uses up energy. "Energy" is intended only in its literal biological sense. The energy we have in mind is the energy depicted in biological measurements. The property of this energy that interests us is its fund-character; the fact that experiencing consumes a portion of it, although the fund may be replenished. This assumption is made in order to allow us to correlate biological facts with behavioral ones. This energy is not causal to behavior nor is it conceived of *in any way* as an impellant of activity. It has no motivational status whatever. Perhaps we can illustrate its status with the metaphor of the radio circuit.

Suppose we say that our actor is like a radio circuit. The characteristics of the circuit would be determined by the characteristics of the tubes, resistors, the wiring, and so forth. However, the battery would be included in the system as a source of electrical output, certain values of which output stood in certain factual correlation with the organizational features that the system exhibited. While these organizational features could be changed by changing the wiring or by varying the nature of the signals, etc. they could also be altered by running the battery down. This then is the point we want to underline; that our actor experiences but that the organization of his experiences depends not only upon what we specify in our behavioral constructs but depends also upon the availability of energy. This is not the same as saying that our actor is to be conceived of as a biological organism, but it is the same as saying that no biological fact is to be ruled out from having organizational relevance for the structuring of experiences simply because it is a biological fact. Neither is it to be given logical priority over behavioral facts. We mean only that biological facts are subject to the same rule of relevance as behavioral ones, i.e. that biological events and behavioral events to be counted as relevant to the phenomena under study must not vary independently of variations in the phenomena. In fact, it would mark a major advance in the discipline if respiration rates or brain waves rather than the clumsy devices obtaining answers to questions could be used to indicate the structure of time perspective.

4. We conceive of our actor as an *animal symbolicum,* to use Cassirer's phrase, (though not Cassirer's usage). This assumption states that our actor is a perceiver who encounters a world of objects through a never ending process of "seeing," "interpreting,"—he is in Burke's phrase "a critic." All objects are for our actor intended objects. Also, under certain conditions of his make-up an experience for him will be an experience of a *something.*

When dealing with objects, he deals with them in terms of their significances for him; such treatment that he affords them he affords in terms of their significances. The world "exists" for him which is to say that the objects he encounters and accounts as existent, real, objective in various ways, as objects of fantasy, of scientific theory, of the dream, of practical affairs have various "modes of Being," or simply put, are of interest to him in ways that differ with variations in Role. He treats an object in accordance with its "mode of Being," i.e. as a unity of meanings.

Stated otherwise, this assumption states that the actor is to be conceived of as a signal transformer. He transforms signals into data. The objects of his world, as unities of meaning, are experienced by him in terms of and only in terms of the data he uses to specify them. His experience of a table is conceived to be not an experience of cues of color, shape, pitch, loudness, etc. but is the experience of a table which may have as the specifications by which he realizes it as a real table the data-specifications of color, shape, position, rights of disposal, hereditary acquisition, and so on. In a later paper we shall take up the theory of the treated object. (Under certain rather rare conditions, conditions that are very difficult to experimentally induce, he will respond to the signal itself rather than respond to his interpretation of the signal.)

Now to return to the figure above. Procedurally speaking there is nothing in the rules of scientific method to prohibit the attempt to correlate signal input with signal output. However, allowing for intervening transformation processes within the "black box" helps predictive matters a great deal. In dealing with systemic order at the *de facto* level, certain constant values of this "intervening variable" are assumed, while attention is addressed to correlations of *data* input and output.

But in order to learn what the most useful kinds of things are for us to conceive that we are holding as invariants, and of course in order to investigate the nature of these signal transforming processes, it is necessary that we represent this "black box" through the use of a set of constructs supplying with them certain operations and a set of rules for combining the constructs under these operations. The result would be a theory of the actor, or, to use a popular term, an "analytical model" of the actor.[9]

Even though there is available a warehouse-full of black-box theorems found in the various theories of personality, there are strictly speaking only two vocabularies that even begin to approximate a theory of the actor: I refer to the theories of Freud and Hull. Even these, however, have properties as their construction, though we shall not go into them here, that reduce their usefulness for our purposes.

Enough literature is available from clinical and experimental studies to permit at least initial specification of these constructions, their operators, and the rules for employing these operators. We'll touch on some of these constructions when we later take up the topic of general areas of research that are relevant to communicative strategies. Role theories will be considered at greater length in a later paper. For the present we shall have to content ourselves with the assurance that the "black box" is not without some considerable chinks.

A brief recapitulation. Our actor is conceived of as a signal generator and signal receiver. These signals are generated and received in sequences, "bit by

---

9. [Editor's Note: Again this is a critical comment, and Garfinkel is very critical of the black box, or analytical model of the actor. But, here it is almost presented as a useful method—unless one reads very closely. The criticisms will come out more in the two following memos.]

bit." He experiences the signals he generates as he generates them. The other party to the exchange who receives may experience them simultaneously or with a time lag. Each transforms these signals into the data of conducts such that he realizes a point of information, a request, a command, a specification of the other person's conduct, and so on. Both are conceived of as experiencing and responding to their interpretations of the signal, though the problem remains of stating the conditions of the actor's make-up and his relationships with others under which this is so, since as we pointed out our actor is capable of responding only to the signal itself.

Our first and important definition: *an interpreted signal will henceforth be known as an expression.* There are three dimensions, all of which must be accounted for in a determinate description of an expression. These dimensions are:

1. The thing or things that the signal signifies. We shall refer to these as the designata of the signal. Again, only under rare conditions of social life does a signal have a single designatum.

2. The "vehicular" character of the signal, i.e. the kind of signal—the sensory media which are the conditions of the receiver's perception. We need to point out that the signal does not "convey" the designata; all designata are assigned to signals through the transforming operations that occur in the black box. This is stated as a matter of methodological principle. Again, we reserve for later papers the assumptions that can be made to loosen the rigidity of this requirement so as to speed the observer's tasks. In talking of persons we shall refer to the vehicular character of signals as the person's "style" or "manner." Style and designata are both analytically and empirically separable. We promise again that in later papers we shall go into the problem of the varieties of combinations and the conditions under which certain combinations are institutionally prescribed.

3. The time specification of the signal, by which we are referring to three things: specifications of duration, and specifications of position or sequential location.

A second crucial conception: *the expressional field.* Our actor stands without ever a moment's escape in a sea of signals that are forever pressing in from the outside. Cues of brightness, hue, warmth, cold, pressure, movement, smell, loudness, etc. Again we make a promise that in later papers we shall consider the big problem of the actor as an "organizer." For the moment we shall simply say that the regularities he experiences are normatively constituted by him and let it go at that. Now this sea of signal material as it stands organized at a point in standard time by our actor and including his own body as a signal source for him will be known in the properties of organization that it shows as a set of sensorial specified objects. For ease of reference such a set will be referred to as an *expressional field at time-n.*

An expression alters the expressional field by the "amount" of its occurrence. The expressional field undergoes unceasing alteration by the amount of expressional activity in it. Because our actor is invested with a memory system, it is necessary to say that an expressional field is altered merely by the passage of time. Hence silences are included in the expressional field.[10]

We shall have to leave for later consideration the task of investigating and describing the properties of the expressional field. Organization and transformability are two that immediately recommend themselves. Whether or not it is temporally irreversible, however—a definite property of the actor's definition of a situation—is not clear. At any rate we have here another problem for future treatment.

Any alteration of the expressional field, i.e. the difference between two states of the expressional field separated by any arbitrary interval of standard time will be known as *a communication* or *a message.* By the general term *communication* we are referring to the alterations of an expressional field.

Because of the redundancy involved, we shall not speak of "communicative actions" but will speak instead of "communicative tactics" or, synonymously and interchangeably, of "communicative devices."[11] Those expressions that the actor orients toward the anticipated alterations of the identified other person's definition of the situation will be know as *communicative tactics.* "Definition of the situation" does not mean the same thing as "expressional field" since much of what comprises a situation of action for the actor, i.e. many of the objects that he is treating and that are relevant to a course of treatment are transcendental to the expressional field as it is constituted at any moment. To state it again: insofar as the actor controls the designata, "style," and temporal ordering of a sequence of his expressions by his assessment of the alterations of the identified other person's definition of the situation we shall speak of the expression or the sequence of expressions as communicative tactics.

There are communicative tactics that are governed by a teleological principle. That is to say, the alterations of the expressional field may be governed

---

10. [Editor's Note: Given the relevance of pauses and silences to later work with Sacks ([1964–74] 1996) and developed by Sacks, Schegloff, Jefferson, and Pomerantz (1974), this early mention of silences is important.]

11. [Editor's Note: As CA developed it made use of the notion of "devices."]

by the projected plan and an intention to realize the plan. (A projected plan is to be conceived of as a set of possibilities of experience that rules of conduct orders with reference to each other according to their specifications of socially standard time. And the intention to realize the plan we already indicated is nothing else than an expectation on the actor's part with regard to the timing of experienced events.) Where the alterations of the expressional field are governed by a projected plan and the intention to realize the plan we shall refer to the configuration of the three as they stand at any given point in time as the actor's *communicative strategy.* Alterations that are governed by an expressional principle of conduct will be known in the configuration of principle and alterations as the actor's *communicative design.*

We have deliberately omitted any reference in the general definition of communicative strategy to the property of calculation in the sense of decision between alternative possibilities made prior to the moment of encountered alternatives. In this respect our sense of strategy differs from the von Neumann and Morgenstern definition which runs:

> Imagine that each player ... instead of making each decision as the necessity for it arises, makes up his mind in advance for all possible contingencies; i.e. that the player begins to play with a complete plan; a plan which specifies what choices he will make in every possible situation, for every possible actual information which he may possess at that moment, in conformity with the pattern of information which the rules of the game provide for him that case. We call such a plan a strategy.[12]

What these authors refer to as a strategy, we shall refer to as a *plan.* However, I leave the naming decision open for the group's considered judgment in the matter.[13]

So much for basic vocabulary.

Our most immediate need is for a descriptive vocabulary of communicative tactics and strategies. I intend as an early task to examine various sources such as trial protocols, books on debating, recordings of precepts that are available at the Study of Education, etc. to build up some sensitization in the matter.

---

12. John von Neumann and Oskar Morgenstern, *Theory of Games and Economic Behavior* (Princeton: Princeton Univ. Press, 1944), p. 79.

13. [Editor's Note: For information regarding the importance of this idea and its later influence, see, for example, Lucy A. Suchman, *Plans and Situated Actions* (New York: Cambridge University Press, 1987).]

V. Illustrative Communicative Tactics

By way of illustrating what they might at least preliminarily look like, the following have been pulled out of a grab bag full that Kenneth Burke presents in the second volume of his delightful *Attitudes Toward History*.[14] These tactics are commonly found in everyday life. Most of these metaphorical designations are Burke's. Needless to say the metaphors are not intended to debunk the tactic, the situations in which they are used or the persons that use them.

Voting for an essence. A tactic whereby when one is faced with a number of features of an action, an event, a person, a proposition—an object—one feature is selected to stand for the definitive characteristics of the object. One person says of another, "I thought all along that X was such and such, but after he did *that* I saw what *really* was." The tactic is commonly employed in strategies intended to effect elevations or degradations of status.

Casuistic stretching. This is a technique whereby the actor stretches the meaning of a term to the point where it incorporates material that would otherwise challenge the integrity of an experiential scheme. Tool Owners, Incorporated, an organization that was formed during the wave of strikes after the war would have called every person with money in the bank a "Tool Owner" thereby making all [i.e., everyone] capitalists, thereby banishing the distinction in interests between workers and managers. The tactic is commonly used in strategies intended to an orthodox definition of the situation.

Ringeleveo with symbols. It is common to stake out property rights to a symbol. It is also common for the opposition to steal the symbol claiming rightful ownership. Counter stealing may then take place. In academic circles the fight rages over caretaker rights to "fruitful work" and Science. In the market place lines are drawn over the rights to oversee the "common good." The tactic is commonly found in strategies intended to legitimize a definition of a situation.

Consulting the dictionary. This is the practice of fixing the meaning of something, an action for example, by referring the action to a set of meaning—conferring criteria that are external to the context of the action. One is thus able to say,

---

14. [Editor's Note: A similar list appears in the 1948 manuscript, but there Garfinkel does not reference Burke, so this is information about that manuscript as well.]

"You said thus and thus, but what you really meant was such and such." Or, "You treat the other guy badly because you think he's a Jew and believe Jews have all the money, but it says here in this book on prejudice that Jews don't have all the money. You lose because you're prejudiced." The use of Freud in the parlor is an instance of "consulting the dictionary." The tactic is commonly employed in strategies intended to maintain an order of status arrangements.

Do not handle the merchandise unless you intend to buy. Another way of saying that one may lose his right to employ a technique, or voice an opinion, or use a particular item of vocabulary through being required by others to take the responsibility for using them in a certain way or of rendering belief in the remainder of the cluster. The tactic is commonly found in strategies intended to effect estimates of deviation from orthodoxy.

Transcending the opposition. Where the terms of one perspective show a poor fit with the reality of requirements of another, the terms may be renamed at another level where, by withdrawing from the specific, a common basis of agreement may be found. In the course of some fieldwork in a small Texas town I had occasion to interview a leading real estate dealer who was also a staunch Baptist.[15] After a pause in our conversation he commented on my name and asked my religion. I told him I was Jewish. He said in return that he was Baptist. Sensing possible hostility and the loss of a good informant, I observed that we were all children of God. I was attempting a "transcendence." (He wouldn't play. He observed after a pause, "there are still differences.") Transcendence upward and transcendence downward. "Upward" means in the direction of increased value; "downward," in the direction of lesser value. Transcendence upward was prevalently employed during the last war in the propagandistic strategies that were intended to effect a unity of diverse occupational, ethnic, and class interests in the face of a situation invested by the communicants with marked unpredictability and threat. Transcendence "downward" could as easily be referred to as "getting down to brass tacks," "calling a spade a spade," "talking cold turkey," "never mind opinions, let's just deal with the facts." The device is a favorite one of status inferiors addressing status peers and against status superiors. It is often used in strategies intended to devalue the status of the opposition and hence impugn the worth of their portrayals of the situation. Despite the appeal to "facts" the device, in accenting the "getting down to," invokes contrast of a lower with a higher morality, the cold turkey being used to effect ironic comparison. The device thus depends

---

15. [Editor's Note: This refers to the study of Bastrop, Texas, printed here as Appendix 5.]

for its effectiveness upon the validity of those tribal myths by which differences in status worth and status interests are positively sanctioned.

The recent Republican attack on Truman's policies in Korea affords a good example of the things that can go wrong when a transcendence downward is attempted in a fluid status situation. The attack ran into considerable dialectical difficulties in its treatment of Marshall for the Republicans tried a transcendence downward in their promise that the inquiry would dig out the dirt-truth, while on the other hand they could seek to fulfill this promise only after making the forensically necessary though strategically troublesome move of publicly allowing Marshall to enjoy a stature that was indistinguishable from that of a certain old soldier whose explicit claim for immortality as a national hero had recently been honored.

VI. Tactics and Their Functions
of Communication and Control

The problem of describing the operations of a communicative system consists of specifying two functions and only two functions that any communicative tactic is conceived of as performing simultaneously. We shall refer to these as the functions of control and communication.

By the *communicative function* is meant that a tactic in its occurrence alters the communicants' definitions of their situations. By the *control function* is meant that a tactic in its occurrence affects the rate and manner of alteration of the communicants' definitions of the situations. These two effects are postulated effects. The empirical task is that of describing the ways in which these effects operate.

Another way of conceiving the control function is to regard the tactic as a measure by which the alterations of these social definitions of a situation are made to proceed in such a way as to maintain the "congruence" between expectations and memories of accomplished events that are sufficiently approximative of each other to permit continuous activity.

Although tactics perform control functions, they are nevertheless not the only means for control, for the actor is capable of intricate and immensely varied covert interpretive devices that serve immediate control functions. Whether we are speaking of tactics or covert control devices, whatever they are, whereby two effects are achieved, though not necessarily simultaneously: control measures correct for discrepancies between expectations and the memories of the event—this discrepancy will be known as *error*; control measures regulate the discrepancy between a prediction as it stands at any moment in the form of a remaining projected path of activity, and the memory of the accomplished path. This discrepancy will be referred to as *discrepance.*

There is of course no one-to-one correspondence between a communicative tactic and the particular function it serves. As we said every communicative tactic serves both.

The problem of stating analytically the conditions under which a system is self-maintaining is the problem of stating those conditions of a communicative system which determine a flow of tactics which in serving the effects of correcting for error and regulating discrepance maintain the conditions that determine the flow of tactics that in serving the effects maintain the conditions etc., etc.

VII. Areas for Investigation

To return now to the general form of the research problems that later papers will specify as theorems, hunches, needed information, and so on. We take them up by "levels."

(A) Suppose we limit the relevant area of questions by holding for central problematical attention how it is possible for communicants to understand each other, and what must be the conditions of the make-up of the participants under which they can go about the business of making continuous sense of each other. Then the statements that we make about communicative tactics and strategies are governed by the statements about the following things:

(1) The conditions of the actor's "role." The following role dimensions will affect what we have to say about the "success" or "non-success" of communicative strategies. ("Success" and "non-success" are misleading since they appear dichotomous. They're not. Temporarily we'll use "success" to mean a tactic or strategy whereby error is corrected for and discrepance is regulated, either by minimizing it or maximizing it. We'll discuss "regulation" further in meeting.)[16]

---

16. [Editor's Note: There is a margin note here. It says "error here— 'success' does *not* refer to a tactic but to an effect served by—." My speculation is that the attempt to give a "fair" appraisal of a *de facto* approach becomes confusing at points in this manuscript. Garfinkel does not think there can be any real "success" in a *de facto* approach— yet he finds himself describing what success would be for such an approach—then corrects in the margin. This point would have been clarified in the seminar.]

   (a) The actor's time perspective.

   (b) The way in which the actor has identified relevant other persons.

   (c) The way in which the actor is given himself to the relationship

   (d) The fact that the actor orients his conduct to the accomplishment of a projected plan compared with activity undertaken for its own sake.

   (e) The rules that specify the accent of interest to be taken in the objects of treatment, i.e. the ways in which the objects of treatment are "real" for him.

   (f) The mode of attention paid to the organized possibilities of experience.

(2) The actor's definition of the situation seen as an organized set of recollections and anticipations that transcend the immediate sensorily given situation, i.e. the order of accomplished and expected experiences that he orients, or, flatly put, the order or definition of a situation as a memory system.

(3) We noted several times that the participant experiences his actions as he acts, incorporating into his definition of the situation his activities as they occur. We need to know the varieties of these "tactics of incorporation"—i.e. the characteristics of the feedback operator. An unavoidable and grossly neglected problem here is that of the "experiential logics," i.e. the rules that govern the way he goes about making continuous sense of what happens to him.

(B) We can assume that our actors do understand each other and hold the above area as unproblematical, and thus address the *de facto* regularities of communicative tactics while assuming the invariant character of the conditions of the actor's make-up, as we do when we say that we shall speak of the market place with its arrays of actors identified as exchange partners.

In such a case we can turn to such structural characteristics of the system as size, turnover of membership, points of entry and egress, prestige, power, and authority hierarchies, primary and secondary grouping arrangements, etc. etc. and consider these as the conditions of the communicative system whose relevance to communicative strategies are of interest; the following problems come up for investigation:

(1) The conditions of a communicative system as they determine the limits of "successful" communicative strategies.

(2) The conditions of a system under which a given probability of occurrence of various types of communicative strategies can be assigned.

(3) Those conditions under which a set of communicative strategies are relevant to the maintenance or alteration of various major effects of the system,

e.g. production levels, profit margins, "morale," security, and so forth. Or, to phrase the problem another way, the conditions under which a set of communicative strategies serve as pre-requisite solutions to the problems that are first order in their relevance for the probability of the system's "survival."

(4) The ways in which communicative strategies operate in their feedback effects to maintain the conditions that determine their probability of occurrence.

(5) The ways in which communicative strategies operate to alter the characteristics of the system in which they occur.

The papers that follow will attempt to rationalize the leading theoretical ideas of this paper and to further specify the areas of problems by presenting specific questions in these areas in their researchable form. Paranoidly speaking, I plan to have by the Spring deadline further papers on theory; an outline of specific research topics; a set of substantive topics framed in terms of the procedures required to research them and documented with relevant bibliography; a set of papers on new research methods, e.g. the method of paradigmatic game, the method of induced incongruity, the method for transforming protocol material into the actor's definition of a situation; the results of pilot studies; and possibly a progress report on a project recently begun (if it works out) concerned with treating the alterations of the definition of a situation as a formal algebra.[17]

---

17. [Editor's Note: This reference to "treating the alterations of the definition of a situation as a firmal algebra" is another reference to the "e" equation that will be elaborated in Memo #3. The reference to "induced incongruity" is recognizable as an emerging EM strategy.]

Appendix 2
WorkMemo #2,
Organizational Behavior
Project, October 4, 1951

Some Problematical Areas in the Study of Communicative

Part VII, "Areas for Investigation," of Memo #1 is the point of departure for this illustrative display of wares. I've tried a free and easy delivery in the hope that though the members may not buy, they will at least know the kinds of things up for sale.

The memo is made up of two parts. The problems considered under each part are illustrative of the kinds of interests we could have in the events of communication if we consider problematical the conditions of the communicant's make-up and the possibility that communicants understand each other. The first part holds these possibilities as open to question; the second part puts these questions aside and addresses itself to the "de facto" regularities of communicative work. In part I, four variables enter the discussion: role conditions, communicative tactics, definition of the situation, and feed-back.

I

Saying that the conditions of the communicant's make-up are problematical is another way of saying that role conditions are conceived to limit the designata, style, and temporal ordering of the communicant's expressions. The previous memo stated that these expressions are regulated by the communicator's assessment of the alterations that he figures they effect in the other person's definition of the situation. Through the effects of feedback, these tactics affect the role conditions under which they occur simultaneously altering the communicant's definition of his situation that regulates the course of his tactics. I'd like now to rationalize this vision holding the characteristics of designata, style, and temporal ordering as a dependent variable, and asking how this variable would be affected by changing the characteristics of the communicant as well as the communicative net.

Suppose we put together a quick and easy frame for our questions. We'll consider the case of a communicant whose communications are governed by some order of projects that his tactics are designed to realize. (We'll put aside the case where the communicant undertakes communicative work for its own sake.) A communicant so conceived entertains an "expectation of timing." That is, he has taken a "position," so to speak, about the way in which both the communicative events that he generates and the events that others produce can, will or should happen. And in accordance with this expectation of timing, he gears his own communications into the world of outside events. While gearing his own communicative work, he is also engaged in the task of scanning the effects of his communications and altering his course in view of the information that he thus picks up.

Now let me introduce a few "new" terms by way of elaborating the scheme a little. In his recent book, *Language and Communication*, G. A. Miller, in talking about communicative nets suggests that a difference be made between the information of the message and the information that tells how the message has been received. He calls the first "primary information" and the second, "secondary information." Any given message may "convey" both types, though not necessarily.

Further, let's talk about two broad functions of messages, which we'll call the functions of "incitement" and "maintenance." By the function of "incitement" we are referring to the motivating effect of a message. Orders, requests, questions, commands, are obvious examples. Although, of course, any message may serve such an effect. Further, there is no one to one correspondence between a message and the incitement or maintenance effect that it serves.

By the maintenance function I am referring to the effect that a message may have in validating the way in which the communicator or communicant has "structured the situation." For example, the student who comes into my office and requests a reading list not only motivates the possibilities for me of a response to the request, but the fact that he has addressed the request to me is in an important sense a "reminder" that we stand to each other in the relationship of instructor and student. If someone were to entertain doubts about the nature of my situation, I might adduce as proof the fact that the student addressed such a request to me. The maintenance functions of messages can be very subtle, of course, as we go about the business of complicating the nature of the makeup and "language" of the exchanges. Any message may simultaneously serve both functions.

Let us assume that the characteristics of the communicative system can be described with reference to the statistical normality of the conditions and the designata, style, and temporal ordering of the messages that the conditions determine.

It is now possible to see some connections between the nature of the project that the communicator is engaged with, the fact that his tactics are geared to the timing and character of the events he encounters, and the success or failure of the incitement and maintenance functions of these tactics. The role conditions listed on page 18 [p. 245 in this volume] of Memo #1 (other than the condition of the teleological or the expressional principle which governs a course of communicative work that we have explicitly included here), are implied as simultaneously relevant conditions. For example, the role condition contained in the statement that our communicant is engaged in project oriented activity which he intends to realize (the expectation of timing being all that such an "intention" means) is by implication accompanied by a pragmatic mode of evaluating what occurs; it is also accompanied by some specific way that the communicant "feels" himself given to his partner (e.g., in terms of public or private identifying materials); it is accompanied by certain orderings of other persons "around him"—reference groups, for example; and it is accompanied by a set of rules that he follows by which the facets of events he encounters are selected to receive by him their particular accent of interest for him, and so on.

We have here a gadget which can serve us as a Dandy Question Inciter. The list of topics is limited only by the amount of time and imagination we want to spend grinding them out. Let's plug in the Dandy Question Inciter by asking; what are the things that we can do by way of altering the facets of the scheme that will imply alterations in the statistical normality of the characteristics of communicative work, our dependent variable. We shall consider only single operations. Those who like to ask hard questions can permute them at their leisure.

1. The factual nature of communicative work would be badly stretched indeed if we were to portray it as consisting entirely of information output and input. Much of what passes between communicants accords with required

and normal communicative expectations although it consists of what might look like unnecessary, tedious, time-wasting repetitions as far as the task of getting simple workaday tasks accomplished is concerned.

But one of the functions of repetitions (we stuck the identifying tag on it of "secondary information") is that of inciting the return of information with regard to the questions of the communicant of not only "How do you *read* me?" but "How do you read *me*?" The first question is clearly provided for in building repetitions into a mechanical system. The second question is not. Radios, even the smartest radios, have yet to act as if they're ego involved with the targets of their messages. Do what you will, they won't be insulted, and this troublesome feature breaks at least one of the legs of the radio analogy.

There are other functions that such "rationally inefficient" repetitions may serve. Occurring in a fashion typical to a socially defined type of communicator, they may help identify the communicator as a bona-fide group member. In a highly formalized communicative setting, such as a conference of diplomats, for example, they may be a sort of ritual "nonsense" that in being observed permits the auditors better to assess the significance of what is not ritually prescribed communication, since the "nonsense" may identify the communicant as one who is acting in his proper public capacity and hence is to be regarded, in the eyes of his auditors, as responsible in *particular* ways for what he says. In this sense, at least, his auditors may regard him as "knowing what he is doing" and thus the auditors can regulate their own tactics accordingly.

For given status arrangements, and especially from the point of view of superiors looking downward, typical temporal configurations of information and nonsense, for example, may be considered the products of "good character." The inferior who "does not repeat himself" may find himself ordered to the status of an aggressive boor.

Such typical arrangements, of information and nonsense, as they occur within a social order to which the communicants are addressed in their exchanges, may serve the further function of facilitating a settled, or better, a *settling* routine.

At any rate, several questions are suggested. First, what are the typical patterns of information and repetition that are found in various social arrangements? In business and industrial arrangements, it is possible to ask what the economics are of such patterns. Since such patterns take time of the sort that is made up of equal, substitutable and additive intervals, it is possible to assign dollar values to them. The common and dissimilar properties of such patterns found by inter-system comparison is suggested as another illustrative question. The question may be asked of how various kinds of alterations of expected patterns alter the characteristics of communicative work in the net, as well as the conditions of the make-up of communicants in the net.

A question that may be tacked on at every point that we shall be discussing is indicated in the suffix, "within what limits?" That is, assume the organized character of communicative expectations, and allow that our communicants have accessible a repertoire of "discounting devices" through the use of which a certain spread of deviation from the expected can, without alteration of the communicant's perspective, be "normalized" by him. We can then speak of a "tuning range" beyond whose limits the communicant's characteristic treatments of what he experiences from the other person(s) gets altered. (Running throughout all these and the questions that follow is the recurring problem of investigative procedure and experimental design as decisions in these matters hinge on the answers to the questions of appropriate time samplings and ways of inducing effects of long enough duration to allow convincing comparisons.)

2. The questions surrounding the characteristics and effects of socially expected and classified information-redundancy ratios can be repeated with regard to expected *procedures* through which the patterns of information and repetition are delivered. The possible variations here are enormous, so we'll talk only of *what* can be varied.

For example, with regard to the communicative relationships that bear upon the range of alternative operations that a communicator in a system is charged with performing, and for which he must rely upon data input from outside sources for making his choices (to use Morgenstern's phrase, with regard to a communicator's "competences"), it might be the case, procedurally speaking, that he receives information and redundancy from a single source. It might be also that he receives both from a number of sources. It might be that the source(s) of information and the source(s) of redundancy are structurally separated. An unlimited number of possible arrangements are possible.

Further it is possible to group messages of information and messages of redundancy in various temporal orderings, and to vary this in turn by numbers of and segregating arrangements of sources, etc. etc.

Suppose we were to establish initially the normality of the procedures. Any such pattern could then be regarded as subject in its variations to the limits set by the "tuning range," and any such pattern, as we pointed out previously, would be experienced by the communicator as relevant to the social order that he orients, with its arrangements of priority of projects, status hierarchies, reference groups, etc. etc.

A big question now comes up. How are such procedures relevant to the chances of successfully accomplishing the tasks of rationalizing factory and office operations? For example, seen from the top down, a re-arrangement of such socially expected procedures might be recommended as a matter of rational office procedure. "Let's cut out the water fountain," says the manager. "All they do is gather there and gossip, and anyway it's the same gossip day after day." Or the executive might be convinced that he's been writing too many different memos on the same topic, a waste of time. "That's got to stop. They're old enough to read and understand it if I say it once. It'll be once and for all." He may thus leave it to subordinates to interpret his statements. On the basis of what we know about social arrangements, his subordinates, in interpreting his statements, knowingly or not, will be interpreting him.

Now seen from the bottom up, such segregation might be rationalized differently. The segregation might increase the phenomenal distance between the worker and his "boss," but will efficiency rise? This depends. For the increase in phenomenal distance may be conditional of either efficient work attitudes or alienation from efficient work attitudes. If the leader does not repeat himself, but if he is vested by subordinates with the capacity of morally backed infallible judgment, the effect of increasing phenomenal distance may be to validate the subordinate's belief in the legitimacy of the hierarchical arrangement and knowing his place he may fall to it with a will. But a leader who decides not to repeat himself in the face of the fact that the legitimacy of his judgment is under question, may by the decision enhance alienation as the complaint gets built into the worker's vocabulary for defining the nature of his situation that "What the hell do the boys upstairs know or care about us?" This is oversimplified, though it may illustrate the way in which the questions about the properties of communicative input may be viewed in their effects as relevant to the various facets of social structure. It is a way of attacking anew, perhaps, the questions about communicative successes and failures as they are the products of arrangements of open and closed channels up and down.

3. The possible manipulations that can be performed on the time behavior of communications gets us an extremely large number of topics even if we consider the case of only a two "person" net (I use person in quotes to underline the fact that a lecturer addressing an audience, or two corporations, or two individuals, etc. come under the heading of a "two person net." In fact, I'll risk the statement for possible argument, that the overwhelming number of communicative situations are two person nets.)

Consider the following diagram. The diagram presents only the logically possible paths of communications in a two person net. These are designated by letters.

1 and 2 are communicants.

The letters a to f indicate all the logically possible paths of signals.

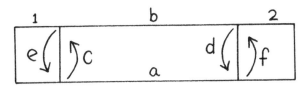

Each path—and all of them are logically independent—can be viewed as a point where eight combinations of the following three kinds of temporal alterations can be introduced, each alteration altering the "normal" properties of the network. (1) We can take a "normal" set of expressions and re-order them as to sequence. We'll call this the *re-ordering* operation. (2) We can take a "normal" set and apply a shift along the time scale of occurrence so as to speed them up or slow them down with reference to the times of occurrence of expressions in other parts of the network. We'll call this the operation of *phasing*. (3) We can alter the interval in which the expression occurs so as to shrink or expand it. We'll call this the *dilating* operation.

This gives us seven *kinds* of alterations for each point, but considering the "normal" as a state, we have eight kinds of configuration. And with six points to combine the eight, we get the figure 8^6, which if one takes the trouble to do the arithmetic gives the figure 262,144 possible configurations of alteration possibilities, each one a topic.

Clearly what we need is for someone to throw a handful of sand into the Dandy Inciter.

Granted that there are 262,144 topics, is there at least *one* to illustrate the kind of information that such investigations might yield? There is and the information it produced is startling and theoretically provocative.

Several years ago—the account was reported in *Time Magazine*—a psychologist at the University of [left blank] played around with the two paths, "a" and "c" by phasing the messages so that the time of occurrence in the path "c" was delayed by a small fraction of a second with reference to the time of occurrence of the message in path "a." He worked this with individual subjects. He used some electronic equipment that had been developed at Fort Monmouth, N. J. (Army Signal Corp Headquarters) where, I am told by an electronic engineer who is employed there, the effect is old stuff. This was the procedure. A pair of earphones was put on the subject—unassorted subjects were used—through which a constant noise signal was introduced. The subject talked into a microphone that fed the signal onto a tape. The distance between the recording head and the playback head for the tape was continuously variable so that the signal output and the feedback signal could be altered in phase along a continuum of zero to quite a long interval. The idea was to isolate the two paths so that the speaker could not hear himself speak except through the signals that he got back through the earphones, the noise cutting out when his voice came through. When output and feed-back were thrown out of phase by minute amounts the subjects showed behavioral changes of intense frustration and a quickly growing and finally uncontrollable rage. The effect was produced even where the subjects had complete prior knowledge of what was going on and even where they had undergone the experience previously.

Were we to limit ourselves to cases of disparity in paths "a" and "c" for individual subjects we'd be hard put to demonstrate the present tactical relevance of such an order of questions to the phenomena of organizational behavior. However, there is a general theorem drawn from some previous theorizing that does make the problem of altering time behavior of communications relevant to the project's interests.

The theorem runs as follows: For any and every role that shows the following properties:

(a) the suspension of doubt that the objects of the world are as they appear;

(b) the assumption of a projected future state with the intention to realize the state by bodily movements that are geared to the nature and timing of outer events;

(c) The assumption of a timing schedule based upon an interpersonally validated scheme of standard time;

(d) a pragmatic mode of attending to the alterations of the situation of action brought about by the communicator's as well as the communicants' bodily movements;

(e) the assumption of a common intersubjective world of communication;

(f) the communicant experiencing himself as given according to some constant disparity between public and private identifying memories.

These are role properties that show up with full prominence and clarity in the work situation of large scale organizations. For roles showing these properties a limit can be stated to the extent of alterations of the time behavior of communications beyond which the properties of organization of the world that is constituted by the role disappear and the probability of continuous activity is reduced to the formal probability of zero. The limits are determined by two things: (a) the repertoire of devices by which the communicator "normalizes" a structural alteration of the net, i.e., the devices by which error can be corrected for and discrepance regulated; and (b) the characteristics of the order of social relationships which serve as conditions under which he can "normalize" to begin with and which set the limits of possible normalizing devices. Offhand I can't think of a better illustration of the ranges of effects, the "normalizing" devices, as well as the structural limits upon these devices that alterations in time behavior of messages induces than those that W. F. Cottrell provides in his article, "Time and the Railroader." I cite this to illustrate the point that the "conditions of understanding" is not a problem in the exquisite minutiae of individual psychology.

We are not quite finished with the discussion of the "time variable." Our scheme points to another kind of time disparity that promises to affect alterations in the typical characteristics of designata, style, and temporal ordering of communications. The first consists of creating a disparity in the kinds of standard time schemata that communicator and communicants employ. Here I am no longer talking about the operations of phasing, re-ordering, and dilation. Rather, I refer to the effects of bringing together various kinds of socially standardized time schemata, schemata that are epistemologically relevant to events in the sense that these schemata are constitutive of the event as a well formed, familiar, and recognizable "categorization" of experiences. Sorokin in the second volume of his *Social and Cultural Dynamics,* and Bateson in a recent letter to the Project in connection with the paper he is preparing for the seminar on model construction make much of the way in which the communicants "punctuate" their experiences with the "grammar" of time, the event being constituted as an event through the time of experience.

An exaggerated illustration may convey what I'm after. We should expect alterations in the typical characteristics of communications if we put a Balinese on a Detroit assembly line.

However, we don't have to go importing Balinese to prove that we have a question. The flow of events is normatively constituted into the "slabs" of the categories of daily life. I invoke the linguistic researches of Benjamin Whorf to make two points: (a) the fact that events are normatively constituted; and (b) the importance of a time schema as the source of the integrals by which a set of possibilities of experience are constituted together through intricate "naming" operations as the specifications of the event.

Now there are marked differences in the way time operates in this regard depending, for example, on psychological characteristics. The anxiety hysteric's use of time in this regard for example is markedly different from that of the compulsive-obsessive. The hysteric tends to relativize his schema, using it and defending it as common currency, whereas the compulsive-obsessive fixes it almost to the point where events stand almost as matters of definition in their requiredness. One is a wastrel in his perceptions of occurrences; the other is so tight that not one thing can occur unless he gives it permission. Both of course have much to learn from the paranoid schizophrenic.

At any rate, we should expect to find these differences present in various mixtures and degrees in any work situation that requires coordination of communications and perspectives. We should also expect to find positional influences in such a system exerting their pressures to "mold" so to speak the "personalities" of the incumbents as, through the ranges of adult socialization that time coordinations effects, one comes to have built into his nervous system the paces and rhythms of the "job atmosphere." Along with the "standardizing" effects for "positional personality" we should find too a whole range of devices by which "slippages" in time schemes between persons are accommodated. I would guess that the least part of the problem of slippage is attributable to matters of bio-physical coordination. I would expect quite a good bit of the unexplained variance to yield to the person's "attitudes toward history." And this touches off another possible topic in this regard, namely that coordinated communication must certainly include a host of devices that serve the effect of informing the communicants of the extent to which they have grasped a definition of the communicative net *that they can assume is common to others.* The relevance of the nature and accuracy of such assumptions to the phenomena of organizational behavior is obvious.

Some further problems are suggested along this same line. For example, the process of rationalizing communicative work may, as it succeeds in "clearing up the channels" also succeed in replacing the efficiencies achieved through the occasional expressions of particularistic interpersonal structures by the efficiencies achieved when one says only what one means, i.e. talks according to the rules of plant operations. This talking according to the language and rules of the plant is frequently considered by managers an ideal to approximate. The machine, for example, except for its expected unexpected balking and breakdowns, communicates no more than is specified as its competence under the rules of efficient production. Those persons who entertain expectations of upward mobility, and who see their personal histories in the industry as proof of the realism of their expectations, should be expected to conform in greater degree to such rational norms of communicative efficiency than those who are otherwise oriented. But one may question the "rationality" of this way of achieving communicative efficiency, for while one may say only what one means, such a communicative flow may buy a simultaneous effect of coordinative fragility, inasmuch as even small deviations from "proper usage" may, because of the rationalizing of the grounds of consensus, render the messages ambiguous or even unintelligible.

So much for the various meanings of time and the relevance of these meanings for the tasks of making communicative trouble.

4. Suppose we turn now to the kinds of operations that can be performed upon the input of secondary information, since the scheme points to this as an independent variable. Secondary information we said is information that can be obtained from a signal that tells the receiver how his own communicative efforts are being received.

An obvious operation consists of depriving the receiver of such information while nevertheless making it necessary for him to coordinate his communications with those of other persons. Personnel interviews, particularly for those occupations that require a man to be suitable in character traits and motives as well as technically competent are locales in which this kind of information is frequently withheld. Pre-medical students, with whom I am partly familiar, build this expectation that they will not be furnished with secondary information nor do they dare request it, into their definition of the pre-medical interview, one factor that makes for considerable pre-interview anxiety. There are many situations that are characteristic to large scale organization that show this structural property as a definitive one: untutored clients dealing with a bureaucratic agency; Army inductees going through personnel classification; front line soldiers subject to a night attack; upwardly ambitious persons (Army, industry, academia, government, business, etc.) who must act at such a distance from those who assess them and are responsible for making rewarding decisions that secondary information is either lost or diluted to the point where it does not sufficiently inform. Anyone who has a student come in seeking redress for a poor exam grade, by assuming a perfectly blank stare and interpreting and answering his questions literally and in strict accordance with public protocol, will witness some intriguing effects of such deprivation, particularly if he doesn't cut the student off from the hope that this is merely a matter of misunderstanding and that the student need only say something more to gain his end.

At any rate here are some possible operations. Life can get complicated because each one in the pile of ways in which deprivation can be effected promises a topic in itself. And by considering only the variations that are possible just in the geometrical properties of communicative nets—e.g., cut it down just to arrangements of channeling, so that one gets stars, circles, forks, lines, etc.—and combining these with deprivation operations, the number of topics becomes astronomical.

What are some of the operations of deprivation?

For one thing communication can be channeled so that the communicant can send but he cannot receive. We simply put in a barrier whether it be physical or psychological. A physical barrier can be achieved in ways limited only by one's ingenuity. We can put the communicator at a distance; put a wall between him and the communicant; make him write his messages that someone else delivers; etc. Psychological barriers can be achieved through status arrangements, rules of procedure, language differences, etc. etc. The range here is in itself interesting, for as we have pointed out, secondary information would appear to be structurally necessary to the human communicative nets of large scale organization, and it might be that various problems of work morale, successes or faults in personnel selection for advancement, the work-a-day efficiencies and economics of plant and office operation, etc., may be studied with reference to the arrangements of barriers that exist to the transmission of secondary information.

Actual barriers are interesting, but there are more subtle though nonetheless practically effective, and I would expect normally present, ways of effecting deprivation in large scale organizations. (1) By giving back contradictory secondary information; (2) by introducing time delays so that though secondary signals are received, the recipient does not know to which question the message refers; (3) by returning only apersonally applicable secondary information ("Good going men of plant 4"); (4) by "overloading" the return path with such a signal density that the recipient must, in sorting them out, make too many sorting decisions relative to the continuity of the transactions that are required; (5) by introducing a "switching point" through which the outgoing message must go and allowing the switching point the right to alter the message without the communicator knowing anything other than that his message may be altered though he does not know the rules that the switcher will employ in altering; (6) by standardizing the range of alternative messages that can be returned as secondary information but making them insufficient to the range of messages that can be sent; (7) by returning secondary information in randomized responses to the message; (8) by randomized temporal re-ordering of the communicator's communication targets that occurs simultaneously with the receipt of the secondary information. (I like this one because it fits a peculiar kind of complaint among enlisted personnel in Army offices at least, that in my experience ran to the effect that one had no sooner built up a satisfactory work history with the lieutenant in charge of the office than the lieutenant got transferred, or the enlisted man got transferred, or the office got dissolved and all got new and different work assignments.) (9) by blocking access to the relevant memory materials with reference to which the assessment of the secondary information is made. These are by no means exhaustive. Again it might pay to investigate the varieties of such deprivations with reference to normal plant operations and problems.

Just as was the case in the areas of problems previously discussed, so it is the case here that each operation that we have cited, and for all those which we have yet to encounter at the site, the introduction of each operation may be expected to alter the "normal" characteristics with which we begin. The introduction of each should call into play devices to effect a fresh normalizing. And for each arrangement we'd expect to find limits beyond which the communicative system begins dealing in "nonsense." I use the term nonsense in communication systems as another term for the behavioral correlates of confusion: anxiety, withdrawal, compulsive repetition, over-determined reactions, etc. As a corollary that is made necessary by the fact that a state of total affective integration is empirically exceedingly rare if not theoretically impossible, and I'm inclined to hold the latter to be the case, every net will have an amount of nonsense that is particular to the characteristics that determine the net. The amount, nature and location in the social structure of this nonsense should throw some light on such phenomena as work discipline, obedience to authority, mobility expectations, alienation and enthusiasm, the operations of trust, the devices by which communicants routinize their situations, the variables that bear on the problem of how perspectival differences get and stay "integrated."

5. Our scheme reminds us now that alterations can be effected upon primary information to get us another array of topics.

Suppose we consider first the places that are built into the communicator, places through which it is possible for the communicator to get communicatively engaged with an outer world. We'll borrow Harry Stack Sullivan's list. He refers to them as "zones of interaction." They are: the oral, the retinal, the auditory, the general tactile, the vestibule-kinesthetic, the genital, and the anal. A point about the list that is particularly intriguing from the standpoint of communication theory is that each of the possible combinations of these eight zones of interaction within the group of them as well as between two or more groups of them can determine a communicative net. The range of topics multiplies quickly when we recall what the clinical psychopathologists have laboriously taught us, namely that each of these zones in the course of a life history becomes "built up" with meanings for the communicant as well as the communities of communicants into variously organized "sending and receptor fields."

Studies of the properties of communicative networks have largely focused on visual, oral, and auditory zones. In fact, one commonly encounters the assumption in the theories of groups that a group cannot be constituted without visual, auditory, or oral exchange. This is open to question, and hence this is a possible topic. As far as I know relatively little work has been done on the properties of communicative networks that arise between persons exhibiting various kinds of organic and functional impairment (which would be a way of isolating these zones,) though of course a considerable literature is available on the characteristic social experiences of such persons.[1]

But again I may be accused of sacrificing a concern for the phenomena of organizational behavior in favor of problems more germane to clinical psychology. I would say in defense that one must not confuse a concern for the literature of clinical psychology with a concern for designing questions that can only be answered in the typical two person situations of the clinic, or whose answers are applicable principally to clinical situations. If we try combining these zones singly there are some combinations that are marked by their typical absence from the observables of organizational behavior, e. g. genital-genital, oral-genital, anal-genital. But when one starts relating them in combinations something very peculiar happens: it becomes literally impossible to define the characteristic types of networks except in terms of combinations of relevant sending and receptor fields that are involved.

Further, it is seen that certain combinations are immediately relevant to the maintenance of typical characteristics of large scale organizations. Further, once these combinations are brought into view they have the effect of freshly and convincingly concretizing the ways in which persons are communicatively engaged with each other. The effect of employing this vocabulary, for me at least, and I invite others to compare their experiences in this regard, is to clarify the nature of as well as the possible structural variations in the communicative lines as these are describable in terms of sequences of designata, style, and temporal ordering. Elliott Mishler put the problem squarely into the organizational setting by pointing out that one should expect that the organizational

---

1. [Editor's Note: Two of Garfinkel's students, David Goode and Brill Robillard, went on to make significant contributions in this area.]

structure will provide the ranges of legitimacy to the variations in the possible combinations of sending and receptor zones that can be employed.

Having attained this vista, we can now proceed to broaden it by calling attention to an area of questions that is so far at least without study. I refer to the study of the properties of the spaces of the objects of the experienced world as the properties of these spaces are determined by the biological characteristics of the zones of interaction. Cassirer reminds us that the work of von Uexhull remains relatively unexploited for the originality and extensiveness of the theoretical statements of this problem. Apart from the work of von Uexhull I know of no major theoretical or experimental work that has been done outside of the unique and very recent work of Luneberg (*A Mathematical Theory of Binocular Vision*) who was concerned with visual spaces, and the work of Ames in following up experimentally the effects that Luneberg's theorizing predicted.

The expectations of common sense are loaded with a traditional stock of knowledge about these spaces. Much is claimed for the autochthonous factors of perception. Common knowledge states that vision can locate at a distance with relatively small irreducible error. Audition can locate at a distance but with larger irreducible error. Audition unlike vision can locate at a distance even around corners. Bodily movements and bodily engagement seem to be necessary to the development of visual skills. Bodily signals seem to be relevant to the construction of instrumentally useful analytical categories. Bateson and Mead in *Balinese Character* remind us of the intricate relationships that exist between bodily experiences in child socialization practices and the time-space orientation of the actor.

But common sense quickly fails us when we press for information that bears on some peculiar anomalies in our experiences. Here the researches of Adelbert Ames and those who have followed his lead violate our usual tendency to say with assurance that we must proceed from the "known" to the "unknown" since the experiential anomalies that they have produced put the "known" at the very frontier of fresh questioning. Rooms that are phenomenally experienced as squared turn out to be a fiendish collection of unlikely angles. Spheres that oscillate toward and away from the viewer turn out to be pulsating balloons. Oscillating windows with rubber rods attached that bend themselves around the window and then fly out straight again with a disturbing jolt—a scene that makes many witnesses ill to watch (I'm one of them)—turn out to be rotating trapezoidal metal lattices with permanently attached plastic cylinders. Rooms that are perfectly familiar in their straight lines and flat walls have people in them that walk through the walls, until it develops that the walls are mathematically determined curved surfaces and the phantom humans are "merely" walking behind a bulge and out of sight. All of which means, I propose, that the phenomenal space of vision—for one case—as the space in which the communicant finds himself and his primary information, has properties that are indeed problematical. The bearing of these problematical properties upon the tactics of communication should be seen without difficulty if one holds in mind the characterizing premise of the action frame of reference, namely, that is in the orientation to the socially defined situation that the premises of the communicant's communications are funded. I am not proposing that we try putting an office in an Ames or Luneberg room. But I am proposing that we can reconsider the relevance of such things as the communicant's work spaces to the phenomena of organizational behavior as the properties of these spaces are relevant to the properties of the zones of interaction through which he engages the objects that he locates there.

With a small further step we arrive at the problem of how these spaces are "integrally" experienced by a communicant. Sylvan Tompkins summarizes the questions by expressing wonderment at the phenomena wherein we hear with our eyes and see with our ears. A host of possible questions center around the peculiar accent of value that the practicalities of life in large scale organizations place upon the visual, oral, and auditory zones of interaction, so that loss of vision or loss of hearing are typically accompanied by severe symptoms of distress. Even the common vocabulary had provided the expression for "I understand," "I see." Academics tend to express this by assuring the other guy that he is clear. The mesomorph "grasps." Those in revolt against the orthodoxy, perhaps as a function of their segregation from the idealizations that the orthodox use in defining the situation, substitute a utilitarian naming with sexual overtones: "I get you," "I dig you." (Don't take this classification too seriously. I'm only trying to illustrate a point.)

Suppose we look at primary information from another angle. We'll turn to primary information in the sense of signal input, considering only the case of visual signal input, and get a look at some ways of operating upon it to effect alterations of the "normal" characteristics of communicative tactics. (Remember "normal" means only statistically typical to a set of determining conditions.[2] The term is a general designator of any conditionally determined state of communicative affairs and is being treated here as a dependent variable.)

---

2. [Editor's Note: Garfinkel is using the idea of statistically "normal" in a very unusual way here and elsewhere in these documents.]

First, visual signal input can be altered by altering the span of the visual field. While this can be done mechanically, it can also be done psychologically, for example, by inducing anxiety. Second, by altering the organizational characteristics of the expressional field. Third, altering the character of the visual cues that are constitutive for the communicator of the defining specifications of the objects he is engaged with. Fourth, altering the cues that are constitutive for the communicator of the defining specifications of the context with reference to which the objects he is engaged with are defined.

The same can be repeated for the other zones of interaction singly or in any of their possible combinations.

Up to this point we have gone over a few of the questions that can be asked about communicative tactics limiting ourselves to the case of the conditions that are relevant to the continuity of the single communicant's experiences. Our scheme shows at least the following topics that would constitute a minimum of topics that would have to be covered to get out at least the most apparent facets of the case of teleologically governed communications. Operations for the altering of (1) the expectation of timing; (2) the devices and the experiential rules that govern the devices whereby information is incorporated; (3) the operations of memory and recall; (4) the structural characteristics of the identities as well as the properties of the "classification" schemes for such identities that the communicator confronts as the relevant "targets" of his communications; (5) the varieties of identities by which the communicant recognizes himself as the perpetrator of his communications; (6) the way in which the communicant is given to the communicative relationship; (7) the variety of accents of interest (or reality) that the communicant places upon the objects of his socially defined situation; the alterations of the relationship of the expressional field and the social definition of the situation; (8) the alterations in the experiential logics whereby objects are compared, contrasted, tested, constituted, created, combined, isolated, in a work, the experiential logical operators of language whereby a definition of a situation is constituted, maintained, protected, changed, etc.; (9) the modes of inducing discrepancies between the expectations and the memories of the accomplished event (error); (10) the alterations of the "normal" devices by which error is corrected; the modes of inducing a discrepancy between the projected path of communication work and the memory of the path accomplished, (discrepance) and; (11) alterations in the devices "normal" to a network whereby discrepance is regulated.

All the points covered so far would have to be reconsidered and the ranges of topics extended as we addressed ourselves to altering the "normal" characteristics of communicative tactics for the case of a communicant who was participant to a communicative net where the communicative work instead of being governed by an expectation of timing, was governed instead only by the motive of specifying through his communications the identifying features of the situation, i.e., the case of communicative work undertaken for its own sake.

Suppose we now shift the accent of our interest in communicative tactics and strategies by assuming the invariant character of the communicator's make-up, and by assuming that our communicants understand each other. These assumptions permit us to address ourselves to the *de facto* regularities of communicative tactics and to seek the structural conditions of a communicative system that determine the characteristics of these regularities.

Appendix 3
Research Proposal, Draft
(undated)

Initial Proposal for Some Studies of the Determinants of the Effectiveness of the Communicative Work of Leaders

When addressing the question of structural determinants of leadership effectiveness, investigators commonly assume a viable system of activity and ask what is going on in the system that contributes to its viability. The structural properties that appear as determinants of viability are then treated as conditional of leadership effectiveness. I, too, have chosen to assume an operative net, but in contrast with usual procedure prefer to ask for the things that can be done to a system to make for trouble.

I choose this tack because, in my interest in the phenomena of social order, I favor the view that the fact of order is not to be assumed or settled by some decision of theory—found, for example, in the various postulates of equilibrium—but requires accounting for in terms of the very activities of the system whose pattern properties are otherwise regarded as "equilibrated." I propose the view, therefore, that by learning specifically how one may make trouble, and in addressing the devices whereby these troubles are prevented from arising or are handled when they do occur, the investigator may learn the "physiology" of the process of self regulation and self-maintenance. I have chosen to address myself to the troubles that can be induced for a set or persons whose activities are mutually oriented and who must act in concert, conceiving of such a "system" as a "communicative net."[1]

Specifically stated, the problem is this: To construct a model that can be used (1) to propose in somewhat systematic fashion the manipulations that can be performed upon a communicative net to undercut leadership effectiveness, and (2) to propose the determinants of the differential empirical occurrence of such manipulations not only within the type of system under scrutiny, but between systems of various types. While the order is a large one, its beginnings are small. The remainder of this Memorandum is concerned only with the illustrating of some relevant facets of this problem.

By way of recommending the task for sociological inquiry, we shall need definitions of "leader," "communicative work of leaders," and "leadership effectiveness." The concept of the "communicative net," as noted in the footnote above, was elaborated [in Memo #3.]

The definition of *leader* to be used here is a revision of Parsons's definition of a leader, found in his book, *The Social System.*[2] He finds the presence of a leader through a description of the allocation of responsibilities in a system relative to the possibilities of action in concert. When the terms of this provocative definition are elaborated under Husserlian phenomenological examination, the key term "is responsible for" involves the following as minimum specifications: (1) An actor is given to an alter as an instance of a socially defined type. (2) As a Me identified according to the resources of communally supported classification schemes, the actor experiences himself as a social object, a Me, in a world of Me-relevant others. (3) The organization of this Me is a scheme of socially typified motives, attitudes, past, present, and future possibilities of

---

1. The concept of the "communicative net" is elaborated in Memo #3 [earlier in this volume, Parts 10–13]. Eight "ideas" are specified there as the constitutive "dimensions" of the concept "a communicative-net-in-general." These are the idea of communicant characteristics, the idea of numbers of communicants, the idea of communicant work, the idea of communicative territory, the idea of communicative scheduling patterns, the idea of social relationships, the idea of normative or constitutive or institutional order, and the idea of communicative paths. When these constitutive ideas are specified through various sets of relevant constructs, e.g., for the idea of numbers, there are such constructs as size, time and rate of replacement, rates of increase and decrease, etc; for communicative work, task relevant, net-relevant, and meta-communicative messages; for scheduling patterns, net-work discipline, and so on, when these constructs are given the alternative values that they can take, and when for a set of possible values a set is specified, the specified set defines the analytic instance of the net. Interest in the memo is confined to nets that show the properties of central direction, self-regulation, self-modification, and boundary maintenance.

2. Talcott Parsons, *The Social System.* Glencoe, Illinois: The Free Press, 1951, p. 100.

conduct, typical plans and history. These may be held, within the socially valid theories of courses of events, as the causal agent of socially defined outcomes. (4) The actor, identified through the "components" of the Me, may be held as a causal agent of experienced discrepancies between expectations and socially defined actual occurrences as agent and discrepancies are relevant within a mutually oriented order of Me-thou relationships.

The terms of the socially typified Me appear inseparable from what Kohler has called the "manifest organization" of the "behavioral field," i.e., the sense that an occurrence has for a perceiver by virtue of its "boundaries of relevance" to past, present, and future outcomes, so that he experiences the event not only in its sense having occurred, but in its sense of "why." The Me for the actor, the typified other from the point of view of the actor's partner, serves for both as constitutive of the outcome as a reasonable or unreasonable, a causally appropriate or inappropriate product. In short, the order of reciprocally entertained relevances and social types is tied hand in glove to the social equivalent of the scientific concern for discovering causes—fixing blame.

Our definition of leader is taken from these considerations. It is postulated that every constitutive order[3] provides a distribution of rights to control the actions of others through a casual review of the other's actions relative to the problem of action in concert, the dimensions of the problem being communally entertained. I shall speak of the fact that a person has an enforceable claim to this right as the sense in which he "leads" the others over whom the constitutive order is binding or can be made binding.[4]

---

3. Out of a set of theoretically possible alternatives of territory, sequences and duration of actions, numbers of persons, status arrangements, prestige claims, etc., etc., these expectations frame a set of required alternatives. By "required" I mean that they are experienced as alternatives that must be chosen regardless of the person's desires, circumstances, purposes, interests, and consequences for himself or others, and so on. The set of expectations will include the required alternative as well that he assumes that the same set of alternatives to which he subscribes, i.e., that he respects, are binding on the other person as well.

From the point of view of the members, these expectations are entertained as invariant to the course of activities actually engaged in. They are in this important sense standards by which the data character of a witnessed event is assessed. As such they serve as the basis by which the member can experience the "strange" or "unnatural" or "erroneous" or "wrong" or "sinful" action that is "outside of the game" so to speak, or better the ground for experiencing the actualization of non-standard alternatives that are incongruous in a most particular and for our purposes important way: their occurrence renders the situation problematical as to its real character, violates the order.

I shall refer to such a set of expectations as a constitutive order.

4. Questions of the emergence, maintenance, change, succession, etc., of leadership consists of inquiring into the structural and operational characteristics of a net that are conditional of the enforceability of such a claim.

From the observer's point of view, putting aside for the time any consideration of phenomenal leadership, to say that a person is a leader is the same as the observer providing an estimate of the probability that such a claim advanced by a member of the net will be honored.

With regard to the term "communicative work of leaders," the position taken is that there is nothing about the communicative productions of the leader that are implied by or that stand by the definition of leader. What varieties of communicative work can in fact be engaged in by persons to whom we assign estimates of high likelihood that a claim to the right to control through causal review will be honored remains to be found out.[5]

For the meaning of the term "leadership effectiveness" I wish to reject any notions of effectiveness that involve matching some outcome against a standard that is found outside of the system whether the standard be furnished by the observer or someone else.[6] I wish, too, to put side any sense of the term that involves the notion that leadership work is by definition effective.

I prefer that effectiveness refer to a property only of the consequences of the treatments that two or more persons, according to their own lights and in their own time, give and get from each other. This means that the term involves some way of conceiving the difference that one person's communicative work makes for another's definition of a situation. This difference is an old friend, being known more familiarity under the name of influence.

By the *effectiveness* or influential character of A's communicative work, I shall mean the likelihood that A by his communicative work and regardless of his intent can so manipulate B's definition of a situation as to restrict B's alternatives of action to those that are for A adequate responses with respect to the relevance for the solution[7] of the communally defined problem of concerted action.

---

5. Not only will we be interested in learning what the varieties of communicative work are for these persons, but we shall be interested particularly in three functions that any communication simultaneously serves. In the "Information" paper cited above (Memo #3), these are discussed as a "motivational function" by which is meant the effect that received communications have upon the grounds of the recipient's actions; the "coordinative function" which means the effects that communicative work has with regard to the establishment and maintenance of an interpersonally valid definition of the situation; and the "control function," which means the effects of communicative work with regard to the regulation and resolution of incongruity, past and in prospect.

6. This involves, for example, putting aside any meanings of effectiveness that involve assessments of the effects of leadership work for the accomplishment of group output or most particularly that involve assessments of effects of his work for the continuity of the group.

7. The scientific observer's analytical problem of concerted activity may be stated as follows: How to conceive the fact of the organized character of interpersonal conduct in light of the fact that this property of organization appears for the observer not only under the aspect of the clock the movements of whose pointers are coordinated to the alterations of bodily

For present purposes, we shall confine our attention to nets, regardless of the numbers of person involved, that show properties of self-maintenance, self-regulation, self-modification, and central direction. The assumption of central direction means that the leader, as the person who has the right to control the activities of others through a causal review of their activities, motives, or attitudes, is simultaneously the status superior to those over whom the right is binding.

Some Troubles, and Some Conditions of Their Occurrence

By consulting the experiences of practitioners, particularly in the areas of politics, industry, and business, it is possible to learn of a host of devices whereby a contender may attempt to get it over a superior. There are such manipulations as withholding information, removing access to funds, by-passing a position, swamping an incumbent with work that he cannot handle within the limits of his available resources while continuing to hold him responsible, there is the frame-up, removal from office, "kicking upstairs," abolishing the office, character assassination, and so forth. The list is limited at this level only by the limits upon men's genius for acting like humans.

What I propose is that current developments in the sociology of communicative work make it possible to rationally order the principles for doing evil, with the result that magnificent new vistas are revealed of ways of conniving the other out of his opportunities for life, liberty, and the pursuit of happiness. For example, communication theory talks about the "secondary information"[8] of a message. By secondary information is meant the information that a receiver gets from a message that tells him how his own message work had been received by the other person.

---

position relative to the body's surroundings, but under the aspect as well of the "clock" of the stream of experience? Any empirical instance of organized interpersonal conduct is a *de facto* solution which calls for rationalization.

Not only is the problem one that is dealt with in various theoretical ways by the scientific observer, but it is one that the participants, too, will entertain various orders of constructs for representing in both the theoretical and empirical sense. These socially defined, maintained, enforced, employed, tested, etc., theories provide for the participants the definition as well as the standards for monitoring socially categorized behaviors that stand within the interpretive scheme of the social theory as solutions, good or bad or whatever as the participant views them. For the leader the problem is one that he defines, talks about, judges, alters, disseminates, etc., in terms that he assumes as binding not only upon him but upon those to whom he stands as a member of collectivity.

8. G. A. Miller, *Language and Communication.* New York: McGraw-Hill Book Co., 1951.

Sociologically conceived, this information may serve the important effect among others, of course, of confirming or authenticating for the recipient the constancies in his relationships to others. Put otherwise, the human communicator is faced not only with the question of "How do you *read* me" but with the question as well, "How do *you* read *me*?" The information that answers this second question we shall call the secondary information message.

From sociological theory we would learn that to the extent that our recipient continues to get such information in regularly patterned fashion, he may be able, because he takes such answers for granted, to take the way he identifies others with reference to himself for granted, and thereby may be able to address his task with some assurance that the ambiguities he encounters in the communications he gets and gives are task relevant and hence "merely semantical." The familiar saw in social psychological theory that if I know with some assurances who I am, I am in a position to know who you are requires for working clarity a statement with regard to pattered reception of "secondary information."

Now if we want to cut this man down, one set way involves operating upon secondary information while at the same time making it necessary for him to coordinate his communicative work with others. That is to say, we might look to the operations whereby the recipient might be kept from obtaining it, or rendering it ambiguous, or not giving it to him in proper time or amount—all of which, for the sake of ease in discourse, we shall refer to as "depriving" the recipient. Though it may appear that deprivation in this regard is too precious an effect to be of practical significance, I would maintain to the contrary that there are many situations of present-day organized life in which the effect is both common and characteristic, with much faltering and anxiety attendant upon its presence. I refer to the cases of untutored clients dealing with a bureaucratic agency; Army inductees undergoing personnel classification tests; front line soldiers subject to night attack; graduate students undergoing oral examinations; upwardly ambitious persons who must act at a distance from and through an intermediary to reach those who are responsible for making rewarding decisions; and so on.

What are some of these operations for effecting a "deprivation" of secondary information?

Obviously, there is the device of simply putting a barrier in the line so that a communicant can send but he cannot receive. A physical barrier might consist of a wall, or by making the communicant send messages that someone else delivers. Psychological barriers can be achieved through status arrangements, routing rules, language differences, etc.

There are, however, more subtle though nonetheless effective and in fact normally present ways of effecting "deprivation" that the model suggests: (1) By giving back contradictory secondary information; (2) by introducing time delays so that though secondary information is received, the recipient does not know to which of his specific questions the message refers; (3) by returning only apersonally applicable secondary information ("Good going men of Plant 4"); (4) by loading the return path with such a message density that the recipient in sorting them out must make too many sorting decisions relative to the time it takes him to complete other transactions that are required of him; (5) by running up the redundant character of the message to the point where it loses its situational relevant significance (an aspect of flattery); (6) by introducing a " switching point" through which the outgoing message must go and allowing the switching point the right to alter the message without the communicator knowing anything other than that his message may be altered though he does not know the rules that the switcher will employ in altering; (7) by standardizing the range of alternative messages that can be returned as secondary information but making them insufficient to the range of messages that can be sent; (8) by returning secondary information in randomized responses to the message sent; (9) by blocking access to the relevant memory materials with reference to which the assessment of the secondary information is made; (10) by randomizing the temporal re-orderings of the communicator's targets that occur simultaneously and without his knowledge with the receipt of the secondary information.

This list, by no means an exhaustive one, is intended to illustrate two points: (1) what I mean by manipulations of a net that can make trouble for any person, and a leader most particularly, since it is a rare leader who can or does in fact take the state of his relationships to others for granted; and (2) that a model that percolates at all should multiply this list by a factor equal at least to the number of ways that the concepts used for conceiving a communicative net can be related.

The second problematic point is that of learning of the determinants for the differential likelihood of occurrence of such manipulations in various structurally defined "situations" within or between systems. To illustrate again:

In its present state of repair, the model proposes that for centrally directed systems the likelihood of the presence of operations that effect the deprivation of secondary information for the case of centrally directed nets is greater (1) where large numbers of persons are involved in the net than where small numbers are involved; (2) where the probability that a status claim will be honored is low than where it is it is high; (3) where status rules are ambiguous than where they are rigid; (4) where the ratio of second order and greater feed-back loops[9] over all feed-back loops is for net A greater than for net B; (5) where the net has undergone a radical and quick increase in numbers than where either the increase has been gradual or where numbers have remained relatively stable; (6) where the periodic alterations of communicative territory are governed by technical preference than by institutional prescription; (7) where the distribution of values of time of occurrence as a parameter that determines the informing character of a message shows small variance than where it shows large variance; (8) where the power of a position is a function of the distribution of power among contending coalitions as compared with the case where the power of a position is fixed by the constitutive rules of the net; (9) where the system for the exchange of information is governed in its operations by tactics for maximizing individual advantage rather than by institutionalized prescriptions for effecting the exchange; (10) where the system for the exchange of information operates to maintain a relative equality of distributed information than where it operates to maintain a relative inequality; (11) where a system is differentiated with reference to the division of labor by the multiplication of incumbents within specialties than by a multiplication of specialties; (12) for all positions and wherever power and responsibility are incommensurate with each other.

Like the first list, this list is a compendium of things written down pretty much as they were turned up through a free and easy consideration of the terms of the model as it stands at this time. The hope is to turn the model into a rationalized gimmick whose ability to generate propositions ideally would be limited only by the amount of time and effort the model user was willing to spend turning the crank. The aim is through a program of researches to develop the present model with this ideal in mind.

---

9. The order of a loop is defined as the number of transformation points between the point of transmission and the point of assessment of a communicator that a communication undergoes. A first-order loop is one with one transformation point. A second-order loop is one with two transformation points. A loop with no transformation point can be illustrated in the case of the person who monitors his own communicative work as he produces it. A first-order loop is illustrated in the case of the person who addresses a question to another and must await a reply, or who awaits the effect of his work upon the behavior of the other. A second-order loop is illustrated in the case of the person who sends a message to a first party who in turn addresses a second party who in turn furnishes the sender with information relevant to the message addressed to the first party. The set of order of feed-back loops is defined by "channeling" rules, i.e., rules governing who can communicate with whom.

Appendix 4
Research Proposal Abstract, June 1953

Predicting the Effects of Time and Rate of Supervisory Succession upon Group Performance

Practical military exigencies make it highly desirable that persons performing supervisory functions be freely substitutable for each other and that when succession occurs it have minimum adverse effects upon the level and stability of group performance. In this connection, we may ask: (1) Why is it that for some task-groups, time and rate of supervisory succession have large adverse effects while for others variations in performance are relatively independent of time and rate of succession? (2) What can be done organizationally to a task-group in order to minimize the adverse effects of succession?

Explorations of these problems suggested an experimental treatment of them. A theoretical model was constructed to handle these questions and furnish a guide for their experimental investigation. Three actual situations, when consulted, showed sufficient correspondence to predictions from the model to furnish encouragement for proceeding further. It is proposed now to put the model to a more responsible test.

The model handles the relations between five variables which are:

1. The organizational characteristics of the task-net.
2. The informational exchange system between the task-net and the situation whose alterations the net is attempting through its concerted activity to keep under continuing definition and control.

3. Time and rate of supervisory succession.
4. The transmittal from one supervisor to another of the "present state of affairs."
5. The chances of adequate performance.

Using a combination of sociological and game theoretic analysis of Chess and Krigsspiel, the model formulates these variables in terms of "geno-typical" constructs and relationships.[1] When the theorems proposed by the model are translated into their coordinate empirical terms, the following leading propositions of the inquiry result:

1. That a leader has perfect or imperfect information about a situation is a function of two variables: (a) the rules of the information exchange system, and (b) the organizational characteristics of the task-net.

2. Wherever there is imperfect information, if the supervisor's activities are controlled by considerations of temporal gearing to the alterations of the situation, then as a matter of formal necessity the leader will not be able to specify the present state of affairs without specifying in its definition how it has come about, i.e., its Present-relevant Past. Put in other terms, under the above conditions, the leader's definition of the present state of affairs is the same as the present-state-of-affairs-as-it-has-developed-so-far.

3. The "historical" character of the present state of affairs is determined in degree by the same factors that determine the imperfect character of the leader's information.

4. The greater the "historical" sense of a present state of affairs, and the greater is the necessity for temporally gearing the operations of the net to alterations in the situation that the net is attempting through its operations to keep under definition and control, the greater will be the discrepancy between any incumbent's and his successor's definition of the present state of affairs under any standard set of measures for transmitting this definition from one to the other.

5. Under these conditions the later in a task a supervisor is replaced as well as the more frequently the turnover of supervisors, the greater will be the discrepancy in transmittal.

6. The larger the discrepancy in transmittal the lower the rate at which a given course of activity can reduce the discrepancy between an intended and an actual state of affairs.

---

1. An addendum to this proposal describes the game of Kriegsspiel and lists the temporal and informational characteristics that distinguish Chess from Kriegsspiel and are the basis for the model that was constructed.

7. The larger the discrepancy in transmittal, the lower the chances of adequate performance if a given standard of performance must be maintained.

The problems cited in the first paragraph of this paper can be framed as follows:

We desire two things: (a) maximum freedom with regard to time and rate of substitution; and (b) minimum adverse effects of substitution. In actual military situations desired effects are defined by performance norms that set acceptable ranges of variation. We shall consider this range as the value that is to be held constant. The two questions follow:

1. The discrepancy between views of the current state of affairs that results from transmittal of these definitions determines performance values. What can be done to the procedures whereby substitution is effected to minimize this discrepancy?

2. We must assume that for most situations a given discrepancy is unavoidable. This would be the case for example wherever there is little that can be done to control the way in which the net receives information about the alteration of a situation (e.g., a combat crew is expected to maintain a given level of performance despite the fact that the enemy controls an important part of the information that the crew needs for adequate performance). What can be done to the organizational character of the task-net to minimize the influence of this discrepancy between the incumbent and his replacement's definitions of the situation upon the performance of the task-net?

When consulted for possible answers to the first question, the model proposed the following possibilities. (1) Make incumbent and successor as alike as possible; (2) Routinize the situation through as much use of SOP's as possible; (3) Loosen the norms of time scheduling of group achieved output; (4) Provide as great an overlap between incumbent and successor as possible; (5) Provide for two supervisors only one of whom is replaced at the time of substitution; (6) Standardize the language for describing typical situations that the net encounters; (7) Construct and standardize a terminology that categorizes time sequences of events; (8) Maintain a log of all information received, inferences drawn, and hypotheses formulated; (9) Minimize opportunities for innovations upon hypotheses and decisions; (10) Shorten the time necessary for the completion of a given task; (11) Effect replacements either at the conclusions of a task or as close to initiation as possible; (12) Rationalize the tasks so that they can be dealt with separately, i.e., in "parallel" rather than "intersecting" time schedules.

The following possibilities were proposed by the model as possible solutions to the second question: (1) Distribute the scanning and monitoring functions among the members of the net so that their performances are autonomously governed; (2) Minimize the performance functions of the supervisor; (3)

Minimize turnover of task-net personnel below the level of supervisor; (4) multiply number of persons performing functions instead of multiplying functions; (5) Simplify the division of labor; (6) Encourage for the supervisor only powers of emergency review; (7) Distribute the supervisor's information among the members of the net; (8) Duplicate the supervisor's "memory" functions of collating, review, and recombination in the net which take over at the time of replacement and during the incumbent's "breaking in" period; (9) Keep the net as small as possible though at a minimum of two persons; (10) Standardize everything in sight.

Both of these lists are partial. Also, it is obvious that not all "solutions" are of equivalent usefulness. While all are partial solutions to the discrepancy problem, some would entail immense elaboration of the structural features of the net which might not be possible or desirable in an actual situation. Combinations of others solve a part of the discrepancy problem though they would make the net unstable as far as internal interpersonal relations are concerned; some combinations would make for stable interpersonal relations but would decrease the speed with which emergency concerted activity could be instituted and still others would permit stable interpersonal relations and insure emergency concerted activity but make the net incapable of dealing with complex tasks.

A preliminary matching of the model with features of actual situations that it is designed to order showed sufficient correspondence to provide encouragement for proceeding further. Three situations were consulted for a preliminary, common sense "test": the experience of Control centers in the Air Defense Command; the message center activities at the Bordentown Reformatory, Bordentown, New Jersey; and the Trenton State Hospital, Trenton, New Jersey.

It is proposed that a program of experimental research be undertaken in order to find out how much truth and nonsense the model is capable of delivering as well as to determine the model's usefulness for dealing with practical "field problems."

Addendum

The Game of Kriegsspiel

Kriegsspiel is sometimes called "double-blind" chess. Two players and a referee are required. Each has a board with a full complement of chess pieces for both sides. The players are not allowed to see each other's pieces. The object of the game, like Chess, is to check-mate the opponent's king. With few exceptions the rules of chess and Kriegsspiel are the same (e.g., in Kriegsspiel there is no case of "en passant"). However, there are additional rules to Kriegsspiel governing the referee's announcements that give the game its particular flavor.

The referee has his own board on which he keeps track of the true state of the game. The information that the players need to carry on the game is supplied through the announcements of the referee. Though there are local variations, commonly he announces the following: whose turn it is; possible captures but by pawns only; only if a pawn can be captured does he identify the pawn as such, otherwise he announces only the location of the threatened piece. He announces possible captures only if the piece can be captured by a pawn, and on any turn he announces all available opportunities. He announces pawn promotions though without indicating where the promotion occurred; nor does he announce the identity of the piece that the pawn has promoted. He announces the loss of a piece and the location of the loss, identifying the piece only if it is a pawn. He announces illegal moves. He announces checks identifying the check by the information that the check comes along a row, a column, or a long or short diagonal. He announces check-mate.

Differences Between Chess and Kriegsspiel

The maneuverings in Chess are governed by the strategies intended to effect control over the opponent's alternatives of play. The strategies of Kriegsspiel are intended also to serve this end, but in addition much attention is given to strategies designed to supply the player with information about the present state of the game for this information is problematical in Kriegsspiel in a way that it is never problematical in Chess. The differences between the two games that were of interest have to do then with the informational exchange system that exists between players in the two games. The consequences of these differences lie at the heart of the model that was developed.

The differences between Chess and Kriegsspiel that result from the rules governing the exchange of information between players result in turn in the fact that the player's definitions of the present state of the game show different temporal and informational properties.

Three parameters describe the present-state-of-the-game-in-general in both games: whose move, the location of pieces, and the identity of pieces.

A. Informational Properties of the Player's Definition of the Present State of the Game

1. Under von Neumann and Morgenstern's definitions of perfect and imperfect information, Chess is a game of perfect information, Kriegsspiel a game

of imperfect information. That is, in Chess a player's definition of the present state of the game always corresponds to a referee's definition of the present state of the game. In Kriegsspiel, there is no more than a chance that there will be such correspondence.

The behavior of this chance, the determinants of its behavior, and the relationships between the size of this chance and the chances of adequate play are elaborated in the model.

2. In Chess the values assigned by the players to parameters of the present state are always the true values, while the messages upon which these values are assigned permit assigning them with full certainty for all times of play. In Kreigsspiel the values assigned to these parameters are true values and known with certainty only for that part of the situation that consists of the player's own position. Otherwise the messages from which information is taken for assigning these values permit only estimates of these values with no better than the probable character of their being correct. The player, for example, must employ typical rather than actual values. Nevertheless, it frequently happens that a player will treat his definition of the present state of the game as if the values were actual and known with certainty. Three "mistakes" are possible: being certain when the player is in fact wrong; being uncertain when the player is in fact right; and being unable to make any estimates whatever even though he had been given opportunities for obtaining the material information necessary to construct a set of estimates.

The model furnishes the conditions of these three types of "mistakes" and shows some important determinants of the behavior of the player's certainty.

B. Temporal Properties of the Player's Definition of the Present State of the Game

1. In Chess the present state of the game can be completely described without reference to the manner in which it came about. In technical phenomenological terminology the present state of the game in Chess is a "monothetic" object. A systematic, atemporal set of rules will completely define it as an actual instance of the set of analytic possibilities that the systematic rules are used to select from. In the model this characteristic is referred to as the "systematic" character of the present state of the game in Chess.

2. In Kriegsspiel the present state of the game cannot be fully described except as the description provides for the present state as the present-state-as-it-has-developed-so-far. The game-as-it-has-developed-so-far is, in fact what is meant in Kriegsspiel by the term, the-present-state-of-the-game. Such an object

is known in technical phenomenological language as a "polythethic" object, or a "time-object." It is to be compared to the description of a Beethoven string quartet which requires in each case a recapitulation of the music in its entirety and is grasped only when the temporally ordered steps have been completed. In the model this characteristic is referred to as the "historical" character of the present state. A "time-object" has the peculiar property that it can be fully specified only after a "final" outcome.

In the model these characteristics are referred to as the C-characteristic and K-characteristic of the definition-of-a-situation-in-general. It is shown that they are general parameters or "dimensions" of the definition of the situation in general. Their formal properties are described and related to the theory of social systems.

2. In Kriegsspiel a present outcome may alter the present view of what the state of the game was at a previous time, which recasts the definition of the present state of the game and with it the grounds for selecting a strategy of play. This effect, which is termed the "retrospective significance of a present outcome," is absent in Chess.

The model shows how this effect generates the complexity of the present state of the game and considers the devices whereby a growing complexity may be controlled or a given elaborated state simplified.

Summary

The model relates these differences, relates the statements describing these relationships to the chances of successful play, and then uses a sociological theory of communicative nets to provide the organizational factors that determine the nature of these relations.

Appendix 5
Research Report
for Wilbert Moore,
July 24, 1942

Bastrop Notes

July 24, 1942
Dear Dr. Moore,

   In the following notes I have attempted to define what I consider to be central problems of the inquiry, and to interpret some of the material in light of these problems. I am certain that we were never agreed as to the specific nature of these problems although we both referred to them in our conversation by use of the summary phrase "community organization." Having different conceptions of the meaning of the phrase, and its uses in research, we put the material collected to different uses, with the result that much that appeared to me to be crucial might have struck you as superfluous, or at the least, too far-fetched considering the time at our disposal. It might be that I have broken too abruptly with the accepted problem models exemplified for instance in Young's Scientific Social Surveys. To your disappointment, perhaps, I did not collect material by "changes in the activities and orientations of the 'institutions' of the church, the school, government, economic activity, and the family"—the currently acceptable designations of institutionalized activity. I came to the project fresh from an examination of this framework that had left me unconvinced of its usefulness for an analytical science of social organization. It was my impression then and further observations during the investigation have convinced me even further that the concept of "institutionalized activity" must come in for such marked revision that the end result is a conceptual scheme far removed from that involved in using the "traditional five" (or six, or sixteen) in the orientation it gives the student as to the key problems of a science of social organization, and the recognition of relevant "facts," a sub-case of which is the manner of interpreting material collected within the former framework. In setting up the problems I attempted to use the conceptual apparatus developed in the writings of Talcott Parsons; with what success remains to be seen, or better yet, "hinted," since the interpretations that follow cover only a small area of the problems investigated. Many of the interpretations and problems are half-baked, this being due to a lack of time, but most important to the fact that I had abandoned one model, or attempted to abandon it, in favor of another which was still too amorphously conceived by me to result in a convincing number and quality of interpretations. This I hold of little matter because of the great promise of the framework, and the prospect that further study will remedy present deficiencies.

I was not interested in the "practical" problems suggested for instance in the sudden increase in school enrollment, or the fact that Bastrop's streets were suddenly torn up to make way for a sewage system, or that workers did not have sufficient houses in which to live with the result that they had to put up with the most abject living conditions. The statements of fact relevant to such phenomena are no more "real," or "sufficient" or "relevant" than the fact that Darby Orgain had hung in his room a poem entitled "Make Me a Man" or the fact that the Methodist Congregation repeated the Methodist creed, or the fact that the women who attended the meetings of the reading circle were meticulously dressed. In the context of the "favored five" an increase in school enrollment is more relevant than Darby Orgain's poem, as I see it, because the former is assigned the role of "sufficient cause" to a complex of changes such as increased expenditures, overcrowding, and mixed into the hash the social phenomena of group realignments, personal adjustments, and the journalistically interesting conflict and "discrimination." In the context I had in mind the "fact" of a sudden increase in enrollment, at its most acceptable point, is background material, necessary perhaps because of the formal requirements in preparing such a report, but having only the most indirect bearing on the problem in hand; it would be a necessary but not a sufficient fact. The poem on the other hand is an objective indication of institutionalized sentiments (the *stuff* of community organization) in the manipulation of which that person's position as a "substantial citizen" is recognizable and acceptable in a community of similar and functionally related sentiments. The women's dress is relevant to the complex of the expressional virtue of competition for social leadership and acceptance. From the standpoint of sociological relevancy, if

"Make Me a Man" lost its affective appeal, or if a representative and accepted woman attended the reading circle wearing a tailored suit such as a stylish businesswoman would find "reasonable," these would be facts which point to far reaching shifts in "community organization," changes which might occur without necessarily being accompanied by the town's accoutrements of torn streets and new store fronts.

For me a study of community organization meant a structural and functional analysis of systems of agents related to each other in time by interconnected modes of appraisal of the objects of their social environment. The key problem was that of fixing the hypothetical nature of social order in Bastrop through the use of constructed types, and then marking social change by comparing successive orders of these types and their properties. The idea as I saw it was to translate such aspects of the social activities of Bastrop relevant to our interest in change into such static terms as would by the fact that they were static permit analysis of the present and future course of the community's organization. This meant dealing with selected aspects of social phenomena rather that attempting to strain for "a reproduction" of the "concrete" phenomena in "all their beautiful complexity." The latter orientation as social research makes good talk but poor philosophy. It is based on methodological hash; its uses in explaining the future course of events are limited to vague and general statements; and concretely speaking, in points of procedure and interpretation it is discouragingly enmeshed in the fallacies of misplaced concreteness.[1] The concept "gestalt" is more "used" than *used.*

The artist and the social investigator employ qualitatively different operations in approaching the "raw material." The distinguishing property of the investigator's procedures being the self-conscious use of conceptualization. The orientation of the investigator toward his material is passive; that of the artist, active. The question is not; "which renders the 'truest' interpretation?" This question is meaningless. The question is: in light of the promise of a scientific interpretation of social phenomena, which system of procedures is most logically bound to the end of the investigation, the end being the recording and prediction of social change.

But what of the limits of time and money? Do not these factors enter as practical determinants of procedure? Yes. But the answer as I saw it did not lie in doing "the best with both in order to guarantee some measure of coverage." More hash. The answer lay in covering the material in hand in the time

---

1. [Editor's Note: This is a reference to Whitehead's fallacy.]

and with the money available as far as possible within the second framework, pointing up the problems that remained for investigation when the allotted period had expired. I am not of the opinion that it is possible to select a problem such as we have here and set up the problem's solution within the limits of a stipulated sum of money and length of time. The limits of each are fixed in unrated contexts. The best that can be done is to say that within such limits we shall gather what is possible. When the limits are reached such interpretations as are scientifically allowable will be made. The rest will be recognized for hypothesis, problems, or whatever it is as defined by the norms of scientific procedure.

I realize that much of the material I have collected does not appear to be in line with the aims I have stated above, and much pertinent material was not touched. This means that a great deal of interpretation will be made by implication and very "unconceptualized savvy." For the "errors of selection" I shall ask excuse by saying that the will was stronger than the means; that I was not sufficiently prepared to carry out the program with professional dash, although I was convinced of the fruitfulness of the procedure over any other in hand. Much was done through casting and recasting, always a time wasting process. The investigation was an immensely important learning experience, though you must find little comfort in such an assurance. The "errors of omission" can be overcome by the ability to recognize a hypothesis when one encounters it.

Again I extend my very deepest thanks to you for the opportunity to work through a series of problems with the aid of sensitive and intelligent colleagues who were, I think, mindful of the same problems although they might not have addressed them to me in the same words.

After all this, then, what do my interpretations consist of?

Garfinkel

Study

It is somewhat misleading to think of Bastrop as a stable and unchanging community prior to the announcement that Camp Swift would be located near it. The major source of its wealth was in agriculture; and its stability in the economic sense was the stability of agriculture. It was supported in its early period by the vast holdings and accumulated wealth of cattle and plantation owners, but this support was removed by the Civil War. A measure of stability was enjoyed when pine and cedar forests were mined, and this in turn was lost. The town boomed during the First World War and for about four years afterward when a heavy demand for lignite was filled by mines located in the immediate vicinity of the town, but this basis was lost in competition with gas and oil. According to W. B. Ransome, president of the First National Bank, the last twenty years were ones in which Bastrop had no support other than that of the surrounding farms, a few families whose fortunes were breaking up as estates were divided, and the little turnover that was brought to the town because it was the county seat. It seems he said, "That nothing we have ever tried has ever worked out." In Dr. E. W. Zimmermann's sense, Bastrop was located on the periphery of the resource hierarchy; and being in such a weak position its stability was that of entrenchment in the face of dynamic and unpredictable circumstances. Yet even this is not strictly true, for such entrenchment as had occurred took place among the large property holders that lived in town. The economic activity of the town reflected their policies, as did the manner in which the town was organized socially. With the range of occupations limited, the movement of the young people was toward the cities. Those that came in from farms unable to support them stayed briefly as clerks, gas station attendants and the like, and then moved out looking for more remunerative and secure occupations. The birth rate fell. Improved roads and the development of the automobile as well as other modes of transportation and communication served further to render the position of the town insecure as competitive influences were facilitated. The increasing rationalization of economic and social activities made entrenchment more difficult; a fact which was brought to keen consciousness by the accumulated stocks of "old-fashioned goods" with which the merchants were tied at the time the camp was announced, as well as the fact that the young folks, of all races, were no longer wont to recognize the affective worth of preachments of the older generations. The city's school had adopted a policy of encouraging the young people to remain in school as long as possible "in order to prepare them better." The Methodist, Episcopal, and Baptist churches reported a lack of interest among such young people as there were in town toward Sunday School. The attendance at church as well as the administration of church affairs was in the hands of "the old folks." The city got along with one man to handle the offices of fire chief, police chief, tax-collector and tax assessor, and he reported no difficulty in handling all three jobs for which he was paid $100.00 a month. Through the policies the true status of the tenants was changed to that of day laborers, the effect of which was to remove them from participation in the economic life of the community to a point where they had to rely upon government support for food, and squatting privileges for places to live, a state of affairs which had repercussions upon the landowners during the boom.

Among the merchants "no one made any money, but no one went broke." The markets for the various products were closely circumscribed by the fixed salaries of the county employees and the prices available for crops. Socially the markets were specifically defined by the merchants in terms of an elaborately maintained system of reciprocities; much of which was marked by the property of gratuitousness, rather than economic need or gain. The available business was "shared." The heavy predominance of staple goods etches deeply the line demarcating the limits of his market beyond which the merchant knew with almost religious assurance he could not go without incurring losses. Within such a stabilized situation the "natural laws" of supply and demand commended themselves to the common sense of the Bastrop businessman. Every cause had its effect; and the model of the universe was monistic in pattern. The premises had long ago been accepted and judged—in the case of some, *by* God—so that non-Euclidean geometry was either prima facie evidence of ignorance or the work of an agitator. The fate of one was the fate of all; let no man untune the string. Deviations were not tolerated or at best were regarded with interested disquietude. So, as Mrs. W. E. Maynard of the Bastrop Advertiser expressed it, "things had reached a point where we were taking in each other's wash," and with the proximity of Austin and its "pluralistic universe" the spiral was inexorably downward, and this was apparent to all. It was not by chance that Cecil Long, George Stavinoha, S. B. May, Amy Standifer, and J. V. Ash organized Trade's Day, a monthly shot in the arm. All were "newcomers" to Bastrop who were attempting to break through the institutionalized procedures of local business in an attempt to extend the natural limits of the universe to include farmers who might otherwise bring their trade to Elgin, Smithville, or Austin. Even so once a month was considered sufficient because it was not possible to tap the source too often without soon running it dry.

Not all economic participants were bound by the system. Federal employees of the Department of Agriculture were outside it by virtue of the external source of income. Dry Bryson, while the most articulate professor of the system, by virtue of his role of physician operated outside the system. The children and late adolescents operated outside it because of the amorphous manner in which their interests were organized, there being some pressure on them in the fact of parental and school teachings, but their decisions were unattached to the compulsions one finds in the sheer business, for instance, of earning a living.

As for the other aspects of the social organization of the town, it might be hypothesized, to begin with, that the status system reflected the instability of the economic basis of the town. There had been times, though not in the last twenty-five years, when the class structure of the community had been sharply drawn, and it was during this period that the tradition of the "Bastrop aristocracy" was established and perhaps unqualifiedly accepted. Some indication of the strength of this acceptance is found in the fact that the offer to establish railroad yards in Bastrop at the turn of the century was rejected by the upper class who according to reports were afraid that such an activity would "spoil the town." "This same group," said Paul D. Page at a Chamber of Commerce meeting, "was opposed to the coming of the camp, but we saw to it differently this time."

As the economic basis of the prestige of the Bastrop aristocracy was removed through the failure of various economic enterprises, agricultural reverses, and a division of the old estates, a realignment of power positions in the town took place. The lignite boom of the World War period from about 1916 to the beginning of the decline in 1925, the erection of the power station by T. P. & L., the developments of United Gas, the installation of an oil pumping station near Red Rock, the prosperity of the ginning and oil mills, saw the influx of young business men from outside the vicinity of Bastrop. Bent on taking advantage of a prosperous condition they made profits the end of their activities, leaving the prestige of "aristocracy" to the old timers, while claiming possession of the town for themselves and establishing their own criteria of acceptance and aristocracy. A Chamber of Commerce flourished during this period, an indication of the importance of business activity at this time. As the lignite boom subsided with the depression, which began around 1927 because of the community's heavy dependence on wealth from agriculture, many of the newcomers left. Those that remained took places as full participants in the economic community.

In the following fifteen years another group arose in social acceptance and power, namely, the old German families. Accepted prior to the war by the aristocracy as "merchants" with whom the aristocracy associated only under the most impersonal of circumstances, the post war period saw the removal of barriers on the part of the aristocracy to social acceptance, with the result that intermarriage and co-participation in running the affairs of the town obscured the former sentimental meaning of "old Bastrop" and such divisions as, "old Bastrop which includes the German families," and "the real Bastrop by which I mean pure Americans whose ancestors came in first and settled the land" resulted. As one woman, Mrs. Powell, put it, "It's the Germans who own all the property and have all the money in Bastrop today. The old timers were just being shoved aside by the new comers and they turned to the German old timers as partners in misery."

Not even the position of the Negroes remained unchanged. Soon after the ear the traditional parallel growth by families of white masters and Negro servants was replaced by a rising generation who were without such ties because of the decline of the large estates which formerly supported them. No longer the traditional servants of aristocrats, they became the commercial servants of a struggling middle class. The generation that followed had some schooling to further disorganize the traditional complex of sentiments by which the position of the "good ----" was fixed, so that today the sentiment is often expressed that the young ones are unexplainable and that they are getting slowly out of hand.

Though they probably did not contend as groups, representatives of the "newcomers" and the "aristocracy" attempted to assert control over the affairs of the town, and it is probable that the participants on each side knew with certainty the issues that were involved. Apparently the descendents of the aristocracy operated at a disadvantage. Their ethic placed primary value on "men of principle status, long run acceptance of position, "culture," background, responsibility, the virtue of being gentle-men. There was no drive for profit unless the drive was possible within the framework of the aristocratic ethic. One did not set himself unabashedly to making money. One made money in a "decent and dignified manner."

The ethic of the new comers placed primary value on the "successful man," the dealer, short run strikes for immediate gain, the conflict for position and the ability to recognize threats, expediency, and use. The end of business is profit, toward which end the merchant should direct full attention.

The means in the case of both types was the available market. When the market was flushed the newcomers were better prepared to explore it. When the market declined, entrenchment took place all around, leaving a sense of prestige that was becoming more and more self-styled. Those that were running the affairs of the town were the new Bastropians. They had, for instance, a sense of belonging to and possession of the town, a sentiment entertained by the aristocracy though somewhat less vociferously; and employed in addition the tactical means necessary to impress upon skeptics the new glory and the timelessness of their ethic by which the new aristocracy was transcendent. Bastropians progress was assured, and their businesses continued to show a reasonable rate of return.

Beginning prior to the depression, about 1927, and thereafter, the frequency and elaborateness of social functions by which the old set asserted its worth and position and the newcomers asserted their credentials declined. Long before the camp came in formal dinner parties, elaborate teas, music functions, a reading circle had already begun to decline to the point where formal dinner parties were rare events, and the music and reading circles had thrown open their rolls in a bid for enough membership to maintain the groups and prevent boredom. The impression is that expressional activities among the women flourished, with bridge clubs and church societies proving most substantial; a fact which may be construed as evidence that upon the women's shoulders devolved the job of defining and maintaining the family status in the non-commercial community. Class and clique lines among the women were more stringently drawn than among the men, which was an indication again of the different orders of "reality" within which men and women operated.

A gap in the research appears when the attempt is made to account for the social structure and changes that were underway among the rather inconspicuous semi-skilled and unskilled workers, small farmers, retired farmers and merchants, widows, minor businessmen, and city and county officials.

With this brief sketch as a guide to the nature of the Bastrop community prior to the camp, the point to be answered now is: What were the problems of the research, and what interpretations regarding the social changes are possible in light of the evidence collected?

There are three central problems: 1. In what manners were the value structures of the different systems of participants related to each other; and what was the functional significance of these relationships? 2. How were the value systems reorganized (a) in their structure internal to a given system of participants, and (b) in their structural position in the community? 3. What are the properties of the action systems during the period January through June that appear significant for predicting the direction and nature of future change?

At the outset the following points should be made clear: First, when reference is made to "merchant," or "sheriff," or "upper-class woman" the reference is made to a role by which is a particular configuration of four constructions, namely agent, norms, ends, and means. The term "merchant" is used by way of a shorthand to designate the institutionalized configuration of these elements, the factor of institutionalization resulting in a more or less consistent body of expectancies and acceptances assigned to and accepted by the actor by virtue of his position in the social structure. The assumption is that order is given a particular meaning when the social phenomenon of institutionalization is present and when such "regularity" is lost—or, to put it another way—insofar as norms are not given common acceptance social order approaches the pole of *anomie*. Second, errors of reification will be avoided if it be understood at the outset that "role," or, more specifically, the term "merchant," is used to designate *one aspect* of the experiencing ego or system of egos under consideration.

For the purposes of this study the following social systems were given the most extended attention:

*Worker's communities represented by trailer areas
*Merchants and transients
*Merchants and residents
*Resident women and workers (roomers during construction period)
*Resident women and camp personnel
*City and county functionaries and townspeople
*City and county functionaries and workers
*City and county functionaries and construction functionaries
*Townspeople and camp functionaries
*Resident women's communities
*Merchants community
*Resident church members and transients
*Resident church members and camp personnel
*Church members communities
*High school community
*Resident high school students and transient high school students
*Professional functionaries and transients
*Professional functionaries and residents
*Occupational functionaries and workers, resident and transient
*(Negro-White-Mexican resident community)
*(Negro-White-Mexican working communities)

*In this paper we shall consider those systems marked by asterisks.

Workers' Communities

The people that came to Bastrop to participate in the construction of the camp had one important element in their orientation that was common to all, namely an appreciation of the fact that their stay was directly dependent upon the length of time it took them to complete their particular phase of the work, and that once this phase was completed there was nothing about the town to detain them, a factor which has definite implications for their relations to merchants, functionaries, and townspeople. Within this limit the group was a differentiated one with regard to community structure, and the properties of their communal actions. We shall consider three types of organization here; that found in the trailer camps such as Roberts', Young's and Nolan's, the Elgin trailer camps, and Kelly Courts. While these do not exhaust the number of arrangements, the cabins in the State Park for instance differed from all three, the first two at least cover the bulk of the transients that lived outside the city proper, while the last touches the professional and highly skilled workers. For a more complete understanding these systems should be analyzed into sub-systems by occupation, for intra-community differentiation in value structure shows up clearly when analysis is made by occupation, while it is difficult to discern when analysis is based on living conditions, recreational pursuits, number of inhabitants per housing unit, wages, or home town.

The picture of social structure within each of the three trailer areas located on Route 95 is that of a discrete series of socially self-sufficient cliques—a "polyp" organized schematically, represented as follows (after the work of J. F. Brown, *Psychology and the Social Order*).

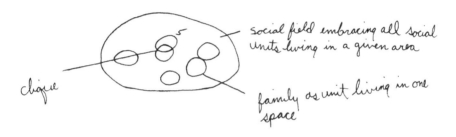

The field was marked by "low potency of membership character." The association of families or groups to the rest of the camp consisted of somewhat extended contacts with friends known previous to the job, with little contact beyond perhaps speaking acquaintance with those living nearby. Identification with the camp appeared to be on a functional basis with interests such as toilet facilities, garbage disposal, a sufficient supply of water, payment of rent etc. being the common objects of consideration. There did not appear to be evidence of expressional identification with the camp community. The community was defined in the specific terms of rational, specific exchange of rights and privileges. Mr. Menly cited his practice of "sizing a family up" when it entered the area and where he thought it called for brought it immediately to the attention of the newcomers that "drinking and carrying on" would not be allowed, often getting the response, he said "that if that's the way you feel about it this is the place for me." Cliques formed on the basis of proximity of persons.

The end of the system was the provision of temporary living quarters acceptable to the inhabitants, a fact substantiated by the frequent references by the women to their "real homes" and their reluctance and sometimes antagonism to being photographed "under these conditions": and the means were the discrete self provision by unit members. The landlord did not feel called on to provide any services or aid beyond those designated by health authorities, and the further norms of order and profitable business procedures. Law violations, for instance, were handled first by the proprietor "and if I couldn't straighten it out then I sent for the law." The tents and trailers were set out in straight lines to facilitate the collection of rents, to make possible maximum utilization of the available space, and to provide access by automobiles to the various living units. The operative norm for the system was that of rational self-concern and self-interest.

The outstanding property of the system was anonymity. In the face of this class distinctions were blurred. Although there were expressions of class differences the affective content of such expressions was relatively low; the women complained less of class snobbery than of "unfriendliness" and loneliness. They expressed their opposition to "butting into other people's business" even when wife-beatings and fights commanded attention by nothing less than the commotion attendant thereto. Some "knew" or suspected that such and such a couple were not married and that women were being brought into camp but there was no inclination to "do something about it" and even reluctance to discuss the state of affairs with neighbors. The impression of the investigator is that only crisis experiences such as serious illness or common misfortune such tainted water supply could have provided sufficient moral power to tie these units into an integrated body of action.

While the trailer camps in Elgin presented a similar "polyp" like organization there were elements in the system that pointed to a more integrated order of community life.

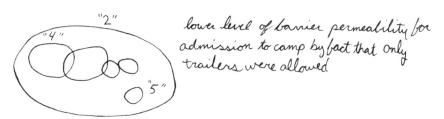

lower level of barrier permeability for admission to camp by fact that only trailers were allowed

While the system was marked by the property of "low potency of membership character" one element at least served to enhance the feeling of difference between members and non-members of the community, namely the requirement that only trailers by admitted to the area. Such a requirement, it appears reasonable to assume, may have operated in the minds of the trailer camp inhabitants as a selective factor the effect of which would be to insure the minimum basis of commonality, with the sufficient conditions of community feeling to be decided later when such factors as place of origin, common acquaintances previous work experience, employer, etc. were taken under consideration.

Cliques in these camps were more extended in nature than were those found in trailer areas. Proximity was not as important a factor in clique formation as it had been at the other areas. Cliques formed by factors of residence and non-residence in Texas and the south, by the same employer, and by similar occupations. Expressional value was placed on employers, for instance one trio of women all of whom were unacquainted when they came to Elgin formed what appeared to be a strong attachment to each other claiming that the fact that their husbands were machine operators for Holland-Page had brought them together. They referred to the "Holland-Page" crowd, saying and agreeing with each other that "You know I believe the Holland-Page crowd is about the finest I've ever seen. They're all friendly and it doesn't matter where they come from," etc. (Mrs. Wilt, Lay, and Sweringer.) Another criterion by which the community was bound was the feeling of difference that the "local people" were supposed to have for those living in trailers. The sentiment was expressed that the local people "think we're different from them," "they think we're not human beings just like them"; "they don't stop to think that if a person wants to follow this kind of work the best way to do it is in a trailer."

A fairly definite code of amenities had been worked out and was insisted upon. It included greetings, visiting rules, the exchange of services. There were some elements of competitiveness in dress; in the arrangement of the trailer, its price, model, availability of conveniences, cleanliness. Visiting was more prevalent than it was among the inhabitants of the trailer areas. There was some evidence of a collective attempt to emulate settled communities by claiming "we have our bridge clubs, our sewing circles, and we even have a reading circle." Gossip was more prevalent, one woman saying "We know where a family is from and what the husband does fifteen minutes after they arrive." The "queer ones" are isolated, indicating again the existence of common standards of acceptance. The trailer model was a commonly accepted prestige criterion, with those having "factory builts" of recent model enjoying or claiming distinction over "home builts." One woman who had just purchased a new trailer which had arrived the day that the investigator was visiting the camp was conscious of a new social position, and that she was not wrong was reflected in the remark by one of the women that "now she is one of us." The point then is that there were elements in the community structure that pointed to a greater degree of differentiation in the organization of the community than was to be found in the trailer areas. The ends of the system were not only the provision of temporary living arrangements, but the expressional end of conferring and maintaining status. We have noted some of the means above. The ends, however, did not have strong moral content with the result that class differentiations were obscure, often self-bestowed, and often had little currency outside the clique that claimed the status.

The same elements of rational, specific exchange of rights and privileges were present here as in the trailer areas, with duties toward the community taking the form of the minor codes noted above, while express and binding obligations were felt only toward the family unit.

As a social system the community at Kelly Courts differed in its structure from both of the systems indicated above. Similar to the other camps in that its form was "polyp-like" it had structural elements that were lacking in both of the previously mentioned systems. Schematically it may be represented as follows:

clique of old timers who put their clique expectations before individual interests as far as community matters were concerned

Similar to the trailer camps where the fact that only trailers were admitted served to accentuate the differences between trailer and non-trailer people, the high rent at Kelly Courts ($15 per week for one room, hot-point, commode, and shower) proved a strong barrier to prospective tenants, and this barrier served as a selective factor by which a "more desirable class of people" was obtained. Differing from trailer and camps, however, the houses and furnishings were already available, with the result that arrangements between tenant and landlord were more nearly on the contractual basis one finds in hotels. Rules and codes were implicitly expected and accepted by virtue of payment for the use of the house. Living arrangements, therefore, were so attached with "mercenary" elements, or, to put it more reasonably, the contractual regard for housing properties made it appear "silly" or "misplaced" to attach a moral content to these properties. Living arrangements therefore were not a particular point of pride or shame; the feeling was that the inhabitants were doing the best they could "under the conditions." This was temporary; a "real" home was located elsewhere, and in most cases the home as given in specific terms. This is to be compared with the references to "home" found in the trailer area where it was given in general terms and in the form of a futuristic myth. There is no evidence that they found anything in the living facilities to codify in expressional form, except for the feeling of difference that was represented by the fence which separated the barracks from the cabin area. The outstanding property of this arrangement was the utilitarian regard for the arrangements that the inhabitants exhibited. Cabin 2 was as good as cabin 12; the difference between push-pin and poetry was non-operative.

As in the trailer areas and camps the landlord was responsible for maintaining order. The operative effect of the norms of "good business" made it necessary that disorderliness such as would seem to call for police investigation would be handled through the agent to the police, or whatever agency was necessary. Kelly Courts, however, was marked by structural differences that modified this arrangement. If one goes by the reports of the women who lived in this area, the high rate of turnover served to set forth and underline a "difference" between those that remained and those that stayed briefly and then went on. "I don't know," said Mrs. Moe, one of the "steadies" "some folks just like to travel, just to be on the go. I'm not like that." This difference in the minds of those that remained constituted a central criterion by which a division was made between "transients" and "old timers." The old timers assumed the role of a ruling clique, the inner nucleus of which was composed of four women one of which, Mrs. Schupbach, was the implicitly designated leader. (She was a *most articulate* woman, even as articulate women go.) Authority was assumed, along with a sense of their primary worth to the manager, and thereby a sense of functional, if not legal, co-possession. Complaints, requests, and demands of various sorts were relayed through the leader, the complaints coming from the more peripheral members of the old timers. Dr. Duncan reports that the group wielded considerable influence citing the fact that Mr. Burroughs, the manager, had asked some families to move after the old-timers had indicated to him that they did not think them desirable tenants, and this action was taken although no overt cause for such action was present.

The extent to which newcomers participated in this phase of the system is not clear. Contacts between newcomers and old timers were limited, and much of the sense of difference and authority was self-designated with little or no attempt to extend "the fruits" of this authority beyond the old timers so that it is reasonable to assume that newcomers hardly participated.

While the trailer camp codes were institutionalized so that the same codes would be operative at the next camp, the system at Kelly Courts was strictly of provincial value, and when another camp was attended the system would have to be built up again from the beginning.

The system operated toward the end of providing temporary and acceptable housing facilities. The lack of development of an expressional code by which social position, for instance, would be defined and maintained limited the affective worth of the expressional ends enunciated by the old timers, and limited their range of effectiveness within the system. The result is that anonymity was a property of the system, and complaints of loneliness and boredom were prevalent.

Merchants and Transients

"Boom-town" suggests profit, and the temptation is to state that the ultimate end of the merchants was profit, and all actions intermediate to this end were colored by this drive. While this end was important, several factors enter by way of qualification which throw the picture into a somewhat subdued light. First is the fact that all the merchants were not so oriented; second, the construction period was so much shorter than had been anticipated, housing facilities were so limited, and other towns were so proximate to Bastrop that the "anticipated boom" did not materialize; third, there were ends served that were non-logical to the schema of the rational pursuit and maximization of profits.

It appears to be true that all the merchants in Bastrop during the construction period anticipated increases in business, but it was the newcomers—by which is meant the merchants who came into town on the promise of the boom—and a very few of the local merchants who had any specific conceptions of what they should expect from their businesses during the construction period. The orientation of the newcomers was that of short-term business, maximization of volume, spread, and plenty of profit. They were out for "killings." Staple items, unbranded merchandise, the cultivation of any means that promised immediate profits and the neglect of any practice that did not tie in logically to the anticipated end were the means. They operated within the norms of calculating competitive enterprise such as are found in the medium sized businesses of a large city. (Attention is called again to the fact that above description is meant as a constructed type. The variations were such that probably no one merchant fits the picture in its entirety; the construction is designed for coverage; it is a summary device by which further analysis is facilitated. It is not an "average," whatever that may mean.) It is in an analysis of the business done by the newcomers that a type case should be developed to represent the popularly conceived "boom town merchant." When volume and profits did not come up to expectations, business was described as poor and the worth of the venture was minimized. It was not enough to make a living. "I can make a living anywhere. Anybody can make a living," was the common expression of the town pawn broker and a dry goods merchant. An Austin concern took a lease for 6 months at $100 a month and never opened the store "because they didn't think there was enough in town to warrant it." One dry goods store closed soon after the construction workers left. The proprietor was moving to Killeen. "He never made money even during the boom. He complained even in March," said the proprietor of a competing house. Had he lost money? No, he simply didn't make what he had expected or anything near it, and having no intentions of settling in Bastrop he moved on to the next opportunity.

(The problem remains of getting a list of businesses in Bastrop by their length of stay and type of business in order to calculate the "death rate" of business by type of management. The County Clerk reported that there were no bankruptcies filed in Bastrop County, and he know of only one forced sale, that of Ronnie Hicks Auto Supply, a merchant who had succeeded Western Auto and had been in Bastrop prior to the boom. The problem remains of checking with the referee in bankruptcy in Austin for cases of bankruptcy and forced sales.)

The newcomers set themselves unabashedly to the task of making money. Unattached to the sentimental structure of Bastrop, the operation of the norm of rational self-interest was unencumbered; and the end of their operations was so clearly perceived that it was possible for them to make immediate differentiation between means that promised gain and means that were long term in effect, indirect, or in a word "impractical."

The manner in which the situation was defined by local merchants shows a somewhat different typical form. While the end was the maximization of profits, the end was marked by the expressional elements of service and propriety. Gain was to be pursued within the sentimental norms implied in the phrase "honorable practices." "The people of this town" said J. S. Milto city marshall and real estate dealer, "have never been money mad. No matter what, they have always put honor, and honesty, and fair dealings above the almighty dollar." Enjoying the status of insiders in the community of Bastrop townspeople, they were "participant sharers" in the communal values, their support of which gave rise to their consciousness of their "responsibilities" as "Bastrop businessmen." Here was another norm that was non-operative in the case of the newcomers. The local merchants had the conscience of the "real Bastropian" to which they answered for their actions. Affiliation with the community also meant long range planning for their businesses; the boom was a "fortunate thing" in the "long trend of Bastrop's progress." When it was over life would continue on. Some had property the care of which constituted an interest that lent power to this sentiment. One property holder expressed disdain for "a certain local man" who was taking advantage of F.H.A.'s policy of insuring building loans for 95% of their value to erect houses "which will only be vacant when this thing is over with." It was pointed out that he was liable though for only 5 percent and this was covered by the fact that he was incorporated so that his loss, whatever it might be, would be limited. He stood to gain with only a small chance of loss; then why hadn't this property holder done the same? "I just don't do that kind of business." Sin ye not today for the inevitable judgement that will come to pass. For the newcomer there was the day that the move would be made to another locality, or escape was possible through bankruptcy or fire, but there was not the press of shame before the "people of Bastrop" by the conflict between "the general" and "the individuum" of which shame is the product, because the individuum was defined relative to a context of values foreign to those of Bastrop by virtue for instance of religious differences. For the local merchant the individuum was the reflection of the Bastrop community. The outsiders therefore could engage in "irresponsible practices" but the local merchant had been circumcised and was no longer ignorant.

Competitive practices did not make their appearance among the local merchants, because "there was no reason for being hoggish; everyone had his share," but nevertheless the newcomers watched each other carefully in stock carried, and number of customers, with each one waiting for the others to make the first move to close the store at the end of the day's activities, one of the dry good merchants being in the habit of visiting the other merchants after he had closed his place, calling to them from the doorway, "Nu, mach' zie," (Well, how about closing up?).

While the anticipations of the newcomers were specific, those of the local merchant were amorphous. The newcomer knew closely what he would pay for rent, what items he would handle, the prices to charge, and what he would have to take in in order to call the deal successful. The policy was "to be ready for it when it came." The local merchant thought in terms of what he *could* pay for rent, being conscious of the press of the *increase.* He ordered cautiously waiting to see what the workers would ask for. Caught between the stable expectancies of the past and unpredictable future demands, old stocks of Bastrop staples and the necessity for stocking large amounts of new worker's staples, old stable inventory values and rising prices with possibilities of shortages the local merchant was unable to anticipate probable profits and was therefore unable to set a value on his business as a going concern in these new circumstances. The policy therefore was "meet the situation as it presented itself." Having no standard by which to measure (few used the experiences of other boom towns as a criterion) the tendency was to set no limit on expectations or else expect nothing and be thankful for whatever appeared. If the newcomers were practically unanimous in their opinion that the boom had not materialized, the local merchants were divided among themselves between disappointment and pleasure, with all shades of each seemingly being represented.

Transactions between merchants and transients were marked by their functional character. The transients did expect and ask however for such extra-business services as housing information and check cashing. The merchants regarded them in a similar functional sense. There is good reason to believe that they regarded the check cashing fees in expressional terms; the complaint often being received that the merchants and banks were taking advantage of the workers by charging them the cashing fee. The sentiment seemed to be that "it isn't the ten or fifteen cents involved; it's the principle of the thing."

Purchase proceedings were marked by their strong secular character, a fact which the newcomers appreciated and took advantage of. Most of their business they reported was done with transients. The local people patronized local merchants and advised such transients as they came into contact with to do the same. The newcomers' attitude was summarized by Mr. Gerhardt of the Fair Store who said that "they (transients) were new to the town. They didn't know one merchant from another. The one that gave them what they wanted, treated them right that's the one they gave their business to."

Strongly oriented to the ultimate, empirical end of "the job" the transients employed the norm system of rational evaluation and procedure in selecting their items of purchase, with sufficient cash to meet the purchase price being the means by which the object was to be obtained. The end of the system was the exchange of merchandise. Purchases were tied closely to the ultimate end; expressional items of sale such as jewelry finding a haphazard market. The system was marked by a minimum of bargaining, self-service or little demand for service, and marked specificity of demand for quality and use. (Note: this does not necessarily mean that they demanded high grade merchandise or even branded goods.) Another outstanding property of the system is the regard that the transients had for the merchants as functionaries.

Resident Women and Workers

Two systems will be briefly considered; first that of upper class women and tenants, and second, the commercial rooming house.

The end in renting by the upper class women was marked by these elements; patriotic service, social acceptance, and profit. The means were high rents, careful selection of tenants, and the manipulation of the sentiments of housing "appropriate" to position. The norms were those of duty, service, sound business procedure, and the proprieties of class.

Skilled workers, professional men, and construction officials were housed, their ends being "appropriate" housing; the means being sufficient cash and the norms those of rational selection and class proprieties. Housing was clearly the intermediate means to the ultimate empirical end of "getting the job done."

The outstanding properties of the system were relative anonymity, rational exchange of rights and privileges in which the sentimental appreciation of property rights and privacy were present.

The end in renting on the part of commercial rooming houses was marked by the elements of providing temporary rooming quarters and profit. The means consisted of filling the house to capacity. The norms were those of sound business procedure.

All classes of workers with the exception of professional and construction officials were housed, their ends being "sufficient" housing; the means being sufficient cash, and the norms those of rational selection, and the institutionalized codes of rooming house procedures. Housing was clearly the intermediate means to the ultimate empirical end of "remaining with the job."

The outstanding properties of the system were the rational exchange of rights and privileges purchased with the payment of rent, few demands by workers, small clique formation on the basis of rooms.

II. How were the value systems reorganized (a) in their structure internal to a given system of participants, and (b) in their structural position in the community?

Under (a):

Attention is called to the brief analysis of the change in values operating within the community of upper class women to be found in the article published in the combination issue of the Bastrop Advertiser. Limits of time make it impossible to do more than point to this as a sketchy example of the type of interpretation that is intended in answering this question, and pointing to the following changes as promising for analysis:

The reorganization of county finances due to the first loss of 350,000 in tax base, and the anticipated further reduction when plans of an addition to the camp are completed, pertinent to the system of county functionaries and townspeople.

The developing shortages of unskilled labor.

The secularization of local business practices.

The return of Negro domestics to the home; and the increasing number of Negros working at the camp.

The return in the importance of bridge clubs, dinners, and other upper class expressional activities since the camp personnel began to arrive.

The organization of a new merchants community.

The organization of formal religious activities.

The threatening decline of the Orgain Memorial Hospital due to acute shortage of nurses and technical help.

The redefinition of the soldier's position in the community due to increasing numbers; disappointments in business; anticipations of sexual promiscuity and feelings of danger to the young girls in town.

Etc.

Under (b):

The following are some suggested problems on which data has been accumulated though not in sufficient amounts:

The redefinition of the place of the church in the community.

The changing role of the adolescent girl.

The increasing importance of secular affairs, especially the "affairs of the market."

The incorporation of soldiers and their families by rank into the class structure.

The increasing importance of rent property; the changing place of rent and business property as the basis for family wealth, security, and social position.

The changing place of unskilled labor in the agricultural and business structure; the redefinition of the codes of race relations.

The redefinition by classes and participant systems of their social problems.

The slow shift in power positions.

The emerging conflict of patriotic and secular functions.

The changing role of charisma in leadership.

The shifts in the definitions of age and sex roles by classes.

The emerging conflicts in authority of premises and means of crime repression.

Etc.

III. What are the properties of the action systems during the period that appear significant for predicting the direction and nature of future change?

The influx of workers, of soldiers and their wives, the installation of a sewage system, the press of activities associated with the war effort, such as the U.S.O. drive, the formulation of a housing program, the installation of a health unit, the influx of new businesses, serve to extend the contacts of the community beyond limits that have been fixed prior to the boom by virtue of the town's previous unimportance. Confronted with new problems, new modes of procedure immediately had to be developed, means hitherto unconsidered had to be employed. While there is no evidence of a sharp break with the heritage, the statement by Bryson for instance, that with the announcement of the camps coming, the old Bastrop died, and a new Bastrop was founded, is a distortion, the sentimental elements in the mode of thought declined in power, being replaced by norms of rational calculation. This, to my mind, is an outstanding property of the system's operation. Attention is called to Max Weber's "law of increasing rationality." The presence in the community of secular ends, the values of which in the minds of the participants have been given priority over former ends marked by their expressional character, implies that as long as the press of circumstances due to the war crisis maintains these secular ends and the importance of these secular ends, social change will be in the direction of increasing rationalization of social actions.

The effect of this trend is suggested in another important property that has emerged, namely, the atomization of the community structure. There is clear evidence that the former cohesiveness of the community structure, marked for instance by the former highly articulated code of social relations, has declined. One is conscious of the growth of impersonalization, a phenomenon that is always attendant to the urbanization of a community. This is not to say that in the course of six months Bastrop has changed from a stable country hamlet to a city. It is possible that the roots of these conditions do not go deep, and that with the support and impetus of the Army camp gone, it will return to a state very similar to that existing prior to the camp. This possibility was suggested when during the period from the end of May until the middle of July the construction people had gone and soldiers had not yet arrived, the expressional character of the community once more asserted itself. That is, bridge clubs, dinner parties, social gatherings, interest in personalities, assumed a position akin to their former importance. However even this possibility must be qualified by the fact that the "second boom" may be marked by altogether different elements than those which marked the first boom. The fact for instance, that camp personnel will constitute a long-term element, bringing with it the unavoidable need for housing, service functions, the development of a new class structure (the merchants, for instance, that came in after the camp's announcement were attracted primarily by the promise that the soldiers would constitute the basis of their prosperity), whereas the construction workers were in only on a short-term basis and participated in community life only at the impersonal level of business contacts, and only in a very peripheral manner in other social functions, suggests that the basis for predicting the direction and nature of future changes remains to be determined from a study of the community in the next six months or year.

Another significant change is suggested in the new position assigned to former values, a concomitant phenomenon to the new norms that asserted themselves. While church membership during the boom rose, the actual importance of the church in the community, as far as Bastrop citizens themselves were concerned, declined, with the rise in secular values. This is reflected in the fact that church attendance by the local citizens declined and did not return to its former level when the construction people left. This would suggest that the importance of the church declined in the eyes of the local citizens, with a rise in secular values. It does not necessarily mean, however, that the support of the church has been diminished. Also, it is undeniable that local people still retain control of the policies of the church and contribute most substantially to its support.

Another illustration is the new importance that the local merchant attached to the value of maximized profits. He came to regard himself more as a functionary than had been true formerly, a new role which he accepted as the logical and necessary one to maximum exploitation of the construction boom, and one which local customers assigned though with some reluctance evidenced for instance in the expressions of unaccustomed strangeness, former demands for service, and in some cases antagonism and withdrawal of business. The end of his activity as merchant prior to the boom had been profit (more concretely "a living") marked with strong expressional elements. The former prevalence of visiting, long conversations, the use of some shops as social centers, casualness, "checker playing" are elements which are non-logical within a framework of "sound business procedures" to the end of maximized gain and are inexplicable unless one assumes that "merchant" and "Bastropian" were inextricably intertwined. "Harry Erhard the druggist" tended to change in the direction of "the druggist." Acceptance of the new end served to minimize the relevance of the old amenities.

At this point I must cut the paper off. It was my intention to point the direction and bend a few sticks to mark the trail. Again I invite your criticism of orientation, theory, statements of fact—and grammar and composition. I earnestly hope you will invite me to write more.

Bibliography

Allport, Gordon W., J.S. Bruner, and E.M. Jandorf. 1941. "Personality Under Social Catastrophe: Ninety Life-Histories of The Nazi Revolution." *Journal of Personality.* 10 (1), 1–22 doi:10.1111/j.1467-6494.1941.tb01886.x

Barley, Stephen R., and Gideon Kunda. 2001. "Bringing Work Back In." *Organization Science* 12: 76–95.

Bittner, Egon. 1983. "Technique and the Conduct of Life." *Social Problems* 30(3): 249–261.

———. "A Theory of Organization." *Social Research* 32: 230–255.

———. 1967. "The Police on Skid Row: A Study of Peace Keeping." *American Sociological Review* 32: 699–715.

Bourdieu, Pierre. [1971] 1977. *Outline of a Theory of Practice.* Cambridge: Cambridge University Press.

Bowker, Geoffrey C., and Susan Leigh Star. 1999. *Sorting Things Out: Classification and Its Consequences (Inside Technology).* Cambridge: MIT Press.

Button, Graham. 1993. "The Curious Case of the Disappearing Technology." In Button, Graham (ed.), *Technology in Working Order*, 10–28. London: Routledge.

Button, Graham, and Wes Sharrock. 1994. "Occasioned Practices in the Work of Software Engineers" in Jirotka, M., and J. Goguen (eds.), *Requirements of Engineering: Social and Technical Issues*, Jirotka, M., and J. Goguen (eds.), 217–240. London: Academic Press.

Cantril, Albert. [1947] 2005. *The Invasion from Mars: A Study in the Psychology of Panic.* Somerset, N.J.: Transaction Publishers.

Coates, D.C. 2003. "Sir! Do You Want Your Change!" Paper presented at the American Sociological Association meetings in Atlanta.

Coates, D.C., and Anne Warfield Rawls. 2004. "The Local Work of Visual Impairment and Blindness." Paper presented at the American Sociological Association meetings in San Francisco.

Coulter, Jeff. Forthcoming. "Rule-following, Rule Governance and Rule-accord: Reflections on Rules after Rawls." *Journal of Classical Sociology.*

———. 1995. "The Informed Neuron: Issues in the Use of Information Theory in the Behavioral Sciences," *Minds and Machines*, 5: 583–596.

Derrida, Jacques. [1983]1990. *Dissemination*. Chicago: University of Chicago Press.

Deutsch, Karl.1953. *Nationalism and Social Communication*. Cambridge, Mass.: Technology Press of MIT and Wiley.

Drew, Paul, and John Heritage. 1992. *Talk at Work: Interaction in Institutional Settings*. Cambridge: Cambridge University Press.

Duguid, Paul, and John Seely Brown. 2000. *The Social Life of Information*. Boston, Mass.: Harvard Business School Press.

Durkheim, Emile. [1893]1933. *The Division of Labor in Society*. Chicago: Free Press.

———. [1912]1915, 1995). *The Elementary Forms of the Religious Life*. Chicago: Free Press.

Garfinkel, Harold. [1948] 2006. *Seeing Sociologically*. Boulder Colo.: Paradigm Publishers.

———. 2002. *Ethnomethodology's Program: Working Out Durkheim's Aphorism*. Boulder, Colo.: Rowman and Littlefield.

———. 1988. "Evidence for Locally Produced Naturally Accountable Phenomena of Order,* Logic, Reason, Meaning, Method, etc. in and as of the Essential Haecceity of Immortal Ordinary Society." *Sociological Theory* 6(1):103–109.

———. 1967. *Studies in Ethnomethodology*. Englewood Cliffs. N.J.: Prentice-Hall. Second Edition, Boulder, Colo.: Paradigm Publishers, 2008.

———. 1964. "Studies of the Routine Grounds of Everyday Activities." *Social Problems* 11: 225–250.

———. 1963. "A Conception of and Experiments with 'Trust' as a Condition of Stable Concerted Actions." In Harvey, O.J. (ed.),. *Motivation and Social Interaction*, 187–238. New York: Ronald Press.

———. 1956. Some Sociological Concepts and Methods for Psychiatrists. *Psychiatric Research Reports* 6:181–195.

———. 1952. "The Perception of the Other: A Study in Social Order." Unpublished Ph.D. dissertation, Harvard University.

———. 1949. "Research Note on Inter- and Intra-Racial Homicide." *Social Forces* 27: 370–381.

———. 1941. "Color Trouble." In *Best Short Stories of 1941: Yearbook of the American Short Story*. Edward J. O'Brien (ed.). Boston, Mass.: Houghton Mifflin.

Garfinkel, Harold, and Harvey Sacks. 1970. "On Formal Structures of Practical Action." In McKinney, J.C., and E.A. Tiryakian (eds.), *Theoretical Sociology* (pp. 338–366). New York: Appleton-Century Crofts.

Goffman, Erving. 1959. *The Presentation of Self in Everyday Life*. Chicago: Free Press.

———. 1961. *Asylums: Essays on the Social Situation of Mental Patients and Other Inmates*. New York: Doubleday Anchor

————. 1963. *Behavior in Public Places: Notes on the Social Organization of Gatherings.* Glencoe, Ill.: The Free Press.

Goodson. James. *World War Two POW Aces.*

Harper, Richard. 1998. *Inside the IMF: An Ethnography of Documents, Technology and Organizational Action.* London: Academic Press.

Heath, Christian, and Paul Luff. 2000. *Technology in Action.* Cambridge UK: Cambridge University Press.

Hershey, John. [1950]. *The Wall.* London: Kindle Books.

Hughes, John, Dave Randall, and D. Shapiro. 1993. "Designing with Ethnography: Making Work Visible." *Interacting with Computers* 5(2) 239–253.

Hughes, J., D. Martin, M. Rouncefield, I. Sommerville, M. Hartswood, R. Procter, R. Slack, and A. Voss. 2003. Dependable Red Hot Action, in K. Kuutti, G. Karsten, P. Fitzpatrick, L. Dourish, and K. Schmidt (eds.), Proceedings of ECSCW '03, Kluwer.

Husserl, Edmund. [1931] 1988. *Cartesian Meditations*, trans. D. Cairns, Dordrecht: Kluwer.

James, William. [1907] 1975. *Pragmatism.* Cambridge, Mass.: Harvard University Press.

Janis, Irving Lester. *Air War and Emotional Stress: Psychological Studies of Bombing and Civilian Defense* (The Rand Series).

Jefferson, Gail (1988) "On the Sequential Organization of Troubles Talk in Ordinary Conversation." *Social Problems* 35: 418–441.

Kitsuse, John, and Aaron Cicourel. 1963. "A Note on the Use of Official Statistics." *Social Problems* 11: 131–139.

Knorr-Cetina, Karen. 1981. *The Manufacture of Knowledge: An Essay on the Constructivist and the Textual Nature of Science.* Oxford: Pergamon Press.

Kogan, Eugene. *The Theory and Practice of Hell: The Classic Account of the Nazi Concentration Camps Used as a Basis for the Nuremburg Investigations.* London: Kindle Books.

Kuhn, Helmut. 1943. *Freedom: Forgotten and Remembered.* Chapel Hill: University of North Carolina Press.

Lewin, Kurt. "Group Decision and Social Change."

————. "Forces behind Food Habits and Methods of Change," *The Problem of Changing Food Habits. Bulletin* 108 (Washington, D.C.: National Academy of Science).

Livingston, E. 1987. *Making Sense of Ethnomethodology.* New York: Routledge and Kegan Paul Inc.

Luhmann, Niklas. 1995. *Social Systems.* Stanford, Calif.: Stanford University Press.

Lynch, Michael E. 1985. *Art and Artefact in Laboratory Science.* London: Taylor and Francis Books.

Luff, Paul, Jon Hindmarsh, and Christian Heath. 2000. *Workplace Studies: Recovering Work Practice and Informing System Design.* Cambridge: Cambridge University Press.

Manning, Peter K. 1979. "Metaphors of the Field: Varieties of Organizational Discourse." *Administrative Science Quarterly* 24: 660–671.

Manning, Peter K. 1979. *Narc's Game: Informational and Organizational Constraints on Drug Law Enforcement.* Prospect Heights, Ill.: Waveland Press, 2nd ed., 2003.

McBeth, Doug. "Basketball Notes." An unpublished paper that has been much circulated for decades.

Meehan, Albert J. 1986. "Recordkeeping Practices and the Policing of Juveniles." *Urban Life* 15(1): 70–102.

Mishler, Elliott G. *Research Interviewing: Context and Narrative.* Cambridge, Mass.: Harvard University Press.

Miller, George. A. 1956. "The Magical Number Seven, Plus or Minus Two: Some Limits on Our Capacity for Processing Information." *The Psychological Review* 63: 81–97

Mills, C. Wright. 1940. "Situated Action and the Vocabulary of Motives." *American Journal of Sociology.* 5: 904–913.

Moore, Wilbert. [1946]1951. *Industrial Relations and the Social Order.* New York: Ayer Company Publishers.

Odum, Howard W. 1936. *Southern Regions of the United States . . . .*

Orr, Julian. 2006. "Ten Years of Talking About Machines." Special Issue. *Organization Studies* 27(12): 1805–1820.

———. 1996. *Talking About Machines: An Ethnography of a Modern Job.* Ithaca, N.Y.: Cornell University Press.

Parsons, Talcott. 1937. *The Structure of Social Action.* Chicago: The Free Press.

Pomerantz, Anita. 2004. "Investigating Reported Absences: 'Neutrally' Catching the Truants." In Benjamins, John (ed.), Conversation *Analysis: Studies from the First Generation,* 109–129. Amsterdam: John Benjamins Publishing House.

Rawls, Anne Warfield. 2008. "Garfinkel, Ethnomethodology and Workplace Studies," *Organization Studies* 29(5): 701–32.

———. 2007. "La Théorie de la Connaissance de Durkheim: Un Aspect Neglige de son Oeuvre." in *Naturalism Versus Constructivism. Enquête.* Paris: Editions de l'École des Hautes Études en Sciences Sociales.

———. 2007. "Théorie de la Connaissance et Pratique chez Durkheim et Garfinkel," in *Naturalism Versus Constructivism. Enquête.* Paris: Editions de l'École des Hautes Études en Sciences Sociales.

———. 2006. "Editor's Introduction to *Seeing Sociologically,*" by Harold Garfinkel. Boulder, Colo.: Paradigm Publishers.

——— (ed.). 2004. *Epistemology and Practice: Durkheim's The Elementary Forms of Religious Life.* Cambridge University Press: Cambridge.

————. 2003a. "Conflict as a Foundation for Consensus: Contradictions of Industrial Capitalism," in *Book III, Durkheim's Division of Labor. Critical Sociology* 29(3): 295–335.

————. 2003b. "Orders of Interaction and Intelligibility: Intersections between Goffman and Garfinkel by way of Durkheim," in Javier Treviño (ed), *Goffman's Legacy.* Boulder Colo.: Rowman and Littlefield.

————. 2002a. "Editor's Introduction," *Ethnomethodology's Program: Working Out Durkheim's Aphorism,* by Harold Garfinkel. Boulder, Colo.: Rowman and Littlefield.

————. 2002b. The *Mauss Review* 19. French translation of "Emergent Sociality: A Dialectic of Commitment and Order." Originally published in *Symbolic Interaction* (1990), 13(1): 63–82.

————. 2001. "Durkheim's Treatment of Practice: Concrete Practice vs. Representations as the Foundation for Reason." *The Journal of Classical Sociology* 1(1): 33–68.

————. 1990. "Emergent Sociality: A Dialectic of Commitment and Order." *Symbolic Interaction.* Volume 13(1): 63–82. (French: Mauss Review 2002 Number 19.)

————. 1989a. "An Ethnomethodological Perspective on Social Theory." In Helm, David, Albert Meehan, Timothy Anderson, and Anne Rawls (eds.). *Interactional Order: New Directions in the Study of Social Order.*

————. 1989. "Language, Self, and Social Order: A Re-evaluation of Goffman and Sacks." *Human Studies.* Vol 12(1): 147–172.

————. 1987. "The Interaction Order Sui Generis: Goffman's Contribution to Social Theory." *Sociological Theory.* Vol. 5(2): 136–149.

Rawls, John B. 1955. "Two Concepts of Rules." *Philosophical Review.* 64: 3–32.

Reisman, David. 1950. *The Lonely Crowd.* New Haven: Yale University Press.

Ruesch, Jurgen, and Gregory Bateson. 1951. *Communication: The Social Matrix of Psychiatry.* N.Y.: Norton.

Sacks, Harvey. 1992. *Lectures in Conversation,* 2 vols. Oxford: Blackwell Press.

Sacks, Harvey, Emmanuel Schegloff, and Gail Jefferson. 1974. "The Simplest Systematics for the Organization of Turntaking in Conversation." *Language* 50: 696–735.

Sartre, Jean Paul. [1938]2007. *Nausea.* New York: W.W. Norton.

Schegloff, Emanuel A. (1992). "Repair after Next Turn: The Last Structurally Provided Defense of Intersubjectivity in Conversation." *American Journal of Sociology* 97(5): 1295–1345.

Schegloff, Emmanuel A., Gail Jefferson, and Harvey Sacks. 1977. "The Preference for Self-Correction in the Organization of Repair in Conversation." *Language* 53(2): 361–382.

Searle, John. 1969. *Speech Acts: An Essay in the Philosophy of Language.* Cambridge: Cambridge University Press.

Seeley-Brown, John, and Paul Duguid. 1996. *Documents as Boundary Objects: Patrolling and Controlling.*

Sellen, Abigail J., and Richard Harper. 2001. *The Myth of the Paperless Office.* Cambridge, Mass.: The MIT Press

Shils, Edward, Talcott Parsons, and Neil Smelser. *Toward a General Theory of Action: Theoretical Foundations for the Social Sciences* (Social Science Classics Series).

Smith, Dorothy. 2005. *Institutional Ethnography: A Sociology for People.* Lanham, Md.: Rowman/Altimira.

Sorokin, Pitirim. [1937–41] 1957. *Social and Cultural Dynamics* (4 vol.). Boston: Beacon Press.

Suchman, Lucy. 1999. *Plans and Situated Action: The Problem of Human Machine Communication.* New York: Cambridge University Press.

Sumner, William Graham. 1906. *Folkways: a Study of the Sociological Importance of Usages, Manners, Customs, Mores, and Morals.* Boston: Ginn and Co.

Turing, Alan. 1992. *Collected Works of A.M. Turing* (4 vol.). London: North-Holland Amsterdam.

Turner, Steven. 1994. *The Social Theory of Practices: Tradition, Tacit Knowledge, and Presuppositions.* Oxford: Polity Press.

Von Neumann, John, and Oskar Morgenstern. 1944. *Theory of Games and Economic Behavior.* Princeton University Press.

Weber, Max. 1968/1921. Economy and Society. Translated and edited by Roth, Guenther, and Claus Wittich. New York: Bedminster Press.

Weider, D. Lawrence. 1974. *Language and Social Reality: The Case of Telling the Convict Code.* The Hague: Mouton.

Weiner, Norbert. 1930. *Extrapolation, Interpolation and Smoothing of Stationary Time Series with Engineering Applications.* MIT Press. (Originally classified, finally published in 1949).

———. 1948. *Cybernetics: Or the Control and Communication in the Animal and the Machine.* Cambridge, Mass.: MIT Press.

———. 1950. *The Human Use of Human Beings.* New York: Da Capo Press.

Whitehead, Alfred North. [1929]1978. *Process and Reality.* New York: MacMillan.

Wittgenstein, Ludwig. 1945. *Philosophical Investigations.* Cambridge University Press.

Index

About the Author and Editor

Harold Garfinkel is professor emeritus of sociology at UCLA and the author of the classic book *Studies in Ethnomethodology.* His most recent book is *Seeing Sociologically: The Routine Grounds of Social Action,* edited and introduced by Anne Warfield Rawls (Paradigm 2006).

Anne Warfield Rawls, an associate professor of sociology at Bentley College, Waltham, Massachusetts, is the author of various articles on Garfinkel, practices, workplace studies, and Durkheim, including the book *Epistemology and Practice: Durkheim's Elementary Forms of Religious Life* (Cambridge University Press, 2004).

CPSIA information can be obtained
at www.ICGtesting.com
Printed in the USA
LVHW08*1230260818
588183LV00010B/124/P